The Way We'll Be

The Way We'll Be

**THE ZOGBY REPORT ON
THE TRANSFORMATION OF THE
AMERICAN DREAM**

John Zogby

RANDOM HOUSE
NEW YORK

Published in the United States by Random House,
an imprint of The Random House Publishing Group,
a division of Random House, Inc., New York.

RANDOM HOUSE and colophon are registered
trademarks of Random House, Inc.

LIBRARY OF CONGRESS CATALOGING-IN-PUBLICATION DATA
Zogby, John.
The way we'll be : the Zogby report on the transformation of the
American dream / John Zogby.
p. cm.
ISBN 978-1-4000-6450-2
1. United States—Social conditions—1980– —Public opinion.
2. United States—Social conditions—1960–1980—Public opin-
ion. 3. Public opinion—United States. 4. Social surveys—United
States. I. Title.
HN90.P8Z64 2008
306.0973′09045—dc222007049644

Printed in the United States of America on acid-free paper

www.atrandom.com

9 8 7 6 5 4 3 2 1

First Edition

Book design by Mary A. Wirth

*To Kathy, my life partner and fellow keeper of the dream,
who has worked on me for more than thirty years
to be more appreciative of what we have now.*

*And to Jonathan, Benjamin, and Jeremy, smart and
talented First Globals all, and my living link
to a better future for planet Earth.*

CONTENTS

INTRODUCTION   ix

1. THE ART, SCIENCE, AND POWER OF THE POLL   3

2. THE NEW AMERICAN CONSENSUS
    Moving Beyond the Values Divide   27

3. DEMATERIALIZING THE PARADIGM
    Leaner, Smaller, More Personal, and Personalized   56

4. GLOBAL, NETWORKED, AND INCLUSIVE
    A Youth Movement That Is Reshaping All of Society   91

5. THE NEW AMERICAN DREAM
    Who I Am, Not What I Own   120

6. ONE TRUE THING
    Searching for Authenticity in a Make-Believe World   148

7. THE WAY WE'LL BE   184

ACKNOWLEDGMENTS   217

INDEX   221

Some people think of pollsters as necromancers, trying to charm trends out of a jumble of dead numbers. Others act like we're con men, unintentionally or otherwise. How can we state with such assurance that Candidate A will win the election or that Product B is doomed to failure when we are talking to only a micro-fraction of the public? I hear so frequently when this discussion comes up: No one ever calls me for *my* opinion!

Still others worry that rather than uncovering the vectors that point to future outcomes, pollsters create them through our surveying, especially on politics. People, after all, like to be on the winning side, and if polling suggests a person is not backing a winner, he or she is more likely to stay home on Election Day. Thus, this argument goes, predictions become, for pollsters, self-fulfilling—and self-glorifying—prophecies. Then there are those who consider us, in essence, glorified meteorologists.

We study the charts and the satellite radar, look for highs and lows, consult the historical data, put a finger to the wind, and venture our guesses: rain or sunshine, a balmy day or a nor'easter.

What's my take? I think there's a little truth in all those characterizations. We pollsters are always looking for the secret incantation that will tease new truths out of the gigabytes of information stored securely in our computers. We also sometimes make astounding assertions—sometimes wrong assertions, even wrong assertions that do affect how people vote or what they buy—based on fractional evidence, although I'm convinced our methods are valid and our mistakes rarely determinative of anything other than our own embarrassment. And like weathermen, we can sometimes be formulaic and predictable in our assertions. Just as you don't need a Ph.D. to know what's going to ensue when an arctic front meets an air current packed with moisture from the Gulf of Mexico, so, too, when Candidate A is leading Candidate B by 40 percentage points with a month to go, it's a pretty safe bet that only divine intervention—or a divine scandal—is going to turn the race around.

But I think the real story goes beyond all that. We are prognosticators, of course; that's mostly what we get paid for. But as I conceive of this work, we are equally priests and philosophers trying to make sense out of the always confusing human condition. To do the job right, *really* right, we have to ask not only the questions that everyone wants to know the answers to—Who's ahead? What's popular? What's on the skids?—but also questions that dive beneath the surface of events and issues, ones that invite answers from the heart, even the soul, not just the intellect. That's where the larger social movements take place, the deep shifts that propel change into and through our daily lives and that are the ultimate subject of this book.

As with priests and philosophers, there's a bit of the ancient soothsayer in us pollsters. Our livelihood involves peering through the veil of time. Unlike priests and philosophers, though, when pollsters make assertions about what's to come, we at least have the data to back us up.

If, for example, you want to see how America is going to relate to the larger world in the decade ahead, look at the eighteen- to twenty-nine-year-olds, the group I call the First Globals. Like all young adults, this newest batch is materialistic and self-absorbed. They want to look richer than they are; they obsess about relationships. But polling we have done for Hamilton College and many other clients tells us that this is in fact the most outward-looking and accepting generation in American history.

These new global citizens are far more likely than their elders to accept gays and lesbians. For all practical purposes, they're the first color-blind Americans and the first to bring a consistently global perspective to everything from foreign policy to environmental issues to the coffee they buy, the music they listen to, and the clothes they wear. First Globals expect to travel to exotic locales such as Cape Town and Dubai in their lifetime. A quarter of them think they'll end up living for some significant period in a country other than America.

Collectively, this youngest voting demographic leans toward the Democratic party, as it showed in the 2004 presidential race when 55 percent of college students voted for John Kerry, compared to 41 percent for George Bush. The trend continued into 2006 when voters age eighteen to twenty-nine voted for the Democratic candidate in 55 percent of gubernatorial races, 58 percent of House races, and 60 percent of Senate races.

On defense and foreign-policy issues, their worldview has clearly been shaped by America's go-it-alone approach to Iraq and the Middle East generally. In polling we did for the Foreign Policy Association prior to the 2004 election, we provided a sampling of one thousand respondents with a broad range of descriptions of the U.S. role in the world today and asked them to rate the properness of the descriptions on a sliding scale. The response to one such description is broken down by age below.

AN IMPERIALIST POWER THAT ACTS ON ITS OWN REGARDLESS OF WHAT THE REST OF THE WORLD THINKS.

	18–29	30–49	50–64	65+
Improper/Somewhat improper	86%	73	69	67
Somewhat proper/Proper	3	13	20	17

No other group we studied—not Democrats generally, not self-described progressives or libertarians, not readers of *The New York Times*—had a greater spread between the two extremes.

But if these First Globals lean left and sometimes act left—they account for the overwhelming majority of the 3.2 million members of MoveOn.org, for example—there is nothing knee-jerk about their politics. Two out of three of them say that abortion is "always" or "usually" morally wrong. They are far more likely than voters age thirty and over to identify themselves as politically "strictly independent." In fact, more than any other generation I've tracked in my polling, Globals seem determined to find a middle ground on the hot-button issues of the day and to decide each one on a case by case basis, not because their party leaders are urging them in one direction or the other.

I like to tell audiences that while First Globals might not be more able than other age cohorts to point to Darfur on a map, they at least know there is a Darfur, and they care what's happening there. That sort of global empathy has not traditionally been the long suit of the young and self-obsessed, but this is a group that has been trained by its own segment of popular culture to look outward, beyond America's borders.

When I described these eighteen- to twenty-nine-year-olds to a small group of high-tech executives not long ago, an IBM representative got so enthusiastic that he asked me to help set up a meeting so the company could introduce this new global generation to IBM's vision of what it calls the "globally integrated enterprise": a place with no one nerve center but rather with pockets and networks scattered across the planet so that workers can do whatever they do best wherever they want to do it. In the months since, we identified some two thousand people who we found fit the criteria of new global citizens. We continued to filter that number down until we gave IBM a specific list of people—Jorge Romero in Austin, Sally Jones in Portland, Kim Li in Boston—to invite to Washington, D.C., for what everyone is planning will be the first great global corporate-citizen symposium of the twenty-first century. In my business, being able to bring such a high concept down to such fine granularity is pure excitement.

▪ ▪ ▪

It was pure excitement, too, back in November 2000 when Al Gore called me from his campaign bus to ask if he was going to win the presidency. Four hours earlier, at three-thirty on the afternoon before the election, Zogby International sent word to our clients, NBC News and Reuters, that Gore had just moved ahead of then governor George Bush by a single percentage point in the popular vote. At six-thirty, I turned on NBC, listened to the ta-doom ta-doom music that precedes the news, heard Tom Brokaw saying "A dramatic new Zogby poll shows Al Gore surging into the lead," and told the person sitting next to me, "If I don't have an aneurysm now, I'm never going to." At that point, I was all alone out there with my finding. An hour later came the call from the vice president.

"Am I going to win?" he asked.

"Mr. Vice President," I told him, "I don't know."

"But you've got me ahead," he persisted. "What about Florida?"

"Sir," I said, "we're not going to know about Florida at midnight tomorrow."

Turns out, we wouldn't know about Florida for more than a month, until the U.S. Supreme Court met.

▪ ▪ ▪

Maybe you have to take a pollster to lunch to understand how I can get as excited by soaps and hair products and cosmetics as I can by a call from the vice president at the end of a neck and neck race, but that's the way it is. Five years ago, the advertising agency for a major foot ointment asked us to measure user satisfaction across a broad range. Why were consumers buying the ointment, or staying away from it? What did consumers think about the container, the size, the packaging, and the retail store placement? How about variations of the product that were then in the research-and-development stage? Among the nearly four thousand responses our surveying generated, about one in three people told us they would be more likely to purchase the product if it were in a cream form rather than an ointment. Our polling also found high interest in a lotion version and in a pumice paste and in cleansing pads. These new product ideas proved so popular in our 2003 and 2004 surveys that by 2005 we were testing customer satisfaction for the actual products. In fewer than three years, a series of questions had turned into on-the-shelf goods.

What's the thrill in such discoveries? This is podiatric care, not the leadership of the free world, and for most of us, the difference between a cream and a lotion is marginal at best. To me, what's exciting is finding the kernels of truth that let us know what's coming, whether the subject is sales or politics or social trends—all of which, by the way, are deeply interrelated. If I didn't think I could do that *and* get a major kick out it, I would be in another business entirely.

▪ ▪ ▪

We pollsters do aspire to tell the future. In fact, we often get the future right, but polling is not a crystal ball. Despite our best efforts and the most pristine methodologies, the unpredictability of events sometimes gets in the way. The chads don't drop, or they don't get counted. (As a matter of fact, First Globals are the only age cohort in which a majority thinks the 2000 presidential election was stolen.) Asking the right questions can reveal consumer desires. The hard reality, though, is that if the foot scrub isn't any good, no polling question in the world can sell it.

But polling does show us the vectors and lay bare the trends. It reveals the values people hold sacrosanct, the shifts in those values, and the deeper meta-movements that always occur when values are in transition, and that ultimately drive society forward. In a very real sense, polling shows the world simultaneously in microcosm and in macrocosm, and in so doing it cuts through the buzz and the fog of the moment. As I write, the Dow Jones Industrial Average is sinking like a stone, and the president and Congress are scurrying to cobble together a stimulus package. By the time this book appears in print, the United States economy might be in recession, or it might again be booming. Either way, the media is certain to be panting after the story, but in a very real sense the public is already ahead of wherever such news is headed. Our polling consistently shows not only that the wealth isn't being shared equally—that's obvi-

1

The Art, Science, and Power of the Poll

Most people think of me as a political pollster, and rightly so. Much of my public profile is tied to politics, especially during presidential and congressional campaigns. But politics makes up less than a quarter of the work I do. The overwhelming majority of my professional time is devoted to measuring and interpreting public opinion for corporations and other business interests and for professional organizations. While voters get to vote only once or twice a year, consumers vote with their wallets every day.

Besides, as different as they might seem, political and consumer polling are pretty much the same thing. In both instances, we make choices based not just on price and value, or promises and policy, but on unconscious signals that we receive and interpret to satisfy our unconscious selves. Business leaders and politicians often miss this essential point. Our minds think in similes and metaphors—we search for comparisons with which we are comfortable to help us understand the unknown. To get to this deeper level of decision-making, good survey research goes beyond simply asking respondents if they prefer Product A or B, or Candidate C over Candidate D.

Good research has to include creative questions that tease out the public's deeper values and identities, and the questions themselves need to avoid whenever possible charged phrasing that can badly skew responses. That's particularly true with political polling. As George Lakoff shows so effectively in *Don't Think of an Elephant,* controlling the language on key issues gives a party a big leg up in controlling voter response. If we had asked a survey sampling in, say, the spring of 2007 whether the United States should "cut and run" in Iraq, the results would have been far more negative—and far less reflective of true public opinion—than if we had asked the same question in neutral language that included a phrase such as "troop withdrawal." On the other hand, if the aim had been to manufacture positive numbers for the president, "cut and run" would have been just the words to use.

The point is that asking questions is only the beginning of good polling: The way you ask them, the language you use, and the effort you make to broaden the connection with those being surveyed all determine the value and ultimately the accuracy of the collective response. Only policy wonks have opinions about HR Bill 313, but if HR Bill 313 happens to concern, say, the quality of drinking water in exurban communities, just about everyone has an opinion on that. The challenge is to put a question in terms people can understand and react to without losing the reason for asking the question in the first place.

An example: On the Saturday before the November 2000 presidential election, I inserted for the first time into our daily survey of four hundred likely voters the following question as a way of leapfrogging past the horse race aspects of the contest to the underlying motivation of voters:

> *You live in the land of Oz and there is an important election for mayor this year. The candidates are the Tin Man, who is all brains and no heart, and the Scarecrow, who is all heart and no brains. If the election were held today, for whom would you vote?*

We could have simply asked voters whether on Election Day they were more likely to cast their ballot for someone who was highly intelligent or someone who was highly empathetic. By then,

ous—but that average Americans have made fundamental adjustments in their expectations, their needs, and their values, and that those adjustments are creating whole new paradigms through which people are making consumption and political choices that will shape the nation in the decades to come.

Polling also reveals generational divides and suggests how the weight of public opinion will shift as one generation yields dominance to the next, and the next. By careful surveying, we can open a window into what buying habits will be like next year as well as a decade and more down the road, when the subsurface movements already in effect begin to take deeper hold on the public's expectations and dreams, its aspirations and fears. Through asking questions that move beyond the present and try to get at how people will respond to situations that might arise in the future, we can anticipate changes in society and in the marketplace, and advise organizations how they must adapt to new realities.

■ ■ ■

That's what this book is about: the current state of America, the likelihoods of the close-in future, and the movement of our underlying social geology. Put another way, this book explores who we are, what's changing, and the way we'll be.

In these pages, you will discover how we spend our money, cast our votes, live our lives, and why. You will read about the great transition my polling has limned—and confirmed time and again—from a nation of excess to one of tangible limits on spending, on the exercise of power, even on our hopes and imaginings. The new American dream is not the same as the old one. The generation now rising to power is fundamentally different in its aspirations and expectations from the "Greatest Generation" now rapidly fading into the sunset. We're still an optimistic people, but in real and deep ways, we have changed the terms of what "optimism" entails, and we have come to accept and even embrace our membership in and responsibilities to the global community.

In all, my research has identified four meta-movements that

separately and together are redefining the American dream: living with limits, embracing diversity, looking inward, and demanding authenticity. These are the new plate tectonics of American society—what opening up the frontier was to early settlers, the shapers of our national character. Just as geological shifts are not readily apparent until they push their way through the earth's mantle in the form of fissures, mountains, earthquakes, or volcanoes, so these social shifts tend to arrive unexpectedly, in the middle of the night or when we are mostly looking the other way. There are, however, signals to help us mark the transitions—signals that polling can uniquely help to reveal. I take those up in the meat of the book: the surprising new consensus that is emerging among Americans (Chapter 2) and the underlying movements that are slowly altering the foundation we stand on as they carry us from where we are to what we will be (Chapters 3–6). Then, in Chapter 7, I paint that future as clearly as I can—not in some inaccessible time where I can never be proved wrong, but just over the horizon, no more than a dozen years from now.

Along the way, I also offer up rules on how to sell everything from automobiles to political candidates in the new American marketplace. The consumers who are most likely to make or break a product in the years just ahead care more about utility than keeping up with the Joneses. They take their cues globally, not locally. They are inner-directed, network connected, and sensitive to the environment. And they are sick right up to their eyeballs of false promises and phony claims. To put it crudely, the bullshit era is over and done. At the end of Chapter 6, I also name my own Zogby Champs and Chumps, the ad and marketing campaigns of recent times that get it and the ones that don't.

First, though, a more in-depth look at the peculiar art and science that has been my life's work and about which we Americans obsess so much and often understand so little: the poll.

The Way We'll Be

the stereotypes were well-established: Al Gore was a master of policy and governmental detail, but he was wooden in a crowd and on the debating stage. George W. Bush, by contrast, was widely perceived to be loosey-goosey on detail work, sometimes tongue-tied in his responses, but empathetic to the heart's core. On the surface, the choice was simple: Do you want a president who was the smartest guy in the class or one who feels your pain? But that's also the problem with basing questions on stereotypes: They reduce what should be complex answers down to emotional responses to a few simple catchphrases.

Instead, we framed the question in terms of what are almost archetypal figures in American popular culture: the Tin Man and the Scarecrow. Respondents for the most part knew which stood for which candidate, but now they had an image and a narrative framework within which to consider their choice. They weren't choosing solely between brains and empathy; they were choosing between two characters found along L. Frank Baum's famous yellow brick road. By phrasing the question as we did, we both simplified the choice and added complexity. Which candidate did voters want to shepherd Dorothy on her journey through Oz? And which one did they want for themselves, waiting, somewhere over the rainbow, when the election was over?

That, at least, is what I was hoping when I came up with the question, and events, as it turned out, agreed. When our results came in on the Sunday before the election, after asking the same question for three days, the precision of the tie—46.2% to 46.2%—told me we were not going to know the winner on Election Day. (Truth in packaging: I didn't reveal this part of the equation when I told the vice president Monday evening that we wouldn't have a victor the next day.) Our seemingly trivial question got at the fundamental image both candidates projected. But the question was about so much more than heart and brain, and about so much more than presidential politics; it was about the soul of Oz itself. Was that fictional world—and was our real one—to be ruled by reason or compassion, by love or by policy? And in the end what the question revealed was both how conflicted and divided we Americans were at the start of the new millennium.

That divide would soon get codified into the artificial construct that came to be known as "red states versus blue states"—artificial because a swing of a few hundred votes in either New Mexico or Florida would have turned those red states blue and handed the presidency to Al Gore. I would see both the divide and conflict in starker relief in my own values polling—polls, for example, that tracked how bitterly separated Americans were on the question of abortion, at the same time that they showed how many of those who opposed late-term abortions believed fervently in a woman's right to choose. And, of course, we would hear and see the divide and the conflict amplified and exploited in the run-up to the 2004 presidential election. But the Oz question is where I saw it first, in unmistakable form, as if someone had cleaved the electorate exactly in two.

All this from one seemingly innocuous metaphorical inquiry that worked so well because it fit the situation and the people so exactly. When I tried the same question four years later, the Tin Man won by 10 percentage points, a big enough margin to suggest a John Kerry victory over George W. Bush, but as our subsequent analysis showed, by 2004 the premise of the question was no longer valid. The president's performance post-9/11 had convinced many voters that he had brains as well as a heart. In the wake of what appeared, initially at least, to be a well-reasoned and forceful response to the attack on the American homeland, Bush's approval rating hit 85 percent in my poll—and as high as 95 in some others—and stayed in the high sixties for well over a year. For Kerry's part, he didn't project pure intellect the way Gore had in 2000. In the end, we realized that we had pulled a question off the shelf and tried to recycle it without first thinking through whether the comparisons still fit.

Here's another example from the world of politics that illustrates what happens if you jump to conclusions and don't focus closely enough on the details. You might recall that on the afternoon of the 1992 New Hampshire primary, CNN caused a great stir when it hinted at and then projected that the underdog conservative commentator Pat Buchanan was going to embarrass the incumbent President Bush when all the votes were counted. To its great embarrassment, CNN got that one wrong, but it wasn't until I got involved in New Hampshire polling four years later that I understood why.

My natural instinct has always been to poll throughout the day, in the run-up to the vote and as people vote. Doing so just makes sense to me: That's how you make sure that everyone is heard from—the late shift and the early one, night owls and day people. All-day calling also leaves you time to redial the people you missed the first time around. Back then, though, the idea ran against conventional wisdom. Polling was basically a two-tier affair: exit surveys earlier in the day and dinner-hour calling when everyone was presumed to be back home. In fact, my upstart round-the-clock polling was so controversial that ABC News refused to air my results. I knew I was right, though, and, sure enough, come primary-election day, Buchanan's voters once again showed up disproportionately early at the polls and skewed the numbers for other pollsters who were relying on traditional methods to make their projections.

I saw the same thing in the 2000 primaries with the younger Bush and John McCain, and in New Hampshire again in 2004 with Howard Dean and John Kerry. In state after state, McCain would be down a few points to Bush, only to come surging back after five or six o'clock. In New Hampshire, Dean appeared to have picked up so much momentum by midafternoon that NBC News was about to wring my neck for insisting the race was still close, but I knew Kerry's voters were going to come out in droves late in the afternoon and in early evening. We had tons of pre-election data showing his numbers spiked after five P.M., and that is exactly what happened. That's why, to this day, we annoy the public by calling all day long.

FROM RED STATE VS. BLUE STATE TO WAL-MART VS. MACY'S: WHERE WE SHOP IS HOW WE VOTE

Annoying, in fact, is probably what pollsters do best, but until you ask the question, you can't find that kernel of truth, and until you chew the kernel, you can't begin to know what's inside. A few years back, I made a big splash by identifying a new conservative political majority emerging among Wal-Mart shoppers. Wal-Mart? What does it have to do with majority anything, other than majority shopping? Quite a lot, actually. Where we shop says a lot about how we vote, who we admire, and what we believe in.

Our polling shows that weekly Wal-Mart shoppers, about a fifth of all those who shop at the store, are far more likely than those who never shop at the retail giant to: be Hispanic, live in a rural area, attend church at least once a week, and—the greatest point of distinction—identify themselves as either conservative or very conservative. In 2004, when John Kerry lost the popular vote by only 3 percent, he lost among weekly Wal-Mart shoppers by a whopping 76 percent to 24 percent. Meanwhile, those who told us they "never" shop at Wal-Mart went just the opposite direction, voting 80 percent for Kerry and 18 percent for Bush.

Even when President Bush's popularity began to slide generally with the populace, it held firm with Wal-Mart's core shopper base. In early 2005, when only 44 percent of Americans retained a favorable impression of the president, 65 percent of the retail giant's most frequent shoppers told us they approved of the way he was leading the nation. Starting in the summer of 2005, all that began to change. As the president's approval ratings were slipping into the thirties with the electorate generally, he gradually fell under 50 percent with frequent Wal-Mart shoppers and ultimately into the low forties. To me, that was a far more telling indicator than any other polling numbers that Bush was losing the American people—including much of his own core.

"Retail politics," in fact, can be taken literally as well as figuratively. If you want to carry your message to liberals, think Filene's with a liberal-conservative ratio of 51–29, Bloomingdale's (48–26), Macy's (42–32), Neiman Marcus (39–30), and Target (39–36). After Wal-Mart, conservatives prefer Sears (16–57), JCPenney (21–50), Kohl's (23–50), Boscov's (26–53), and Kaufmann's (29–46), which has since been bought by Macy's. If it's a perfect balance you're seeking, Marshalls is the place. I found that 34 percent of Marshalls customers lean liberal and 35 percent conservative, with the rest undecided or independent. These political alignments with particular stores are so consistent that I've come to think of retail locations as a cluster of mini-precincts—and these mini-precincts are very definitive marketing opportunities.

Shopping destinations, it turns out, are equally as useful as predictors of political leanings as the red state–blue state paradigm and ultimately may prove more effective. I have a far easier time envisioning a "red" state such as Virginia or Colorado or Florida going "blue" in 2008—or a "blue" one like New York going "red" had Rudy Giuliani gotten the Republican nomination—than I do Wal-Mart voters deserting the GOP despite their current disenchantment with George W. Bush. Indeed, I have a not-so-far-fetched vision of a time in the near future when election night TV maps will be peppered with store logos, and instead of swooning over which way Ohio votes, we'll swoon over which way Target and Kohl's have fallen. I have an even clearer vision of candidates making media buys not through TV or radio stations, but through store catalogs. Why not take the ad where the swing voters are shopping?

Equally, the political leanings and related sociological background of store shoppers tell us enormous amounts about what will move off the shelves and which products will sit forever. Remember when Wal-Mart tried to launch its designer label line? The thinking was obvious—there's no point losing sales to label-conscious shoppers when volume guarantees you can undercut the competition's price—and it was obviously wrong. People don't shop at Wal-Mart out of snob appeal. That's for limousine liberals and Wall Street conservatives. They shop there for the breadth of offering (everything from foodstuffs to prescriptions to ammo and beach balls) and because Wal-Mart knocks down underwear that normally costs $5.97 to $2.95. Forget that populist appeal, and you've forgotten everything that matters. So definitive are these retail affinities and loyalties that when Macy's purchased the midwestern Kaufmann's chain, I found myself wondering if the New York–based retailer was as interested in broadening its ideological base as it was in strengthening a thin regional presence.

FROM RED SKELTON TO RICHARD PRYOR: WHAT A GOOD LAUGH SAYS

As a pollster, I believe in casting the broadest possible net because you never know where an answer might be hiding, and I believe in parsing the data that comes in to the nth degree and looking for unusual connections, because sometimes it's in the strange crevices where interesting truths begin to emerge. A case in point: Back in December 2006, in surveying for AOL, we threw in almost as an afterthought the following item:

> *Who do you consider to be the funniest comedic performer of all time?*

Respondents were given sixteen comedians to choose from, ranging from Lucille Ball, Jack Benny, and Jerry Lewis, to Jeff Foxworthy, Chris Rock, and Jerry Seinfeld. Of the roughly four thousand respondents, more than a thousand picked "other," and another 774 opted for "not sure," standard reactions to such an open-ended question. That narrowed the sampling for a question that already seemed to be of narrow interest. Still, the more we chewed on the results, shown here and on the following pages, the more interesting they proved.

BY TOTAL RESPONSE

Red Skelton	7.1%
Bill Cosby	6.9
Richard Pryor	6.8
Robin Williams	5.8
Bob Hope	5.7

Inevitably, spreading responses over so many candidates made for some marginal victories, as well as some counterintuitive ones.

The overall winner, Red Skelton, is virtually unknown to younger Americans. But the results did establish a clear dividing line between the first and second tier. The number-six finisher, Jerry Seinfeld, received fewer than half the votes of Bob Hope, who brought up the bottom of the top five. (For the record, Chris Rock finished last among the sixteen, just behind Lucille Ball and Steve Martin.)

Breaking the results down by age and gender didn't produce any great surprises. The youngest respondents favored Robin Williams; the oldest, Bob Hope. Red Skelton was the favorite of those from age fifty to sixty-four, whose coming-of-age years paralleled Skelton's remarkable twenty-year run on prime-time TV, from 1951 to 1971. The lower middle-agers (thirty- to forty-nine-year-olds) went with Richard Pryor, whose edgy routines and high-wire life caught the spirit of a generation that has never really been able to settle down. Pryor was also the favorite of men generally, while women preferred the avuncular humor of Bill Cosby.

Once we added income level to the mix, though, things grew interesting:

BY ANNUAL INCOME

Less than $25,000	Bill Cosby
$25,000–$35,000	Richard Pryor
$35,000–$50,000	Bob Hope
$50,000–$75,000	Robin Williams
$75,000–$100,000	Bill Cosby
More than $100,000	Richard Pryor

Surely it's legitimate to speculate that Hope's $35,000–$50,000 fan base consists largely of older Americans on fixed incomes and to further speculate that Skelton doesn't appear on this list because his fans are more spread out than Hope's among the lower three tiers. But if Robin Williams is the favorite comedian of the young and the well educated, why does he win an income level that seems too high for those under age thirty and too low for those with B.A.'s and beyond? This is not a case of averaging.

What about Pryor's and Cosby's appearances at both the bottom and top of the income charts? The bottom of the income-distribution chart inevitably is overrepresented by African Americans, who might feel a cultural kinship with Pryor and Cosby, but both comedians also command the top of the income chart, where whites are certain to dominate. Are both men's low-income fans laughing at different aspects of their humor than their high-earning ones? Or are Americans at both ends of the income spectrum united in humor, if little else?

Finally, we broke down the results by self-proclaimed political affiliation, and at that point, for me, things got truly fascinating, and a glimmer of sense, maybe, began to emerge.

BY POLITICAL AFFILIATION

Progressive	Richard Pryor
Liberal	Richard Pryor
Moderate	Bill Cosby
Conservative	Red Skelton
Very Conservative	Red Skelton
Libertarian	Bill Cosby

What do we know now, in the light of political affiliation? Or more accurately, what can we speculate with some reasonable assurance? That progressives and liberals are drawn to Pryor's angry humor of discontent. That they represent a broad income range but one with little middle. And that the majority of progressives and liberals are male and younger middle age and below. With similar assurance, we can speculate that those who describe themselves as conservative and very conservative are older than the progressive-liberal bloc, less educated, more likely to be solidly middle class in income, and given to a nostalgic, even sentimental worldview.

That, in turn, tells us something about how to appeal to them as a voting bloc, and it also suggests where they shop and what they shop for. An ad campaign for Wal-Mart built around clips of old Red Skelton routines could be a great hit—the two have virtually the same demographic. Meanwhile, and almost counterintuitively given his strong appeal to the poorest Americans, the late Richard Pryor might be used to draw high-end shoppers into left-of-center retail strongholds such as Bloomingdale's, Filene's, and even Target. It's worth repeating: Voting and consuming are not unrelated; they are often parallel expressions of the same mind-set.

Finally, what of that odd marriage in the political affiliation table above—the one that unites moderates and libertarians in admiration of Bill Cosby? The answer this time might be ideology: Cosby has been outspoken in recent years on the need for personal accountability within the African American community, a stand with powerful appeal to libertarians. Or it might be geography: The libertarian movement is generally stronger in the West, where Cosby has the greatest appeal. But I suspect the answer also is that libertarians and moderates are not so far apart in core beliefs and that together they could be a vital new political force waiting to happen, one that shuns both the God-talk of the religious right and the let-government-solve-it mentality of the traditional left.

Other polling we have done also suggests as much. When we asked respondents what measures they had taken in their personal lives to ease pressures on the environment, and then parsed the answers by political affiliation, moderates and libertarians were far closer to each other than to any other political bloc on issues such as driving more fuel-efficient cars and using public transportation and energy-efficient lightbulbs. Who knows, if Bill Cosby can get them to laugh together, maybe he can lead them to polls together, too.

All of this admittedly is only a pyramid of assumptions and assertions, some of which will undoubtedly go up in smoke under harder scrutiny, but without suppositions, inquiry doesn't get started, and without inquiry, all we know is the same old thing.

FROM HOMER'S *ILIAD* TO HOMER SIMPSON: IGNORANCE IS NOT BLISS

What else do we learn from polling numbers? Enormous amounts, useful and not. I was amused, for example, and somewhat dumbfounded to learn that Atlantans are only semiliterate about TV Homers and almost completely illiterate about classical ones. In surveying we did for AOL of metropolitan statistical areas, only 57.4 percent of adult residents of Atlanta knew that the name of Homer Simpson's son was Bart. That compares to more than 67 percent of the adult residents of Chicago and Dallas, and 66 percent of Minneapolis adults. Only Los Angeles adults scored lower, with a bare 55 percent able to name Bart Simpson. When we upgraded the Homer question to the classics—asking respondents to name just one of Homer's two epic poems—Atlanta took the booby prize. One in three Bostonians could come up with *The Odyssey* or *The Iliad,* but only one in five Atlantans.

Is this pairing of disparate subjects a pollster's stunt? To an extent, sure. It's fun to think up these questions. A little surveying quirkiness also lightens the load when people are being asked to answer a long list of queries. We want our respondents loose, not tense. But pairing the mundane with the more consequential also gives us a context for looking at the results. Probably no one without a financial stake in *The Simpsons* ultimately cares how many Americans know Bart's name, but when four in five adults can't come up with the title of at least one of Homer's great epic poems, some of the seminal works of ancient Greece, something important is being said about the transmission (and fragility) of Western culture and about what it means even to be "educated" in our time.

Have a look at the tables below, which analyze by race and ethnicity the responses of Atlanta adults to the two Homer questions.

KNEW THE NAME OF HOMER SIMPSON'S SON

White	51%
Hispanic	65
African American	69
Asian	72

DIDN'T KNOW THE TITLE OF EITHER
OF HOMER'S EPIC POEMS

White	70%
Hispanic	88
African American	94
Asian	86

Here we have essentially two ladders going in opposite directions. The TV Homer breakdown suggests either that white adults are less in touch with popular culture or that adults of color are overdosing on the empty calories of television, oddly enough in this instance a cartoon show about a white family that pokes frequent fun at ethnic and racial stereotypes and just about everything and everyone else. Again, there's almost certainly a mixture of the two at work, and maybe a third element as well: Atlanta whites as a group might simply be more humor-challenged than Atlanta blacks, Asians, and Hispanics—less able to laugh at *The Simpsons'* irreverence, less appreciative of irony and satire generally.

About the ancient Homer breakdown, there's less ambiguity. When seven in ten white Atlanta adults can't name either of Homer's epics, we can safely speculate that either (a) schools aren't passing on the canon of Western culture, or (b) when schools do, students aren't listening very hard. But when nineteen in twenty black Atlanta adults can't do the same, we begin to see numerically the tragic and long-term consequences of the miserable educational opportunities that have been available to African Americans in this country and—to return to Bill Cosby—the consequences of the failure of too many African Americans to take advantage of what is available, meager though it might be.

It's not a matter of knowing anything specific about *The Iliad* and *The Odyssey.* In the larger picture, having a command of the details of, say, the Trojan War is mostly immaterial. But I for one am willing to bet that a lack of any knowledge of Homer's works, even

the titles, correlates as powerfully as any other single factor with annual earnings at or below poverty level. In our survey, one in eight
of those earning under $25,000 a year properly picked *The Iliad* as
the title of one of Homer's epic poems, compared with better than
one in four of those earning over $100,000. Among those earning
$25,000 to $35,000 annually, only 3 percent identified *The Odyssey* as one of Homer's works even when the title was put in front
of them, compared with 11 percent of those earning $75,000 to
$100,000 a year.

One of the things I love about polling is that you never know
where the answers might lead you.

FROM NECROMANCY TO ADVANCED MATH: HOW SAMPLING, WEIGHTING, AND MARGIN OF ERROR HELP US GET IT RIGHT

This book is the culmination of both specific surveying and a professional lifetime of asking questions such as those raised above and
then dissecting the answers. In the search for where we have been,
who we are, and where we are headed, I've pored through the
polling literature and consulted the work of every survey organization I thought might have something useful to offer. To tease out
specific answers, we've done dozens of special overnight polls and
added hundreds of questions to our regular rounds of surveying. I
don't mind saying that nobody does such work better than Zogby
International.

I've also designed a series of extensive surveys to help identify
the underlying movements that are pushing us forward. One such
survey of almost four hundred questions was completed by almost
sixteen thousand people selected randomly from a list of nearly two
hundred thousand Americans with e-mail addresses. In the polling
business, that's the big time. And of course we have our own vast
data bank to mine. My organization does three hundred to four
hundred paid projects a year for everyone from Fortune 500 companies to regional utilities, universities, charities, and politicians and
their parties. Add to that the regular monthly political polls we've

been conducting over the last seven years—polls that include on average about twelve hundred likely voters—flash polls, Zogby Interactive polls that tap the opinions of thousands through the Internet, and the like, and it's safe to say that we are querying at least half a million people a year. That's a huge sampling.

Many of the questions we ask are straightforward ones about items purchased and preferred, political leanings, and basic demographics. But many questions are designed to probe into respondents' aspirations, concerns, desires, and beliefs, and their behavioral and attitudinal characteristics. I want to know what magazines they read, what their hobbies are, whether they are better off or worse off than they were before some benchmark event, and how they define the meaning of life. Does the one with the most toys win in the end? Or is it true that you can't take it with you? I'm also curious to learn if males have a female boss, if whites have a black coworker, and if people generally have been to a party recently where other races and ethnicities were present. This isn't just nosiness. These kinds of issues affect "votes," whether they're shopping votes or political ones; they give us a sense of how people identify themselves, how they see themselves in relation to others and to the world around them, what motivates their decisions, and what their core values are.

All of that sounds nice, or at least I hope so, but I'm also sure it raises larger questions for many readers—and the largest for some: Can we really just interview by phone or e-mail such a small number of people and make broad generalizations about how millions and millions of people will think, behave, vote, or shop? Are we really the bunko artists dressed up in good suits that many suspect us of being? The answer to both questions (and here I feel free to speak for the entire profession) is no, and the reason is something I've alluded to before in these opening pages: the tried and true principle of sampling.

Probability sampling is the fundamental basis for all survey research; in fact, without probability sampling there would be no polling industry. Imagine a huge jar filled with a million marbles, some white and some black. If I want to find out how many of each color are in the jar, I have two choices: (a) I can spend virtually the rest of my waking hours counting each and every marble, or (b) I can draw a sample of, say, a thousand and get a very close approximation of how many of each color are in the entire jar. I need to ensure that my draw is done randomly—no peeking, no cheating—but if I enforce the simple rule that says each marble in the jar has the same chance of being selected as every other marble, then I "know" (a) that if I repeat the sample one hundred times, I will get the same result ninety-five times out of a hundred, and (b) that the results of any single sampling will not vary in this case by more than three percent, plus or minus, from the norm.

This variance, known as margin-of-sampling error, can sometimes seem almost whimsical from the outside, but it's calculated using a well-established statistical formula—the MOE, as it's known in the trade—that calls for dividing the number 1 by the square root of the sampling size. Thus, if my initial count of the thousand-marble sample yields 55 percent black marbles and 45 percent white ones, the laws of probability, not to mention near infinite experience, tell me that if I repeat the count one hundred times, in ninety-five instances I will have between 52 percent and 58 percent black marbles and between 42 percent and 48 percent white marbles. This 95 percent confidence level doesn't preclude the possibility of a bad sample or other error, but it gets us close to certain.

People, of course, are more complicated than marbles, but the same principles apply, which is why a randomly selected small percentage of a population can represent the attitudes, opinions, and projected behavior of all of the people *if* the sample is selected correctly. A good sample will reproduce the characteristics of the population being polled as closely as possible. If the U.S. Census Bureau tells us that 55 percent of adults in a particular community being polled are women, then the sample should represent that figure. Or if we know from past presidential elections that 20 percent of likely voters are under age thirty, then any sample of one thousand likely voters should have approximately two hundred people in that age group.

We don't hit our target percentages exactly, but so long as we're not too far off, we can bump some groups up and knock others down. This is not voodoo math: We just apply multipliers—"weighting" as it's known in the business—to bring underrepresented groups up to what we know their representation should be and, similarly, to reduce groups overrepresented in the sample. Example: Since we know from past experience that normally 10 percent of likely voters in any national election will be African Americans, any sample of a thousand should include about one hundred African Americans. If we end up polling eighty African Americans, we can multiply their responses by 1.25 to "weight" their representation up to one hundred. An initial sampling that included only, say, thirty African Americans would be a problem—weighting can be stretched only so far—but we've never had to deal with that at Zogby International, and in fact such problems are a rarity at any legitimate polling organization. The only instance I can recall at Zogby was a Tennessee poll where we initially "weighted up" a limited sampling of black voters to represent all African American voters in the state, then realized that, through some odd circumstance, two in three of the African Americans we had surveyed were Republicans. But even there, additional sampling brought the percentages into line with known norms and corrected the problem.

One area where I have diverged from many of my colleagues over the years is in applying weights for party identification. When I do political polling, I want the sampling to reflect the known percentages of voters who identify themselves as Democrat, Republican, or independent/no party. Other pollsters, but by no means all, see "party ID" as a "trailer variable"—a softer factor based on how people feel at a given moment in time. I don't agree. I think party identification is a strong determinant of how people see their world and how they are likely to vote. Of course, it changes over time, but only in response to large events and significant mood shifts. Watergate and the Vietnam War tipped the scales dramatically for an earlier generation of voters. In our time, 9/11, the Iraq War, and the federal response to Hurricane Katrina are having the same effect, individually and collectively, but none of this happens overnight. Any poll that shows wide swings in party affinity over very brief time spans comes decked out in red warning flags so far as I'm concerned.

Another tool that I and just about all my colleagues use in our political polling is the so-called rolling average. If we're closing in on Election Day and the target sample is twelve hundred likely voters, we might poll four hundred on Monday, four hundred on Tuesday, and another four hundred on Wednesday. Then, we'll add another four hundred on Thursday and throw out the Saturday figures. That way, we keep the numbers fresh and reflective of the rush of events.

FROM LANDLINES TO CELL PHONES: SEARCHING FOR ANSWERS IN A MOBILE WORLD

When I founded Zogby International back in the mid-1980s, polling was actually a fairly simple business. No more. Back then, we could routinely count on an average response rate of 65 percent—for every three people we reached on the telephone, about two would agree to answer the survey. Long-distance calls, our basic means of surveying, still commanded attention in American households in those days. Far more households than today were single-earner intact nuclear families, so someone was likely to be home and have a few moments to talk on the phone. Just as important, answering machines were an anomaly and caller ID did not exist.

A multitude of factors have caused response rates to nose-dive in recent years, to less than 10 percent in many instances. Cell phones, which we were once not allowed to call by law and I am still reluctant to dial, have become prevalent, especially among younger Americans. Depending on the source, anywhere from one in four to one in three adults under thirty-five no longer even has a landline. The National Do Not Call Registry, while it doesn't apply specifically to our industry, has also emboldened telephone answerers who suffered for years under the constant onslaught of telemarketers. Beyond doubt, we pollsters have to work harder for good and reliable results, but the fact that our election predictions generally line up so accurately with actual results proves that we can still get them. But for how much longer?

In truth, I think telephone surveying could be reaching the end of the line. That's why Zogby International and a few other pollsters have turned increasingly to the Internet. While home Internet access hasn't yet reached the same level as home telephones, nearly three in four adult Americans do use the Internet at home, and about nine in ten likely voters—close to universal Internet penetration for that group. Just as important, minorities, always underrepresented in telephone surveys, make up one of the fastest growing segments of the Internet population.

We still do a lot of telephone surveying and will continue to do so for many years to come. You don't throw out a proven system just for the sake of doing something new. But increasingly we are using our Internet wing, Zogby Interactive, to take advantage of shifting communication demographics. In a typical nationwide Interactive survey, we randomly select the sampling from our vast database of e-mail users who have registered to participate in polling—rather like the million marbles in the jar!—and offer an invitation to a secure website to take a poll. Registered individuals don't get to choose which polls to participate in, and security measures keep them from voting more than once so they can't skew the results for their candidate or product. Once a survey is conducted, about 2 percent of respondents are telephoned to confirm their personal data.

E-mail polling does require some weighting for party affiliation—Democrats are slightly overrepresented among the people who respond in our database—but it requires less adjustment for age differences than one might imagine. Yes, younger voters disproportionately outnumber older ones among all those we could possibly contact, but because the young are generally not as civic-minded as older voters, they are less likely to respond to our polling initiatives. What really matters is that the reliable results are quick to arrive and quick to tabulate, and ever since we introduced Interactive polling in the 2004 elections, the results have shown themselves to be highly accurate. In fact, in the 2006 midterm elections we used Zogby Interactive to correctly call the winners in eighteen of nineteen Senate races, including four of five races that were won by single digits. The only race that Zogby did not pick correctly—the Missouri contest between Jim Talent and Claire McCaskill—was still safely within our announced 3 percent margin of error. We had Talent winning by a razor-thin 1.3 percent. When he finally conceded, early the next morning, McCaskill had prevailed by 2 percent. To me, such blue-ribbon results are all the evidence I need that the future of polling can be found through the Internet, and in fact much of the new surveying for this book was done through Zogby Interactive.

Text-messaging offers many of the same advantages as Internet polling, with the added advantage that it allows us to focus in tightly on the eighteen- to thirty-four-year-olds who are by far the most likely users of text-messaging among eligible voters. Shortly before the 2004 presidential election, we teamed up with Motorola and Rock the Vote (launched in 1990 by members of the music industry in part to bring younger voters to the polls) to test the efficacy of text-message polling. Motorola provided us with a list of forty-two thousand subscribers who had signed up for Rock the Vote. We then sent out two text-messages to all forty-two thousand: Are you going to vote? If so, who will you vote for? The results showed Kerry winning by 14 percent, exactly his final margin of victory among eighteen- to thirty-four-year-olds.

Do we ever get it wrong, by phone or online or by text-messaging? Indeed. In 2006, to cite one particularly bad day, I completely blew the calls in gubernatorial races in Colorado and Arkansas. Postelection analysis showed that we had put together incomplete panels of likely voters in both states. To be more specific, we had based our weighting, and thus our voter panels, on 2004 presidential results rather than on the results of the previous gubernatorial races. Only afterward did we realize that in both states the turnout for these two types of races is very different. In Colorado, for instance, 31 percent of presidential voters in 2004 were between thirty and forty-four years old, while 24 percent were age sixty or older. Had we looked to earlier contests for governor, we would have been better able to predict the actual age breakdown in 2006, when 41 percent of voters were age thirty to forty-four and only 16 percent were over age sixty. We've taken steps to assure that doesn't happen in the future—this business is a constant learning process— but human error is always the wild card. Still, if you are one of those who have long thought that polling was only a step or two removed from necromancy, I hope you'll realize now that this black magic takes place on a solid foundation of science and math.

FROM SELF-INDULGENCE TO QUIET ACCEPTANCE:
COMING TO TERMS WITH A CHANGING WORLD

Collectively, the results of all the polling and investigation undertaken for *The Way We'll Be* have been more revealing and uplifting than I could have hoped for or predicted. Some social critics have used recent books such as Gregg Easterbrook's *The Progress Paradox* and Arianna Huffington's *Pigs at the Trough* as proof that the prototypical American is a rapacious vulture hell-bent on destroying the planet. I think both books are miscast in the effort—they are far more nuanced than that—but my work paints a different America. My surveying shows that we are in the middle of a fundamental reorientation of the American character away from wanton consumption and toward a new global citizenry in an age of limited resources.

Beneath the surface, I have found, millions of us live in quiet acceptance of the new boundaries that have been placed on us. The angry white men who led the Republican revolution in Congress back in 1994 are still around—talk radio and TV couldn't survive without them. The superrich haven't disappeared, either. In fact, their numbers have swelled under the tax policies of the current administration, which is why there's still a market for two-hundred-dollar cigars, thousand-dollar bottles of champagne, and spec houses the size of the Taj Mahal. But in basic ways, both groups are becoming marginalized. The majority of Americans have mellowed in recent years. They've modulated their desire to acquire material things, adopting lifestyles that respect the environment and human rights, and they take a more critical attitude toward progress. Just as Americans rose to the occasion in World War I and World War II, so we have found they are again willing to sacrifice for the broader public good, so long as—and this is key—they are certain the sacrifice is shared. That's especially true of such hot-button issues as global warming. Our polling consistently shows that the people are well ahead of political leaders in their willingness to tone down acquisitiveness in order to reduce greenhouse gas emissions. But it's true more broadly, too. People want better lives, not more things to fill their hours with. Surprisingly, in ratcheting the dream downward, Americans are finding contentment in a land of less plenty.

Don't misunderstand. Modesty and dampened expectations have not turned us into a nation of moralistic, boring, one-dimensional, or penurious people. Americans still love to shop, love to own beautiful things, and love to fantasize. We're still too apt to fall for a pretty face in ads or a silver tongue in politics. And we are still, to me at least, wildly unpredictable in fundamental ways. More and more, though, for all our differences and oddities, we are coming to agree on a simple set of principles, equally applicable to candidates, products, politicians, and businesses: Be fair. Be honest. Practice ethics; don't just talk them. Appeal to what is best in our character, not what is worst in it. And never forget that for new Americans as well as for the descendants of those who arrived here on the *Mayflower,* the seedbed of our beliefs can still be found in the meritocracy the founding fathers worked so hard to create. I found that confirmed in a Gallup poll taken early in 2007 that asked respondents how satisfied they were with the opportunity Americans had to get ahead by working hard. More than 70 percent said they were at least "somewhat satisfied," and 40 percent said they were "very satisfied."

Despite all the dire predictions that we will fall into hopeless self-indulgence, despite even the raw greed that seems to grow like mold inside so many CEO suites and corporate boardrooms these days, the United States is inhabited by a sober, caring, honest, ethical people. The media has a penchant for doom-and-gloom headlines that send precisely the opposite message. I remember one from a July 2007 edition of *USA Today* trumpeting that 13 percent of American adults have credit card debt of $25,000 or more. That's a lot of money to carry on plastic, at hideous interest rates, but the larger story goes unreported: 87 percent—seven out of eight of us—aren't carrying a debt load like that despite the constant encouragement of the credit card industry to max out our cards. To paraphrase Dwight Eisenhower, we are a great nation because we are a good people. But we are also a nation in great transition.

I am no Pollyanna. If you're searching for a coming world where war is no more; global warming disappears; divisions of economics, race, and ethnicity no longer haunt us; and leaders always lead and never pander, look somewhere else. I've spent my career teasing honest answers out of often recalcitrant data for clients who need to be told the truth. That kind of work tends to produce realists, not dreamers, and the real future is always messy and unstable. What gives me heart is that we are heading toward all the complications that lie ahead with so many of our best values intact.

Not long ago, Starbucks did me the honor of asking for a quote for its "The Way I See It" series, which features coffee cup quotes from the famous and not so well known. In truth, I was thrilled. Contributors have ranged all over the place since the program was begun in early 2005, from former George W. Bush speechwriter David Frum ("In politics, partisanship is a force that can make things happen"), to actress Goldie Hawn ("Searching for more joy is not a frivolous pursuit"), to popular pastors (Rick Warren), bioethicists (Wesley J. Smith), the political humorist and candidate Al Franken, and Starbucks's own customers and employees.

Inevitably, with a range that wide and with Starbucks's great visibility, the quotes haven't been free of controversy. The San Francisco–based writer Armistead Maupin, for example, enraged the Christian right by using his moment of coffee cup fame to encourage gays to come out of the closet earlier so they would have more time to pursue meaningful love. I've found that I don't have to go searching for controversy for myself; it seems to find me okay on its own. But I did have something I wanted to say where every coffee and latte and cappuccino drinker in America could see it, so I sent Starbucks the following quote:

> In three decades of polling, I've found that while individuals make mistakes in judgment, America as a whole rarely does. A collective wisdom emerges from a poll or vote that is far greater than the sum of its parts.

That indeed is the one thing I do know for sure.

A QUICK GUIDE TO READING POLLS

- Majorities are important in polling, but the intensity with which even small groups respond to questions tells us more about the deeper values that drive decision-making.
- "Retail politics" can be taken literally as well as figuratively. Where people shop and how they vote are both self-reinforcing and mutually illuminating.
- God is in the details. Don't stop with overall results. Demographic and behavioral-group breakdowns are the true gold in almost any poll.
- Don't be afraid to riff, either. Reading poll results creatively often leads to discoveries that we pollsters have missed.
- Keep in mind that humans are complex and multidimensional. The deeper you dig with your questioning and analysis, the closer to the truth you are going to get.
- Always ask how the poll was done. Was the sample randomly drawn? Is it large enough to represent the diversity in the universe being questioned? Not all poll numbers are created equally.

The New American Consensus

MOVING BEYOND THE VALUES DIVIDE

For a nation that endlessly conducts, reads, argues over, and bashes polls, we Americans know so little about ourselves. What divides us is often painfully obvious—from the great divide of slavery and the Civil War to the divide over such social issues as abortion and gay rights that has fueled what often seems to be a second, less bloody civil war in our own times. We know what we don't like, and whom, but what unites us, what pulls us together and makes Americans one people, is harder to pin down. Every generation, it seems, subscribes to some new definition of what it means to be us.

The astute French aristocrat Alexis de Tocqueville, who visited the New World in the 1830s, came away convinced that the distinguishing characteristics of American society were its classlessness, the engagement of ordinary citizens in civic and political life, and our boundless optimism. "America is a land of wonders, in which everything is in constant motion and every change seems an improvement," de Tocqueville wrote in his classic study, *Democracy in America*.

"The idea of novelty is there indissolubly connected with the idea of amelioration. No natural boundary seems to be set on the efforts of man; and in his eyes what is not yet done is only what he has not yet attempted to do."

The homegrown poet Walt Whitman loved our classlessness, too, and the democratic institutions that stood behind it and so powerfully formed the American character. As Whitman wrote in *Democratic Vistas,* "It is native personality, and that alone, that endows a man to stand before presidents or generals, or in any distinguish'd collection, with aplomb—and not culture, or any knowledge or intellect whatever." A few decades later, Henry Adams, who had culture and knowledge and intellect to spare, bemoaned the very classlessness and democratic institutions that de Tocqueville and Whitman had celebrated. And thus the battle has gone ever since.

To W.E.B. Du Bois, one of the greatest observers of our fundamental nature, America's inability to get beyond the "color line"—by which he meant race and racism—inevitably held us back from the greatness to which we aspire. For Richard Nixon's feisty and ultimately disgraced vice president Spiro Agnew, the "nattering nabobs of negativism" stood in the way of fulfilling our national character. All of which leads to the questions of who we really are and what distinguishes us from the citizens of anywhere else.

Answering those questions is not a new pursuit. Nor has the pursuit been without debate and controversy. In the 1790s, the Hamilton Federalists and Jeffersonian Democrat-Republicans waged a holy war over which party truly represented the spirit of the American Revolution. Anyone reading the party newspapers and pamphlets of that time can easily see the similarities between that era and the hyperpartisan rhetoric of the religious right and liberal left that has so dominated politics in these early years of the twenty-first century.

For the party of Thomas Jefferson, the revolution was defined by the principles of freedom, tolerance, and equality. Its slogan was a familiar one: no taxation without representation. For the party of

Alexander Hamilton, principles mattered, but the revolution was for naught if a strong government could not be established to protect these principles and the people. Both parties believed they were fighting for American values, but the values themselves were so diametrically opposed that the election of 1800 was contested as if Armageddon were at stake.

To be sure, American values are enshrined in that great document the Constitution of the United States of America and, in particular, in the Bill of Rights. If a sacred text has run straight through American history, the Bill of Rights is it, more so than the Bible. We are the people of rights. Unlike any other nation, we are defined not by geography, by arts or letters, by cuisine or sensibilities, by religion or ethnic background or war; we are defined instead and quite simply by the rights we have. Our rights are our history; they are why the first European settlers came here and why millions upon millions more settlers have come in the centuries since. The values expressed in the Bill of Rights are what we all aspire to—the metaphorical foundation on which rests Ellis Island and the Statue of Liberty; the U.S. Congress, the Supreme Court, and the White House as well. Those rights are the one great constant in the evolving American experience.

Yet even that nearly biblical text—the Constitution with its Bill of Rights—is not immune to the values divide. In the name of the Constitution and the values articulated therein, John Adams jailed and fined French sympathizers for violating the Alien and Sedition Acts. Under the banner of the same Constitution, Southern states seceded from the Union in 1861, an act of defiance that brought on the bloodiest war in American history. In defense of America and its rights, ways, and customs, Chinese were excluded from immigration from the 1880s through the 1940s, German Americans were victimized during World War I, and Japanese Americans were interned during World War II.

What does the Bill of Rights mean when it says in Amendment One that "Congress shall make no law respecting an establishment of religion" or when the authors write in the next amendment that "the right of the people to keep and bear Arms, shall not be in-fringed"? Is the Constitution a living document or one set in stone? Is "original intent" to be taken literally or figuratively—another way in which our founding document and the Bible converge at the horizon? And how does "promot[ing] the general welfare" square with the right to life or the right to choose? In the abstract, these sound like questions for a panel of learned elders. In practice, such issues rend the country and its people every day.

The truly remarkable aspect of this, of course, is that the na-tion has endured and prospered despite our sometimes violent dis-putes over what this right or that one means and whether American "values" are being preserved or destroyed by the actions of the body politic. America survived the Jefferson-Hamilton wars and the great Civil War, too. We struggled our way through the civil rights struggles of the 1960s and the horrible assassinations of that decade—including the Kennedys and Martin Luther King, Jr.—and through the painful denouement of the Vietnam War in the decade that followed. We have careened over the last half cen-tury through a succession of presidents that in retrospect couldn't have been more different from one another: Eisenhower, Kennedy, Johnson, Nixon, Ford, Carter, Reagan, George H.W. Bush, Clin-ton, and George W. Bush. With little more than our common val-ues to unite us, we've reeled from "gate" to "gate"—Water-, Iran, Monica, WMD—and yet, for all the drama, we've been left stand-ing at the end.

What's the common denominator? What's the ballast in what would otherwise be this wildly yawing ship of state? I'm convinced it's our shared values. We roll this way. We roll that way. But our values steady us. They are who we are, who we want to be, and what we want for our children and their children. Even though we often cannot express them coherently or without shouting from the other side, we hold those values sacrosanct, and we look to our can-didates for the presidency and the House and Senate to express them in ways relevant to our times, our economic and social conditions, and the ongoing drama of our politics.

FROM UNDROPPED CHADS TO DUG-IN POSITIONS:
THE ARMAGEDDON THAT DIDN'T HAPPEN

Still, there are moments that seem to be off the charts, times that rise above the business-as-usual life of the nation. The year 1800 was one such time, a moment when the fundamental structure of the still-forming nation was being decided. The year 1860 was another instance. Would the Democrats win and either appease the South to the point where the Union was insignificant or let the South go and let the great New World experiment crumble? Or would the victory be Lincoln's and war inevitable? One has to look only at the state by state results to see how brightly red and blue America really was in that crucible year. To cite one small example, Lincoln drew a little more than 2 percent of all the votes cast in Maryland in the presidential election of 1860. Across the Mason-Dixon Line in Pennsylvania, he won 56 percent of the vote. Nothing in modern elections even approaches a state by state spread like that.

I thought 2004 was such a time again, another Armageddon election, and I said so in speech after speech around the country. There was, first of all, the history of the previous election, particularly the recount of votes in Florida—a state then governed by one of the candidate's brothers—and the U.S. Supreme Court intervention that effectively handed the presidency to George W. Bush. When we asked about the election in December 2003 polling, feelings were still running high, especially among the youngest voters. The table below shows the results, broken down by age. (Note that throughout the book, columns might not total 100 percent because of rounding.)

CONSIDERING THE RECOUNT OF VOTES IN FLORIDA
DURING THE PRESIDENTIAL ELECTION THREE YEARS AGO,
DO YOU REGARD THE BUSH PRESIDENCY . . .

	18–29	30–45	46–65	OVER 65
As legitimate	44%	57	58	55
Election was stolen	57	38	36	38

Among all voters, significant numbers were not being simply unsupportive of a sitting president; they were denying the very legitimacy of the process that had brought him to office in what is purported to be the most stable democracy in the world. That worried me, as did the generational divide between the youngest voters and the rest of the electorate. If the election then less than a year away was as close as the previous one, and if the Supreme Court or Congress again intervened on behalf of George W. Bush, I thought it quite possible that an entire generation of voters—the generation with the most elections ahead of it—would retreat to cynicism and effectively abandon the most basic function of democratic government.

I saw an even greater generational split when we asked in the same survey if respondents agreed or disagreed with the "political, economic, and social values espoused by former President Bill Clinton and his wife, Senator Hillary Clinton." Among eighteen- to twenty-nine-year-olds, the approval of the Clintons was overwhelming: 59 percent agreed while only 30 percent disagreed. With every other age group, the results were almost the polar opposite, but nowhere was the gap wider than with the generation just above the youngest voters. Among thirty- to forty-five-year-olds, 56 percent disagreed with the Clintons, while only 37 percent agreed. These are not casual differences. These are numbers that reflect fundamentally different worldviews in generations that rub side by side against each other.

But a longitudinal divide was only one of many factors that suggested 2004 stood to be an Armageddon moment. By March of that year, my polling was showing John Kerry, the likely Democratic nominee, running a few points ahead of the incumbent. That didn't say much more than that, all things staying equal (and they almost never do), the race would be Kerry's to lose. What was really telling, though, was that at such an early point, a full eight months before Election Day, only 5 percent of likely voters were still up in the air over how they were going to cast their ballots. Such a narrow window of undecideds is pretty much unheard of with the primaries just winding down and the general-election campaign yet to heat up in earnest. It told me (a) that the battle for that swing 5 percent would be down in the trenches, no-holds-barred, and (b) more important, that America had become a deeply polarized place, where voters were evenly split and so heavily dug into entrenched positions on the large issues of the day that no matter who won the vote, just about half the electorate was likely to be mad as hell about the outcome. The values divide, in short, had become the dividing line between what was becoming two separate Americas.)

That alarmed me, as did the depth of the divide as it appeared in our polling. Those who owned a gun, for example, were 22 percentage points more likely to vote for George W. Bush than those who didn't own one. Eight years earlier, Bob Dole had outpolled Bill Clinton among gun owners by a relatively narrow 13 percentage points—51 to 38 percent, with Ross Perot capturing 10 percent of the gun vote. Those who attended a place of worship at least once a week favored Bush by as many as 25 percentage points over those who never attended services, the same margin by which Bush trounced Gore among the same subset of voters. Bush trounced Kerry in our polling among married voters. Kerry trounced Bush among singles and never-marrieds. (The married–never married gap, by the way, is far more pronounced than the gender gap among voters today.) Whether one believed in an active, ever-present God or believed in no God or a remote, removed one was a far more powerful determinant of how one was likely to cast one's vote than whether one believed Bush or Kerry would be more effective in prosecuting the war on terror. So was whether or not a likely voter was a NASCAR fan. (No surprise, race car fans were overwhelmingly for Bush, while those who wouldn't be caught dead at a NASCAR event were Kerry supporters through and through.)

As never before in my experience, we saw these value-laden differences looming huge in our state by state polling. Even when some states barely fell into the Bush camp or the Kerry one, the differences between their residents on questions such as belief in God or gun ownership were profound. Like the North and South states of

1860, the red and blue states of 2004 were diametrically opposed in terms of demographics, behavior, and ideology.

We saw the differences in equally stark relief whenever we added political questions to our consumer polling, and not just among the predictably polarized Wal-Mart frequent shoppers and those who don't shop at Wal-Mart. America had polarized coffee shops as well. When the voting was all tallied, Dunkin' Donuts regulars gave Bush a 60 to 39 advantage over Kerry. Starbucks lovers— 17 percentage points more likely than the Dunkin' Donuts base to be from large cities, 18 points more likely to be under age twenty-five, 16 points more likely to be female and/or Jewish, and 7 points more likely to never attend church—went for Kerry by an almost equal spread: 57 to 42.

"A house divided against itself cannot stand," Lincoln said famously at the Illinois Republican state convention in 1858. (He was borrowing from the Gospel according to Mark at the time.) That's what America was in 2004, a house deeply divided by differing values, and the election to come played out in almost perfect-storm fashion. Bush won by 3 percent of the popular vote, enough of a margin to keep the results out of the courts and Congress but not sufficient to prevent suspicion about everything from slow voting in Ohio to the political loyalties of the top management of Diebold, manufacturer of many of the voting machines used to determine the outcome. And at the end of it all . . . the perfect storm never broke. Armageddon didn't arrive. Within two years, a political house so deeply divided had healed itself with such efficiency that a center that once seemed unable to hold in any form had reasserted itself with enough authority to alter the leadership of both houses of Congress.

What happened? Certainly the divisive rhetoric didn't die down. The shouting heads on FOX didn't stop shouting. Lou Dobbs and his anti-immigration campaign on CNN didn't suddenly go mute. On the left, the jeremiads about America's racist society that took flight after charges were brought against three members of the Duke University lacrosse team barely abated even after it was concluded that the Duke players had merely behaved badly, not criminally.

Other flash points were still plentiful as well. Recall that it took a 2006 court order to force Wal-Mart to start selling the contraceptive morning-after pill in the face of objections from management and shoppers. And all this, of course, took place against what was fast becoming perhaps the most unpopular war the nation has ever engaged in, under the direction of a president whose approval ratings have hit and maintained historic lows.

With so many factors in place, the values chasm should have been able to sustain itself for years. It should have widened over the last election cycle; instead it narrowed. Specific reasons are many. Corruption dispirited many Christian conservatives, and as that happened, the volume got ratcheted down on some of the most divisive screaming matches, including those on the topic of gay marriage. The increasing unpopularity of the war in Iraq gave opponents on the right and left something to agree on. Libertarians in particular found themselves troubled by civil liberties abuses both here and abroad, and just about everyone was embarrassed by the Terri Schiavo case. But I think there was a more general reason in play as well: We had gone too far; it was time to find another way.

FROM TOP-DOWN TO BOTTOM-UP:
DITCHING THE DEMAGOGUES AND FINDING COMMON GROUND

Here's what I'm convinced happened. Americans stopped listening to their leaders—there was too much noise coming from both sides, and too much wasn't working, whether it was the war, the health care delivery system, the inequitable distribution of wealth, or post–Katrina New Orleans. Instead of being seduced by the old labels that for so long had characterized the political debate—God! Guns! Gonads!—people began to look for more enduring qualities in their elected representatives. Competence, it turned out, did matter, and values, although not specifically Christian ones. As that happened, new areas of commonality arose among people who had been trained always to look first for points of division. Finally, out of this inchoate groping toward a middle ground, what James MacGregor Burns calls the vital center began to reassert itself—the same migrating majority that cre-ated mandates for presidents as diverse as Franklin Roosevelt and Ronald Reagan. A new American dream characterized by lower ex-pectations, less want, and more civility has begun to emerge; and as that has happened, a new American consensus is being born.

Case in point: the Investor Next Door (IND), a broad group of self-identified stock-market stakeholders who range from Warren Buffett to blue-collar workers nursing small 401(k)s. Like the mil-lionaire next door in Thomas J. Stanley and William D. Danko's bestseller of the same name, this investor group is virtually invisible. Its demographics are those of the American people as a whole: young and old; men and women; union members and nonunion workers; whites, African Americans, and Hispanics; affluent and struggling.

Compared to non-investor voters, investor voters are more likely to fall into the thirty- to forty-nine-year-old age group (50 per-cent compared to 40 percent), to be married (67 to 53), to have completed college and perhaps gone on to do graduate work or earn a graduate degree (67 to 44), and to have household income in the $50,000 to $75,000 range (19 to 15) and especially in the $75,000-and-up category (51 to 28). But the group defies easy generalities. One in nine investors is under age thirty, one in three has never com-pleted college, and a little better than a quarter have household in-comes under fifty thousand dollars a year. Racially, investors and non-investors have virtually the same representations.

What sets this group apart isn't that the members own stocks or that they own certain classes of stocks or mutual funds. That can be said of virtually everyone who has any sort of retirement plan. What really sets this group apart and makes it a vital element of the build-ing American consensus is twofold. First, these people think of themselves as investors. When asked "Do you consider yourself to be a member of the investor class?" these investors answer "yes." That might sound like a thin reed on which to hang a demographic bloc, but as I wrote earlier, self-identification counts for a lot. It af-fects how people vote and how they look generally at the world and their lives. Simply put, the Investors Next Door have a capitalist mind-set, but with an important caveat. For a growing percentage of them, money is not everything. Time and again in our surveying, many of these investors show a willingness to forgo maximization of wealth if doing so will serve the greater public good.

Rather than being one-dimensional, today's investor class has to be viewed on a split screen. On the one side are the heirs of J. P. Morgan and the whole *New Yorker* cartoon tradition of fat cats in top hats. On the other are the tens of millions of Americans who were forced into the stock market by the collapse of defined-benefit pension plans and by the rise of 401(k) plans, IRAs, and IRA-type investment programs. The latter group is the Invisible Investors Next Door to most of us. Many of them, in fact, are reluctant market players, and they bear almost no relation to traditional investors. Nearly two in five self-identified stock market participants have portfolios of less than fifty thousand dollars. Roughly three in five have portfolios worth less than $100,000 in value. Fewer than one in three self-identified members of the investor class follow the stock market daily, and more than four in five say they invest in stocks primarily to "save for retirement." Their expectations are modest: About half expect to use their investments to maintain their current lifestyle, and another one in five is just hoping to "provide for a simple retirement." Ten percent are saving for their children's college education. All in all, only 9 percent hope to use their investments for "some luxuries such as vacations and boats."

When we ask investors generally to define success, three in four say it means nothing more than eliminating all credit card debt. To one in three, success is the freedom to make a large charitable donation. Fewer than one in five (18 percent) define success as the ability "to travel anywhere in the world whenever I want," and even fewer (12 percent) think of buying a larger home. Fewer than one in ten say success means owning a luxury car, buying a second home, hiring household staff, mingling with celebrities on an equal basis, or belonging to an exclusive country club.

What wealth is not to them is all-determining. In a 2004 poll we conducted for the PBS show *Wall Street Week with FORTUNE,* we presented alternative investment scenarios to a sample of 652 self-identified investors nationwide. One question went as follows:

WHICH BEST DESCRIBES YOUR VIEWS?

Statement A: The biggest responsibility for a company I own stock in is to make sure that the stock price continues to increase, making a profit for the shareholders, even if it means outsourcing good-paying jobs to countries overseas.

Statement B: While it is important that a company I own stock in makes sure that the stock price continues to rise, it should not be at the expense of good-paying jobs to countries overseas.

Almost three in four (72 percent) agreed with statement B— a company has a social responsibility that simply goes beyond pleasing its stockholders. Subsequent scenarios involved companies that were socially responsible but showed only modest stock performance. In every case, the investors opted for companies that are loyal to their communities, pay fair salaries, hire women and minorities, and maintain good environmental standards over simply strong market performance. Many of these people are, after all, corporate employees themselves, small business owners, and citizens of hard-hit communities. They know who feels the pain when management will do anything to pump share value. And while they care about profit and generally favor pro-business measures, they are also far more likely than commonly assumed to invest their funds in ways that satisfy both their pocketbooks and their consciences. Largely propelled by the Investors Next Door, the number of so-called SRI mutual funds (for Socially Responsible Investing) nearly doubled over the ten years ending in 2007. Total SRI assets under professional management grew more than fourfold, from $639 billion to $2.7 trillion.

My first introduction to the broad dimensions of the investor class came in the late 1990s when Reuters asked us to find out how many Americans owned stocks, mutual funds, and other financial instruments. I kept asking the same questions in subsequent years and pushing deeper into the responses, and as I did, the outlines of a new and important subset of Americans began to emerge, including what to me were some serious demographic surprises amidst all the prevailing camouflage. These investors, I came to see, included substantial numbers of African Americans and Hispanics and other people of generally modest means. That's part of what made them so invisible—they were hiding out in places we don't normally look for stock market participants. Then in 2000, Americans for Tax Reform, led by Republican strategist Grover Norquist, hired Zogby International to do a very detailed poll on investors. Who are these people who call themselves investors, and what do they want? By the time we crunched those numbers, it was clear that these self-identified investors were approaching a majority of the American public, and in fact that number has continued to grow, to as high as 52 percent in polling we did in July 2007.

To Norquist, understandably, this represented a potentially powerful political force, and he and the George W. Bush administration moved quickly in those opening months to exploit the situation by touting what they called the Ownership Society. The idea was brilliant and, in its own way, revolutionary. While the New Deal and the Great Society addressed the needs of the nation's poor and forgotten through an aggressive welfare state, the Ownership Society promised liberation for millions through jobs, home ownership, and a stock portfolio. And despite intervening events that threw the Ownership Society into the shadows, Norquist's inspiration paid off spectacularly in the 2004 presidential contest, across a wide range of demographic groups. The results below are from a Zogby Interactive poll of thirty-seven thousand voters conducted immediately after the election.

OVERALL RESULTS—2004 PRESIDENTIAL ELECTION

	INVESTORS	NON-INVESTORS
Bush	61%	42
Kerry	39	57

**2004 PRESIDENTIAL ELECTION RESULTS BY
DEMOGRAPHIC GROUPS**

	UNION MEMBER		18–29		WOMEN		HISPANIC		$50K–$75K		SINGLE	
	INV	NON	INV	NON	INV	NON	INV	NON	INV	NON	INV	NON
Bush	57%	36	52	32	55	37	60	43	64	45	45	25
Kerry	42	63	47	67	45	63	37	56	36	55	53	73

The trend continued into the 2006 congressional elections when self-identified investors chose Republican candidates over Democratic ones by a 57 to 40 margin, while non-investors went for Democratic candidates by an identical margin. So, do these results suggest that investors will now be a reliable Republican constituency for decades to come? Maybe, but I think that's looking at matters from the wrong end. Investors aren't anyone's constituency. Increasingly, they are defined by a set of values that grow, first, out of their attempts to cope with the new reality of the American experience that has been building for more than a decade—a nation of less, not more—and, second, out of their own sense of social duty and justice.

If the Republicans assume they can continue to force-feed investors generally the same low-tax pro-business policies that traditional Wall Street Republicans clamor for, they will ultimately lose them. To repeat, this is not a one-dimensional group. Many Investors Next Door are in the stock market because they feel they have to be, but on the whole they are not materialistic. Their goals are modest. It's not *things* they want so much as it is *security* for themselves and their families. It's not *politics* they care about so much as it's *fairness* for workers and communities. As much as they supported George W. Bush in the 2004 presidential race, investors also supported the Democrat Eliot Spitzer in his 2006 New York gubernatorial campaign because Spitzer, before his disgrace, had built a record as state attorney general of going after malfeasance that most traditional Wall Street investors would just as soon ignore. Perhaps they're only making a virtue of necessity, but so many investors have moved beyond defining their lives by the size of their paychecks or their estates. Their lives are driven more by purpose than profit or possessions. Indeed, in our 2005 consumer survey, fewer than one in twenty-five members of the investor class agreed that "he who dies with the most stuff wins."

Similarly, if the Democrats assume that the people of color and female segments of these new investors will ultimately come around to them for no other reason than that they are people of color and female, the Democrats are wrong, too, and disastrously so. That this group will go to the Democrats is basically the thesis of an otherwise compelling book, *The Emerging Democratic Majority,* by liberal political activists John Judis and Ruy Teixeira. According to the authors, the future belongs to the Democrats because the fastest growing demographics in the early twenty-first century are those that have historically tended to support the party: Hispanics, African Americans, women, South Asians, and so on. The math is right, to be sure, but the reasoning is all wrong. Demographics are not destiny, in politics or in life.

An example: By and large, election after election, African Americans vote about 90 percent Democratic, but in the last presidential election, only 74 percent of black investors voted for John Kerry. That's a huge difference, and if you'll look to the table on the previous page, you'll see the same vast swing with Hispanics and union members and women, although those margins mostly disappeared in the 2006 congressional races when nearly all things Republican sank like a stone. The point to be made is that assuming anyone's vote because of race or ethnicity or gender is the short road to political oblivion. Self-identification will always trump imposed labels in the end because labels are slapped on from above while self-identification grows out of daily experience, and daily experience forges our values. It's values, not demographics, that finally determine how people vote, what they want, and what kind of America they dream of, for themselves, their children, and their grandchildren. That's really where the action is in America today—not in politics but in the American dream itself. Of all the tectonic plates that are shifting beneath us, this is the one that is driving everything else forward with it.

FROM THE LAND OF PLENTY TO LIVING WITH LIMITS:
THE *REAL* REALITY SHOW

The old American dream never strayed far from the promise of un-fettered capitalism and those still-stirring words from the opening paragraphs of the Declaration of Independence: "We hold these truths to be self-evident, that all men are created equal." This was the land without artificial boundaries: of caste, of place of birth, of parentage. With enough hard work, a man could become a king, every family could own the roof over its head, and each new entrepreneur had a shot at being the next Rockefeller or Ford or Carnegie.

Even for those who didn't crack the big time, there was a chicken waiting in every pot, two cars in every driveway, a television in every bedroom. For our children, the future was boundless. America, the beautiful. America, the meritocracy. America, the land of endless optimism—a place where, as de Tocqueville wrote, there was "a lively faith in the perfectability of man."

The new American dream, I've found, is far more textured be-cause the American experience at the start of the twenty-first cen-tury is so different from what it was just a half century ago. We still dream great things for our children, but today we do so within the context of the new limits in our own lives. Fifty years ago, housing was cheap. College was within financial reach of most middle-class Americans—and just about all World War II veterans. The Ameri-can workforce was hierarchical and predictable; and thanks to pen-sions, labor unions, and Social Security, the future was taken care of, at least the basics.

Today, so much of that has evaporated or is quickly vanishing. Watch the morning television shows, for example, and you'll be swamped with stories about our citizens' growing indebtedness. And in fact, in our polling, four in five Americans say household debt is a serious problem. Almost half call it a "very serious problem," and a high percentage of those have lived so long in debt or at the edge of debt that they no longer dream of palaces or even home ownership. Combine this with the fact that in excess of 25 percent of adult Americans earn less than they once did, up from 14 percent in 1990, and you'll see why people are feeling less optimistic.

I find those to be breathtaking statistics—this in what has so long been the land of plenty!—but what I find even more startling, and more telling, is how broadly the numbers apply. In a Zogby Interactive poll conducted in late February and early March 2007, we asked respondents to choose which of the following three statements best applied to their credit card debt:

Statement A:	I don't worry about it. I can handle payments and know I'll pay off the balance eventually.
Statement B:	Sometimes I worry a little that it will take me a long time to pay down my credit card debt.
Statement C:	I'm very worried about my credit card debt and sometimes feel like I'll never be able to pay it off.

In all, 55 percent of respondents chose either statement B or statement C, and there was amazing agreement across the subgroups. Geographically, 57 percent of Easterners went with B or C, 51 percent of Southerners, 56 percent of respondents from the central and Great Lakes states, and 58 percent of Westerners. Union members compared to nonunion workers broke down even more closely: 57 percent of union cardholders and 54 percent of noncardholders were either a little or very worried about their Visa and MasterCard debts. That narrow pattern held throughout. Fifty-three percent of those who described themselves as born-again worried about credit card debt, as did 54 percent of non-born-agains or those who weren't sure whether they had or had not been touched by some divine hand. Fifty-two percent of married people answered in the affirmative, as did 54 percent of those living in civil unions. For those serving in the armed forces, 54 percent said yes; 46 percent said no, they didn't worry. The spread grew slightly larger when we segmented the results down by political affiliation: 59 percent of Democrats fretted about their credit card debt compared with 53 percent of Republicans and 51 percent of independents. But when it came to worrying, a majority of all three groups said, yes, they did. The one group not alarmed by credit card debt was the one least likely to use the cards and the one protected by Social Security: Roughly three in five of those age sixty-five and older told us they don't sweat their credit card balances at all.

We saw the same broad pattern of agreement when we asked in a February 2007 poll "Can you imagine yourself becoming poor?" Fewer than half of the elderly said yes. That's in part the Social Security factor, but it's also reflective of life-cycle issues. The elderly aren't buying $125 sneakers in triplicate for their children, they have probably made their last mortgage payment, and while their incomes tend to be low, their net worth is often higher than other age cohorts. Among all other age groups, roughly three in five or more said, yes, they could imagine themselves in poverty. Large- and small-city and rural residents were within two points of one another. Slightly fewer self-described suburbanites said yes, but even in the supposedly happy golden streets of suburbia, 54 percent could see themselves impoverished. When we broke the results down by religious affiliation, the rate was highest among those who never or rarely attend church, but only 3 percentage points separated those who attend church at least once a week and those who go only on holidays, and born-agains and non-born-agains were closer than that. The same tight formation held for Wal-Mart shoppers: 61 percent of those who shop at Wal-Mart weekly could see themselves in poverty, as could 59 percent of those who shop at the famous discounter only once or twice a year. Amazingly enough, this exercise in poverty imagining extended even to 53 percent of those who earn in excess of $100,000 a year.

These aren't numbers that can be laid at the feet of a single demographic or geographical niche. It's not a red or blue state phenomenon. It's not just spendthrift large-city East Coast atheists who are worrying about credit card debt, or born-again Hispanic Wal-Mart regulars who dream about tumbling into poverty. The one positive result of all this insecurity is that it's uniting us around a set of shared values.

FROM JOB SECURITY TO JOB ANXIETY:
TAKING THE PUNCHES AS THEY COME

America, we're told, is a knowledge society; education is the key that unlocks the door. Yet over the last thirty years, in-state tuition and fees at public four-year colleges and universities across the country have grown ninefold, while already high private university fees have gone even higher. Today, under these economic pressures, so many Americans are shown the path to success and simultaneously denied access to it—unless they want to incur crippling debt or go through what has become a perilous back door into higher education and technical training: the all-volunteer army and National Guard. Little wonder our society sometimes seems bipolar, or at the least suffering from cognitive dissonance. We are a land of constant mixed messages.

Job security that once appeared to be an American birthright is increasingly rare. When we asked about the subject in June 2006—not long after the unemployment rate had dipped to a five-year low of 4.7 percent—40 percent of respondents said they were either concerned about the future or in unstable work situations, and another 9 percent said they could lose their jobs at any moment. This isn't security; this is high anxiety. But the point is that people aren't in revolution; they're not marching in the streets. Yes, as I write, some politicians are posturing all over the place about immigration and protecting American jobs, but the people who are losing the jobs, as opposed to the ones who are talking about the people who are losing the jobs, are adjusting. They're altering their ambitions; they're tweaking their values to bring them in line with the realities of their lives because those realities have been going on so long and because they have so little choice.

My own workplace serves as an example. I still live in the town where I grew up—Utica, in beautiful upstate New York. Zogby International operates out of twenty thousand square feet in a large brick building that began life as a textile mill, then became a GE Aerospace facility, and is now home to among other businesses my globally driven information company. Plenty of people in Utica still remember the previous two tenants, and some felt the whipsaw effect each time one of them closed down, and endured the tension of waiting for a new tenant to move in and start hiring. As with my brick building, so with the community as a whole. Since the 1970s, we've lost defense contractors and aerospace firms, and we've seen a huge air force base, Griffiss, close down. My own home in the city lost 40 percent of its value as the local economy sank and then seemed on the edge of collapsing. But the men and women who come to work at my place every weekday or the ones I see walking into O'scugnizzo's Pizzeria on Bleecker Street for the best damn pizza on the North American continent aren't broken or dispirited. They've redefined themselves as service workers; they've learned new skills and found employment in back-office businesses and photonics development and, for that matter, in polling. I just expanded my own workforce by one hundred fifty people.

Often, the pay isn't as good. Job security is nowhere near what it was thirty years ago, or at least what we all thought it was and would forever be back then. Outside of a few precious spots such as Washington, D.C., and its ever-expanding bureaucracy, that's the way things are in America. But every day in Utica, I see people picking themselves up off the floor, making the adjustments they need to make to compete, and jumping back into the battle in whatever ways they can. It's nothing short of heroic, and it's happening all over the country.

In our June 2006 polling, a third of respondents said that in order to adapt to a more dynamic job marketplace, they would be willing to change workplaces, take courses to stay abreast of developments and gain new skills, or change careers. Almost two in five said they would be willing to do all three, and only 12 percent said they would do none of the above.

One other thing people, unlike politicians, aren't doing: They're not throwing blame all over the place—at immigrants for wanting to come to America or at Hispanics for not speaking English. To be sure, many communities are split on the subject. You don't have to channel surf long at the evening news hour to find screamers with steam pouring out of their ears as they decry the jobs lost to illegal workers. But this is one of those issues where majorities matter less than intensity. The loudest voice wins airtime, and airtime shapes the debate. But the people intuit what the polls show—that 80 percent of Hispanics want their kids to learn English—and for the most part, that's good enough for them. They've got more important things to worry about.

FROM PRADA TO DOLLAR GENERAL: BUYING DOWN, NOT UP

The American dream still exists; it's not going anywhere. But in so many ways, it's being refashioned and repackaged to reflect the new circumstances of so many of our lives. Americans work differently from how they once did. Job hierarchies have been flattened. Especially in the high-tech sector, old formalities have disappeared. Whatever their product, multinationals are 24/7, synchronous with financial markets and workplaces around the world. Jobs come and go, and for the many struggling to make ends meet, jobs turn into two minimum-wage shifts a day with barely time to sleep in between.

Even many of those who make enough money to participate in the old aspirations are showing shifting priorities, to establish and commit to a broader purpose. Instead of keeping up with the Joneses, they're plugging into a growing global consciousness that emphasizes a greater sense of what is truly valuable and what is not, what they must have and what they can let go.

As the table below shows, a surprising number of Americans say they shop, even for the necessities, with the same sense of social responsibility they bring to their stock portfolio and to the ballot box.

IMPORTANCE OF POLITICAL VALUES IN CONSUMER DECISIONS FOR WOMEN

FACTOR	% SAYING VERY IMPORTANT
Environmental friendliness	44
Human rights record of country	37
Child labor used	51

A March 2007 Gallup poll turned up similar results, with 70 percent of respondents saying that the environmental record of a company was "an important, but not the most important factor" in determining whether they would buy one of its products. Do such sentiments translate into direct action? Do people who talk the talk of social responsibility actually walk the walk when they get into the store? The evidence there is largely anecdotal—the roaring success of the environmentally friendly Toyota Prius, for example, or the growing demand for fair-trade coffee. But to me the anecdotal evidence is becoming powerful enough to suggest that, yes, the answers people provide to such questions do indeed have, in the aggregate, a direct effect on where they shop, what they buy, and who they buy it from.

There's also an accompanying shift to focus on functionality rather than form. We see it time and again in our surveys of shopping motives. Whether it's refrigerators or stoves, men and women say they buy first for utility and performance. "Look and feel" comes far down the line, roughly half as important for both sexes. Far below that is the old shopper's high: "Just gives pleasure." Even with a fashion statement like coats, men *and* women select based on utility and performance more than look, feel, and pleasure.

None of this is to say that luxury shopping is dead, or that every label will eventually have to read like a U.N.-approved promise of social responsibility. There will of course always be a market for the one-of-a-kind designer items displayed in full-page ads in the "Sunday Styles" section of *The New York Times*. Prada and Hermès might die from mismanagement, but they won't perish from an atrophying customer base. But (if you're looking for a market that's going to grow ahead of the population curve, you would do far better to study the "dollar" retailers that are undercutting even Wal-Mart and Costco.)

With their jumble of low-price items spilling off overcrowded shelves, Dollar Store, Family Dollar, Dollar Tree, and especially Dollar General, the largest American retailer with 8,260 outlets, are where the rubber meets the road in the new American dream. In effect, Dollar General and the others have turned themselves into a loosely organized seven-day-a-week yard sale, a bargain hunter's bonanza, and to great success. Henry Kravis's KKR private equity firm not long ago paid $6.9 billion to take Dollar General private, the largest buyout ever of a U.S. retailer. For its part, Dollar Tree has seen net sales grow fourfold and outlets threefold since 1998, while Big Lots—a discount retailer of otherwise discontinued goods—has doubled net sales over the same time frame.

One of my first jobs was at a Utica grocery store chain called, strangely enough, Chicago Markets. After bagging groceries for a while, I became one of several produce clerks. Early each day, we would stack the lettuce heads and oranges, and just about every morning a little old Italian guy named Tony would stand there watching us and give us the same advice: "Looka, the only thing you ever gotta learn—pile 'em up high, sell 'em low." That's what is happening with the entire economy now: It's being driven from the bottom. Social scientists describe "cultural lag" as a phenomenon whereby the population is slow to perceive the reality of change on the ground. In this case, quite to the contrary, the public understands the new American dream just fine. While political leaders seem to stumble from day to day in near-utter dark, the public is trimming expectations, making do with less, and finding a subdued peace in the process.

FROM DIVIDE AND CONQUER TO UNITE AND LEAD:
WHAT VOTERS WANT TODAY

In the spring of 2007, Zogby International released the first "values" poll tied to the 2008 presidential campaign. Based on a telephone survey conducted May 17–20 of nearly a thousand likely voters, the poll carried a margin of error of ±3.2 percentage points. The results follow:

TRAIT IN A PRESIDENT	% OF LIKELY VOTERS WHO RATE TRAIT AS "VERY IMPORTANT"	% OF INDEPENDENTS WHO RATE TRAIT AS "VERY IMPORTANT"
Is a competent manager	82	79
Can bring the American people together	80	77
Can command the military	76	70
Has personal morality	76	77
Can promote the image of the U.S. abroad	73	71
Can cross the aisle to win support from the opposition	58	60
Has Christian values in his or her personal life	46	38
Has diplomatic experience	46	39
Stands strongly with his or her party	42	26
Has successful business experience	36	28
Has state experience	35	28
Is a charismatic speaker	32	30
Has been a legislator	21	16

Breaking down the numbers provided a valuable snapshot of the various campaigns at that moment in time. Rudy Giuliani and Hillary Clinton ran well ahead of their competitors when we asked who would be the most competent manager among the Republican and Democratic candidates for president. On the subject of bringing the American people together, Giuliani again topped the Republicans, with 22 percent. On the Democratic side, Barack Obama also drew 22 percent but from a broader base. Nine percent of Republicans saw him as the candidate best positioned to bring the American people together. As for leading the military, John McCain stood all alone. A third of all those polled named him as the best choice, including nearly half (46 percent) of those who identified themselves as moderates.

For political pollsters, that kind of data is like mother's milk: We can live off it for weeks until the ground shifts, a campaign implodes, and we have to scramble for the next new thing. To me, what was more interesting and less ephemeral about this particular poll was what it said about the desire of voters for a middle way. Seven years after first electing a president who promised to be a "uniter, not a divider," Americans were thirstier than ever for just that. "Competent manager" and "command the military" are prerequisites for the presidency, especially in troubled times and after four-plus years of a war that seems to have been mismanaged from the beginning. In every other instance, when voters were given a choice between a divisive trait and a uniting one, they chose the latter.

Among all likely voters, about two in five rated "stands strongly with his or her party" as an important trait, while three in five gave high marks to "can cross the aisle to win support from the opposition." That's a big enough spread in its own right, but if you look to independents, the margin between the two statements is more than double—26 percent to 60 percent. Experience as a legislator counted nearly for nil among all those polled. What institution in American life has been more bitterly partisan over the last decade than the U.S. House and Senate, from the Republican attempt to impeach Bill Clinton to the Democratic attempt to impose a timetable for troop withdrawal from Iraq? Meanwhile, seven in ten voters rated as very important the ability to promote the U.S. image abroad—this after seven years of go-it-alone foreign policy, and an in-your-face U.N. ambassador in John Bolton. In polling we did in April 2007 for the group Business for Diplomatic Action, seven in ten respondents endorsed the need to change U.S. foreign policy; six in ten said the U.S. needed to "build bridges" to the rest of the world, not "build fences" between America and its neighbors; and three in four said they were very or somewhat concerned about America's reputation in the world. What was telling, in that latter figure, was that those who were very concerned outnumbered those who were somewhat so.

Even on the subject of personal behavior, voters chose the milder, more centrist path: About three quarters of all those polled ranked "has personal morality" as very important, but only 46 percent were willing to put a specifically Christian face on that morality. Among independents, twice as many opted for personal morality as chose Christian values. In 2004 Election Day polling by Harris Interactive, highly divisive Christian right agenda items such as "marriage protection" and "pro-life" outranked even "honesty" as "very important" reasons for voting for George W. Bush, and "belief in God" and "biblical values" finished not far behind a simple dedication to the truth. (The results of my polling tell me that the coalition of angry Christians is in sharp retreat. People want more from their president than a perfect attendance record at the local prayer breakfast.)

Far from being an exception, results like these are becoming commonplace. Left and right, conservative and liberal, Wal-Mart regulars and Wal-Mart nevers aren't suddenly going to agree on all of the hot-button issues. The American people were not meant all to sing from the same hymnal. But they are showing more of a willingness to listen to one another and attempt to find common cause. They are reasserting a center, not only in politics—although, that's certainly what happened in the elections of 2006—but in the great moral and issue debates of our time as well. And as they do, the broad margins of a new national consensus are starting to form.

Over the years, I've had plenty of opportunity to ponder the conflicting values of Americans as they show up in my polling. I can remember back in 1994 asking New York State residents if they agreed or disagreed that destroying a fetus was tantamount to manslaughter. A majority agreed that it was. Five questions further on, a majority also endorsed a woman's right to choose. Five years later, a majority of respondents were telling us that they disapproved of Bill Clinton's personal behavior but thought the nation's moral compass was fine and that even presidents have a right to privacy.

Those conflicting values go on, but now for the first time in decades, we actually have discussions going on about some of the subjects that most conflict us. Pro-lifers are talking about poverty as one of the consequences of having unwanted children. Pro-choice people are willing to discuss adoption as an alternative to terminating pregnancies. Meanwhile, as I mentioned earlier, eighteen- to twenty-nine-year-olds both approve of a woman's right to choose *and* think abortion is almost always morally wrong. Granted, that's a conundrum, but thinking through such seeming contradictions is how we'll get beyond the intractability that has plagued the abortion discussion since the *Roe* v. *Wade* decision.

Recall the unmitigated stink that has been raised by religious right leaders such as James Dobson of Focus on the Family over everything from abortion to homosexuality and Terri Schiavo, and then remember the vast outpouring of approval when Rick Warren invited Barack Obama to his twenty-thousand-member Saddleback Church in Lake Forest, California, to discuss AIDS and world poverty. And then ask yourself who is the future of the evangelical Christian movement: Dobson or Warren? I think the answer is obvious. Since early 2006, Zogby International has been tracking the growing moderation among evangelicals and born-agains. It's a very real phenomenon.

Ask simple questions on stem cell research, and you'll get simple answers. Pro-lifers oppose it because they believe that harvesting stem cells will result in the destruction of fetuses. Pro-choicers are for it although certainly many of them would welcome some alternative technology such as the recent experiments on "reprogramming" skin cells of mice to become stem cells. But if you drill down into the answers, things change. When I ask conservatives if they have in their household or immediate circle of friends someone who suffers from Parkinson's, ALS, Alzheimer's, or other diseases that might be amenable to stem cell therapy, I discover that people who say yes to that question are as much as 25 percentage points more likely to support research, whatever their feelings about abortion and fetus harvesting.

FROM BLOC VOTING TO WEB SURFING:
WHY THE INTERNET IS MAKING US BETTER CITIZENS

So it goes with question after question and poll after poll. Time and again, faced with rants and posturing from both sides, Americans are finding their own solutions, in their own ways, through their own reasoning. They're using the Internet and other technologies to access information that would have been unavailable to most people as recently as twenty years ago. They are reaching out through e-mail and chat rooms to other views and other life stories.

Overall, about three in four adult Americans have Internet access. Among likely voters, the ratio rises to nine in ten. Before long, we will have almost full Internet penetration among voters, and they will be doing more—much more—than checking their e-mail occasionally. Two in five Americans already spend more than ten hours a week online, including about a third of Americans age sixty-five or older. Another one in five spends six to ten hours weekly—more than an hour a day for most of those people. A little more than half the time people go online, we've found, they head first to their e-mail accounts, but that means that just about half the time, they don't. They check the news or sports. They research using Google or Yahoo! They check in with their own affinity groups—from politics to hobbies to medical issues.

Inevitably, a good deal of Internet activity merely reinforces points of view already deeply held—the Internet is a great place for radical points of view to cocoon with one another—but as often as not, I'm convinced, the Internet also broadens us. It exposes us, sometimes painfully, to other views. The Al Jazeera website (english .aljazeera.net), to cite one example, can be maddening to many Americans, but if you want to learn how the U.S. is seen and portrayed in a key part of the Arab media world, there are few better windows. Even the BBC website (www.bbc.co.uk) gives a view of the world much different from that of mainstream American news purveyors. More so than it divides and isolates us, the Internet empowers us with knowledge. It allows us to take our curiosity global. And as that happens, old stereotypes start to break down, dialogue begins, and new solutions emerge.

That's where we are now—at the start of a new dialogue, in the midst of one huge tectonic shift, and sliding along four subsidiary tremors. I take up the first of those four subsidiary tremors next.

A QUICK GUIDE TO MARKETING TO THE NEW AMERICAN CONSENSUS

- Don't let niche marketing and micro-targeting blind you to the many ideas and values that most of us share. Market with the medicines that heal, not just with the sharp objects that cut.
- Appeal to the best in us, not our baser instincts: Washington and Lincoln emphasized common goals when we were perilously split; Wilson and Franklin Roosevelt promoted the quest for freedom; Kennedy and Reagan issued calls to a higher order. Marketers can do the same.
- Respect the public. Americans are moving into a better future on their own. Help them.
- Social responsibility counts, for investors and consumers.
- Common sense counts, too. People today are less interested in luxury and extravagance than in comfort, convenience, costs, and the dictates of a growing global consciousness.
- Remember: *reasonable,* not *big.*
- And forget about the bumper sticker: Americans are *not* spending their children's inheritance.

3

Dematerializing the Paradigm

**LEANER, SMALLER, MORE PERSONAL,
AND PERSONALIZED**

Seismic shifts can be slow, but they are seldom gentle. The underlying plates grind together, or they pull apart. Mountains are thrown up. Rifts open, whether they are the literal chasms of geological shifts or the metaphorical ones of social change. That's where America is today: Old paradigms are toppling; new ones are rising out of their rubble as the future begins to take shape and form.

In fact, America often seems bipolar these days, trapped between two competing views of what it is and what it will be. At the one extreme stands the Yale historian Paul Kennedy, who argued in his controversial 1989 tome *The Rise and Fall of the Great Powers* that the era of the superpower is dead and gone. By Kennedy's reasoning, the Soviet Union simply imploded first, more exhausted than America by the forty-year cold war. The United States, Kennedy contends, is sure to follow. Neoconservatives take the opposite view, envisioning the broad spread of U.S.-style capitalist democracy throughout the world—a fulfillment of national destiny that, despite occasional setbacks (Iraq, for example), will ultimately usher in a global Pax Americana.

My polling and that of many others paints a middle ground, but with a distinct twist. A majority of Americans do want the United States to be a force for good—good for other nations, good for the environment, good for the global economy—but they neither relish the role of a superpower nor expect their leaders to act unilaterally in pursuit of national objectives. Whatever abstract world the Paul Kennedys and neoconservatives might live in, these Americans see the real world they occupy as a constrained place, not one of imminent decline or limitless opportunities, and they are rapidly losing faith in the large institutions that traditionally have shaped American society, most notably the largest mega-institution of them all: the federal government.

Here are some numbers to consider in the continuing drama of the ever-evolving American spirit. These come from the Gallup Organization, which has been doing this work well for a long time.

In a May 1972 poll, 70 percent of those surveyed said they had either a great deal or a fair amount of trust and confidence in the federal government's ability to handle domestic problems. By 1998, and again in 2000, that combined total had slipped to 65 percent. According to the most recent Gallup poll on the subject, conducted in September 2007, fewer than half of all Americans—47 percent—expressed at least a moderate trust and confidence in Washington's ability to cope with domestic problems.

The news is no better on the international side. In May 1972, three in four of all those surveyed by Gallup expressed confidence in the government's capacity to deal with problems around the world. By 1998, roughly three in five said the same. In September 2007, a bare majority—51 percent—expressed such trust.

Not surprisingly, the executive and legislative branches have seen their ratings fall in tandem with those for the overall efficacy of the federal government: for Congress, from 71 percent in 1972 to 61 percent in 1998 to 50 percent in 2007; for the executive branch, from 71 percent in the first year of the second Richard Nixon administration to 43 percent in the third year of the second George W. Bush administration. Of the three governmental branches, only the judiciary has seen an increase in public esteem over the same thirty-five-year time frame: a slight bump from 66 percent in 1972 to 69 percent in 2007. When Gallup asked in more general terms how many respondents had at least some trust and confidence in the men and women who occupy public offices or seek them, the numbers slid from 65 percent in 1972, near the height of the Vietnam War protests, to 55 percent in the fall of 2007.

More specific polling on some of the leading issues of our time offers up an equally dispiriting picture. When Zogby Interactive asked roughly ten thousand adults in a February 2007 poll for United Press International whether the U.S. health care system functioned properly and needed no reform, functioned adequately but needed minor reform, or functioned inadequately and needed major reform, only 6 percent chose the first option. The rest were evenly split between minor and major reform. When we broke the responses down by type of health insurance, no group gave the current health care system higher than a 7 percent approval rating.

A month earlier, in January 2007, Gallup surveyed a little more than a thousand respondents on how satisfied they were with the quality of public education in the nation. A mere 11 percent answered "very satisfied" and another 30 percent "somewhat satisfied." On the negative side, 29 percent said they were somewhat dissatisfied and 28 percent said they were very dissatisfied. As we'll see shortly, my polling on environmental matters yields similar results. On question after question, a plurality of Americans expresses dissatisfaction with energy policy; they worry about degradation of the air they breathe and the water they drink; and they fault the Bush administration for failing to embrace international cooperation on such potentially devastating issues as global warming.

From Hurricane Katrina, Americans carried away the dual lesson that their government (a) could not protect them from natural disaster, and (b) wouldn't succor them much when disaster did strike, especially the most needy among them—one large reason why I'm convinced historians will ultimately treat Katrina as a more significant moment in American history than 9/11. From the seemingly endless war in Iraq, Americans are also learning that to be a sole superpower in the world today is perhaps more burden than blessing.)

So what's going on here? Have the American people fallen, justifiably or not, into a permanent state of depression? Instead of the American Century, are the years ahead fated to be the Zoloft ones? Or the Bitching Time?

In fact, something different, deeper, and more structural is going on. Yes, Americans are abandoning government and other dominant hierarchies of society as a directive force in many aspects of their lives. They recognize clearly, even if their leaders don't, the new limits on the exercise of American power, on the resources we consume, the waste we generate, the stuff we have. They know in their bones that the land of seemingly inexhaustible plenty their fathers inherited is not the land they will be passing on to their children. But rather than being depressed by all this—and far from the arrogant, self-centered, my-way-or-the-highway image of Americans so many beyond our shores believe in—these are people willing to search for ways to live more gently and collegially on the planet. Not only are they assuming personal responsibility for many of the decisions long forced on them by the mega-institutions of American society; they are redefining the institutions as they do so and finding themselves empowered in the process.)

While Americans watch their president being dragged kicking and screaming into acknowledging that global warming might have a scientific basis, they are already making adjustments in their own lives to cut down on energy usage, to make do with less. And they are rewarding the companies that appear ready to help them along the way. In their book *Green to Gold,* Daniel C. Esty and Andrew S. Winston cite studies that show the British petroleum giant BP has increased its brand value by a staggering $3 billion simply by positioning itself as the environmentally sensitive "Beyond Petroleum" company.

Americans see their leadership pursuing a lone-wolf foreign policy when what they long for is power-sharing, not power-grabbing. The public wants the nation to be a force, not use force in the world. In my polling, clear majorities of Americans favor acting in concert with NATO and the United Nations to cool down global hot spots. In the relatively few years since 9/11, patriotism has declined dramatically as a marketing tool for selling everything from wars to autos.

Americans look out at the wreckage of the hierarchies that for so long sustained them—bureaucracy-encrusted public school systems, the great industrial giants that curtailed or abandoned pension obligations to their employees, a Roman Catholic Church more interested in hiding aberrant priests than in seeing them prosecuted—and they have been voting with their feet there, too. Roughly two million children are being homeschooled in the United States, an enrollment that is growing by about 10 percent annually and now includes over 15 percent minority students.

In polling we did in September 2007, overwhelming majorities of all age groups and all political persuasions told us they would prefer to work for a lean business over a large corporation. The only subset that bucked the trend were Republicans age eighteen to twenty-nine. Otherwise, Democrats, Republicans, and independents young and old were united in believing that, in the workplace, small is beautiful. A 2005 Harris Interactive survey of nearly eight thousand American workers age eighteen and over produced similar results. Despite vast discrepancies in compensation, bonuses, and stock options between large and small companies, employees of the latter reported far greater job satisfaction. More than half of those who worked for companies with fewer than fifty employees said they "feel passionate" about their jobs. At companies with five thousand or more employees, only 36 percent of workers could say the same.

People are seeking less hierarchy today, not more. They want choice, not imposition, and they are demanding to be treated as individuals. Using the Internet, Americans are democratizing access to universities and breaking up the hegemony of what was once a handful of dominant news organizations. Old delivery systems of knowledge and information are being reduced to electronic demate-rialized blips, and in the process the public itself is forcing the old paradigms that stand behind those delivery systems to reinvent or die. This is life in the opening decade of the twenty-first century: smaller, leaner, more personal, and personalized, and Americans seem to be adjusting to it just fine.

FROM CONSPICUOUS CONSUMPTION TO SAVING PLANET EARTH: BUILDING NEW CONSTITUENCIES IN A RESTRICTED WORLD

Because energy usage touches on so many issues—personal com-fort levels (how high is the heat in winter, how low the AC in sum-mer?), the monthly budget, environmental concerns, geopolitics (where's the oil going to come from?), and more—polling data on energy provides an especially useful barometer of broad shifts in public attitudes and behavior. In February 1979, the Gallup Orga-nization asked a series of questions exploring people's adjustments to rising energy costs. With the revolution in Iran under way, the newspapers were already raising the specter of a replay of the 1973 OPEC embargo when crude oil prices had almost tripled. Twenty-eight years later, with per-gallon prices hitting three dol-lars and higher, we repeated the Gallup questions, adding "hybrid car" to the first one since such cars didn't exist in 1979. Here's the comparison:

OF THE FOLLOWING ENERGY-SAVING MEASURES, WHICH HAVE YOU ADOPTED IN YOUR PERSONAL LIFE TO CONSERVE ON ENERGY?

	GALLUP 1979 (BY %)	ZOGBY 2007 (BY %)
Buying more fuel-efficient (or hybrid) car	5	29
Making sure lights are turned off when leaving the room or house	27	89

**OF THE FOLLOWING ENERGY-SAVING MEASURES,
WHICH HAVE YOU ADOPTED IN YOUR PERSONAL LIFE
TO CONSERVE ON ENERGY?** *(continued)*

	GALLUP 1979 (BY %)	ZOGBY 2007 (BY %)
Adjusting heating or air-conditioning to use less power (or be off completely when not home or at night)	44	86
Using less water (for example, not letting water run while brushing teeth, or taking shorter showers)	2	60

Shifts of this magnitude simply aren't explicable in purely economic terms. The energy price gaps between then and now don't justify multiples of two and three, much less of thirty. Instead, the shifts are reflective of a fundamental rethinking of American consumption patterns, coupled with a self-criticism of our excesses, national and individual, and underlined by the continuing geopolitical consequences of our dependence on foreign and particularly Middle Eastern oil.

When we asked in a September 2006 poll whether the United States should (a) sharply reduce oil imports from the Middle East to avoid indirectly supporting groups that mean to do harm to American interests, (b) sharply increase imports to encourage the establishment of democratic institutions in the region, or (c) continue current import levels because our reliance on Middle Eastern oil has nothing to do with the political or military conflicts in the region, fewer than one in four respondents went for the last choice. That number varied by no more than six percentage points when we broke the answers down by age, party affiliation, region of the country, gun ownership, and active-duty armed forces.

Americans, in short, are mostly united on the larger consequences of our oil consumption, and they are equally united on the need to do something about it on the home front. On page 63 are the responses to an Interactive poll we did in January 2007 for UPI. This is not the profile of Americans who are determined to remain an unchecked "people of plenty," or who even think that is possible any longer.

DO YOU . . . THAT THE U.S. IS TOO RELIANT ON NONRENEWABLE FOSSIL FUELS (OIL, COAL, NATURAL GAS)?

Strongly agree	64%
Somewhat agree	25
Total Agree	**89**

THINKING ABOUT AMERICA'S USE OF OIL, WHICH OF THE FOLLOWING STATEMENTS BEST REFLECTS YOUR THINKING ON THE SUBJECT?

Statement A:	America should use as much oil as it needs to keep it growing.	30%
Statement B:	America should balance its oil consumption with that of other important economies to make sure that everyone has enough to meet their needs without shortages or price spikes.	50
Statement C:	America should now reduce its oil consumption to spare more for other nations who are trying to grow their economies and provide jobs for their citizens.	10

REGARDLESS OF THE TYPE OR SOURCE, DO YOU THINK THE UNITED STATES USES . . .

Too much energy	64%
Not enough energy	3
The right amount of energy	27

DO YOU . . . THAT THE U.S. GOVERNMENT SHOULD ACT TO REDUCE ENERGY USE IN THE U.S. EVEN IF THAT MEANS SIGNIFICANT CHANGES IN YOUR LIFESTYLE?

Strongly agree	26%
Somewhat agree	33
Total Agree	**59**
Somewhat disagree	14
Strongly disagree	23
Total Disagree	**37**

In other polling, we asked if oil drilling should be allowed in the Arctic National Wildlife Refuge as a way of easing our dependence on foreign oil. Respondents were split just about evenly on that issue, for and against, but then we brought the issue closer to home and to the pocketbook by asking respondents to agree or disagree with the following statement: "The U.S. government should decrease environmental regulations governing oil refineries so the American oil industry will build more of them, making it easier for the industry to meet consumer demand for gasoline." The results: Only 24 percent strongly agreed and another 18 percent somewhat agreed. On the negative side, 13 percent somewhat disagreed and 42 percent strongly disagreed, even though more refineries would almost certainly lower fuel bills and shorten gas lines. Among eighteen- to twenty-nine-year-olds, the divide was even sharper: Fewer than 15 percent strongly agreed that environmental regulations should be eased, while 52 percent strongly disagreed.

In still other polling, 42 percent of respondents told us that the United States should sign the Kyoto global warming treaty. Half that amount, 21 percent, disagreed, while 35 percent answered "not familiar enough"—which was not surprising, given the complicated terms and the warring sound bites that have surrounded the treaty. Again, one could dismiss all this as the normal fluctuations of a hot-button political issue if the numbers were even close, but the fact that double the people with opinions support a treaty that the Republican party in general has stridently opposed suggests that GOP strategists may be losing touch not only with the rank-and-file of the voting public but with the party's own base supporters, including the most religious among them.

The late Jerry Falwell liked to belittle concerns over global warming as "Satan's attempt" to divert Christians from evangelism to environmentalism, but to most Americans, including many younger evangelicals, environmentalism and global warming are very real concerns. In a February 2007 survey by the Pew Forum on

Religion and Public Life, two in three evangelicals under age thirty agreed that the United States was "losing ground" on pollution, as did nearly two in five evangelicals thirty and over.

In surveying done prior to the 2006 congressional elections, 51 percent of white evangelicals told Pew that "scientists agree on global warming," while only 37 percent felt the scientific opinion was still unsettled, a contention reluctantly abandoned by President Bush and one still pushed by industry leaders such as former Exxon-Mobil CEO Lee Raymond. (The comparable numbers for white mainline Protestants were 58 and 30 percent.) Sixty-eight percent of white evangelicals (as opposed to 79 percent of all Americans) felt global warming was a "serious" or "very serious" problem; and while 38 percent of white evangelicals felt that stricter environmental regulations would "hurt the economy," 47 percent said the regulations would be "worth the cost." (For all white Protestants, the split on "hurt the economy" compared to "worth the cost" was 34 percent to 53 percent; secularists split 14 to 76.)

With the religious right, it's not just talk, either. The Evangelical Environmental Network made a big splash with its What Would Jesus Drive? campaign that targeted gas-guzzling cars. At a 2006 antiabortion rally in Washington, Richard Cizik, chief lobbyist for the thirty-million-member National Association of Evangelicals, carried a banner that read STOP MERCURY POISONING OF THE UNBORN. Far from spurning science, Cizik and others at the rally handed out literature citing federal government studies that have found one in six babies in the nation are born with elevated mercury levels. In his PBS documentary *Is God Green?* Bill Moyers profiled evangelical West Virginians who have formed Christians for the Mountains to combat the environmental degradation caused by mining. The evangelical magazine *Christianity Today* has weighed in on the issue, too, urging Christians to "make it clear to governments and businesses that we are willing to adapt our lifestyles and support steps toward changes that protect our environment."

Even on the subject of the environmentalist movement generally—one of the longtime whipping boys of the political right—white evangelicals are parting ways with their old leadership. Nearly half, 49 percent, said they had a "favorable" view of the movement, while 40 percent had an "unfavorable" view. That 49–40 split put white evangelicals closer to self-identified moderate and liberal Republicans (54–29) than it did to conservative Republicans (43–50).

FROM THE AMERICAN CENTURY TO AMERICAN PARTNERSHIPS: IT'S NOT ALL ABOUT US ANYMORE

In our polling and related research, we have seen the same broad pattern repeated time after time. Fixated on the paradigms of yesterday, our leaders—whether military or civilian, government or industry—keep marching armies onto the wrong battlefields, with outdated strategies, in pursuit of missions that have failed before they are undertaken, and with ever-dwindling support from a public that has already looked over the horizon and adjusted its own hopes, ambitions, and expectations to a newly configured world.

The war in Iraq is perhaps the most obvious and tragic example of this divorce between leadership and those being led, between old paradigms and the new ones. More than four years after George W. Bush touched down on the deck of the USS *Abraham Lincoln* beneath a banner declaring MISSION ACCOMPLISHED, his administration found itself bogged down in the sands of Iraq, so short of manpower that it was calling up forty-year-old navy reservists to man street checkpoints in Baghdad, and increasingly bereft of outside support and isolated in world opinion. Meanwhile, virtually every poll we have taken on the matter over the past three years shows that Americans have tired of the lone-wolf superpower mind-set that still holds such sway on Pennsylvania Avenue. Americans of all ages expect the nation to play a lead role in the world today, but they also want the United States to share power and responsibility with allies and through the United Nations. More diplomacy, less bellicosity—that message rings out from our surveys.

In fact, the Muslim world wants much the same. In June 2000, we polled Iranians and found a high receptiveness to America and to things Western generally. Almost two years later, after Iran had been branded part of George W. Bush's "axis of evil," we again surveyed Iranians, as part of a ten-country poll that included two other non-Arab Muslim nations, five Arab nations, and France and Venezuela. This time, Iran led all other nations surveyed in its lack of receptiveness to such traditional American virtues as freedom, democracy, and diversity. That same pattern of converting would-be allies in the Muslim world to ardent enemies goes on to this day. Almost as I was writing those words, Iranian president Mahmoud Ahmadinejad, in New York City for the opening of the United Nations General Assembly, was being lectured on his many sins by Columbia University president Lee Bollinger. Ahmadinejad is indeed a man of bizarre beliefs and sometimes buffoonish behavior, but according to *Newsweek,* his shabby treatment at Columbia, where he had been invited to give a talk, was sufficient to drive even hardened expatriate opponents of his government to vow to defend their homeland should the United States ever attack it. This is not diplomacy but its reverse.

In polling for the Foreign Policy Association, we asked a broad national sampling of adults to tell us which of the following two policy statements came closest to their own view of how the United States should conduct itself in the world:

Statement A: Favors diplomacy over strategic power in international disputes, and actively seeks out the assistance of international bodies like the United Nations and the North Atlantic Treaty Organization to work together with the U.S. in crisis areas

Statement B: Favors the U.S. acting alone if necessary, and playing the role of both moral force and superpower in such disputes, all with the intention of protecting U.S. interests

The results: 70 percent chose statement A and only 25 percent statement B. More than half of respondents—55 percent—also agreed that the United States should sign on as a participant in the International Criminal Court, another opportunity for global cooperation that the Bush administration and its predecessor as well as Congress have resisted in favor of writing their own rules of conduct. When we turned the questioning specifically to budgeting options for the wars in Iraq and Afghanistan and for homeland security, 72 percent of respondents said the United States should limit its defense budget and ask for financial assistance from world allies to complete the rebuilding process in Iraq, while only 22 percent felt the nation had no choice but to allot most of its own budget to those causes.

The depth of the longing for a more cooperative approach to foreign policy making almost certainly reflects the public disenchantment with the progress of the war in Iraq, but we were seeing similar responses back in 2003 when victory still seemed easily attainable and when the memory of 9/11 hung heavily over the nation. What's more, we were seeing it especially among young adults, a group that might otherwise be expected to have the most emotional response to the tumultuous events of those early years of the twenty-first century. Even as newspapers trumpeted photos of Saddam's toppled statues lying facedown in the streets of Baghdad, almost four in five members of this generation agreed that the "proper role of the United States in Iraq should have been to seek help from the United Nations and other allies" before intervening—10 to 20 percentage points higher than any other generation. The same pattern has held with the ongoing nuclear weapons dispute with North Korea and on a whole slew of other international issues, big and small: The younger the respondents, the more likely they are to favor a cooperative approach.

Collectively, the message from the street couldn't be more clear. Americans want to share power; they are prepared to forge new alliances to combat everything from global warming to ethnic cleansing. And they want institutions that throw their weight around less and listen better. The stumbling block isn't the American public. Again and again, it's the leaders who would have to sacrifice some share of their own power to make the alliances work. The results of the 2006 congressional elections, I'm convinced, were less an ideological statement and more a repudiation of the inertia that dominates the current governmental paradigm on both sides of the political divide. As Americans have shown in subsequent polls, they are as ready to blame Democrats as Republicans so long as the status quo goes unchanged.

FROM MASS-PRODUCED TO MICROBREWS: ONE SIZE DOESN'T FIT ALL

Social shifts of the sort I am describing don't happen overnight. They bubble and perk quietly for years; sometimes they retreat again before pushing forward. Unlike geological shifts, social ones are also event sensitive. A sudden uptick in the good news from war-torn Iraq would almost certainly dampen a desire to share power on the world stage with the U.N. or other individual world powers, at least for the short term. Likewise, a sharp down-tick in gasoline prices would leave us driving more and worrying less about where the next gallon of crude was coming from. For the moment, the environmentalist and evangelical lions and lambs are lying down together, or nearly so; but that's a marriage with a built-in high volatility factor.

Consumer choices are less tied to wavering political, military, and diplomatic fortunes and thus offer more immediate tests of the same principles, and unlike political choices, these get voted on every day. Well within the living memory of most of us, institutions—whether they were manufacturers, retailers, HMOs, or any other monolithic organization—had the upper hand in virtually any exchange. They knew the rules. They made the goods. They sold and controlled the service. It was up to consumers to adjust to their whims, their regulations, and their product lines. In recent years, that control has been torn apart by the Internet—

by the knowledge base it offers as well as by its commercial potential.

Not long ago, I was waiting in line at my local drugstore while an elderly woman in front of me argued with the pharmacist. She was worried about the interaction of several medications she was taking. "No," the pharmacist kept saying, "that's wrong. There's nothing to worry about." Finally, steadying herself on her walker, the woman pulled a printout from her purse and shook it in his face. "I downloaded this information!" she told him triumphantly. Was she right? I don't know. But the Internet had definitely empowered her.

So it goes on all sorts of fronts. Technology gives us the strength to push back against the megas, and the modalities to punish them if they don't listen. Popular music offers one quick example. For most of their still brief lives, twenty- and thirtysomethings were force-fed the overproduced cookie-cutter ear candy that pours out of the major recording studios. Now they're using iPods, MP3s, and pirated downloads to gain access to the far greater range of sounds available from indie studios and, through the Internet, from all around the globe. Simultaneously, popular rock bands such as Radiohead are circumventing the major labels entirely by selling their albums, using digital downloads, directly from their own websites. Together, customers and performers are remaking the recording industry from the bottom up and the top down.

Meanwhile, the simple miracle of Netflix—millions of DVDs, hundreds of shipping centers, a great website, and monthly fees equal to movie theater admission for two in most major metropolitan areas—means that none of us has to rely on MGM or Disney for great cinema, or on Blockbuster or Hollywood Video to be our middleman. We select what we want to see, and we get to keep it as long as we want—a one-to-one relationship that is the exact opposite of the old movie paradigm of, basically, take it or leave it.

The beer industry is being similarly transformed as distinctive-tasting microbrews steal market share away from domestic mega-brands such as Budweiser and Miller Lite. These microbrews are simultaneously forcing mega-breweries to respond with a barrage of in-house "craft beers," such as Frederick Miller Classic Chocolate Lager, that together constitute one of the largest growth sectors within the big-brand beer industry. Today, we have in effect a two-tier beer drinking system. High-end beers are enjoyed in the plurality by thirty- to forty-nine-year-old white male college graduates who voted in 2004 enthusiastically for John Kerry (60 to 39 percent) and who, if they could shop at only one store the rest of their lives, would choose Target. The lowest-end beers are enjoyed (again, according to our polls) by thirty- to forty-nine-year-old white males who may have attended some college, voted overwhelmingly for George W. Bush in 2004 (71 to 29 percent), and are wild about Sears.

Probably anyone could observe the same thing by hanging around the beer aisle at the local supermarket in states that allow such sales, and after all, it's only beer we're talking about. But it gets, I hope, at a larger truth. One of the things emerging out of the collapse of the old paradigm is choice. Today's beer drinker and movie watcher and rock music fan can personalize his or her refrigerator or DVD or iPod playlist as never before. Oddly, in an age defined by narrowing limits, people are gaining options galore. Smaller is not only beautiful; it also can be liberating.

FROM JINGOISM TO JUST GOOD VALUE:
THE DECLINE OF PATRIOTISM AS A MARKETING TOOL

Nothing is more redolent of the old American industrial and consumer paradigm than Detroit and the auto industry. The Big Three manufacturers—GM, Ford, and to a lesser extent Chrysler—produced a relatively narrow range of models, segmented more by size, horsepower, and bells-and-whistles than by technology, and the car-buying public responded to the siren call of look, feel, sexiness, and speed as able and/or needed. Nothing, too, suggests the meltdown of both the industrial and consumer paradigm more than the state of the domestic auto industry today. Utility reigns, the Big Three reel, choice is everywhere, and except for a die-hard segment of auto consumers, point-of-origin has all but disappeared as a car-buying determinant.

Like energy usage but even more so, cars can be both a pollster's dream and a pollster's nightmare. Why we shop for autos the way we do, the choices we make, the motivations that push us along, are interwoven with so many overlapping issues: cost; practical needs (number of children, commuting distance, soccer team transport); status aspirations; even midlife crises. Back in 2005, in our massive consumer poll of nearly sixteen thousand randomly chosen respondents, we first segmented out those who told us it was either "important" or "very important" that the car they owned made them feel equal or superior to their peers. Then we broke those figures down by the actual cars they drove. Those results appear below. (Only the highest percentages are shown.)

PERCENT SAYING IT IS IMPORTANT OR VERY IMPORTANT THAT THE CAR THEY DRIVE MAKES THEM FEEL EQUAL TO THEIR PEERS, BY CAR MAKE

Infiniti	24
Volvo	23
Jaguar	20
BMW	19
Land Rover	18
Audi	16
Pontiac	16
Cadillac	15
Mercedes	15
Porsche	15
Saab	15

**PERCENT SAYING IT IS IMPORTANT OR VERY IMPORTANT
THAT THE CAR THEY DRIVE MAKES THEM FEEL SUPERIOR TO
THEIR PEERS, BY CAR MAKE**

Land Rover	36
Jaguar	14
Saab	14
BMW	13
Mercedes	13
Pontiac	13
Porsche	12
Audi	10
Lexus	10
Volvo	10

To me, results like these are bursting with whys. Why are more Pontiac owners than Cadillac owners interested in feeling equal to their peers, and how does owning a Pontiac make them feel that way? How, for that matter, did Infiniti finish four points higher than Jaguar on the same scale? (Four points, in this case, translates into Infiniti having 20 percent more snob appeal than Jaguar. Did Ford know that when it bought the struggling British manufacturer as opposed to the struggling Japanese one?) And *what* is it with Land Rover owners and their need to feel superior—and with the ad campaign that convinced them this could be so? (In this instance, the gods seemed to have wreaked a sort of left-handed revenge: In the 2007 Initial Quality Study by J. D. Power and Associates, Land Rover ranked worst in problems per one hundred vehicles.)

What's really interesting to me in all these figures, though, is how low a percentage of the auto-buying public these numbers actually represent. In all, only 15 percent of car owners told us that feeling equal to or superior to their peers really mattered to them. By contrast, 85 percent ranked "utility of the car" as "important" or "very important," and almost exactly the same number, 84 percent, said "performance of the car" was what counted.

In May 2007, we repeated roughly the same question in one of our Interactive polls, this time adding "environmentally friendly" to the mix. Here are those results:

WHICH OF THE FOLLOWING BEST DESCRIBES THE REASON OR REASONS YOU PURCHASE A PARTICULAR CAR?

It reliably gets you there	69%
The cost	55
Like the overall style	48
It's environmentally friendly	26
It makes you feel powerful	5
It makes you feel sexy	4
It makes you feel patriotic	3

In still other polling, we asked about the influence of political concerns in purchasing products generally. Below are the results of our question on patriotism, broken down by age. As you'll see, patriotism motivates buyers in proportion to age along an incline that ascends in an almost perfectly steady slope.

PERCENT SAYING "PATRIOTISM: MADE IN AMERICA" WAS VERY IMPORTANT TO THEM

Age 18–29	27
30–45	39
46–65	49
Over 65	59

So, what does this morass of numbers ultimately tell us about the present and future of the auto industry? For starters, it's no wonder the hybrid Toyota Prius is the gold standard for consumers newly conscious of their global responsibilities. Not only does the Prius reliably get you there; it does so in an environmentally friendly fashion. And it does both those things so efficiently that customers have been willing to wait for delivery and pay a steep premium on top of that.

In our May 2007 Interactive polling, only 3 percent said they owned a hybrid vehicle, but when we asked "How likely are you to consider purchasing a hybrid vehicle the next time you are looking to purchase a vehicle?" 29 percent said very likely and 27 somewhat likely. Collectively, that 56 percent amounts to an obituary for the old look-feel-sexiness-power quartet by which auto manufacturers once sold their wares. Significantly, the "very likely" responses to our hybrid-vehicle question included 40 percent of eighteen- to twenty-nine-year-olds and 36 percent of big-city dwellers. As so often happens, Toyota was in front of the market, waiting with the Prius, when social forces finally coalesced to make the market viable.

The numbers also tell us, if the stock market hasn't already, that Detroit is still slow on the uptake and too often moving in exactly the opposite direction from where the marketplace is tending. General Motors, for example, continued to trumpet the road-hogging, gas-guzzling, in-your-face aspects of its Hummer even as environmental concerns mounted and the brand itself became inextricably linked with an increasingly unpopular war at a time when Americans were becoming more, not less, globally aware. Little wonder that the indie band Trans Am in 2006 spurned a $180,000 offer from Hummer to use the band's song "I Want It All" in a TV ad campaign. Inevitably, GM had missed the song's irony.

GM and other American auto executives also missed the point when they descended on Capitol Hill in early June 2007 to once more lobby against proposals to raise gasoline mileage standards for cars sold in the United States. The argument is both an old one— that American car buyers wouldn't pay the sticker price needed to retool plants to build smaller, more fuel-efficient automobiles—and so wildly out of touch with the broader concerns of consumers that it suggests an almost pathological obtuseness on the part of what used to be called the Big Three. More recently, green initiatives have begun to sprout in Detroit, but the Big Three will still have to convince buyers that they mean it.

When we last asked consumers to pick their fantasy car from a list of at least thirty makes, Toyota won with nine percent overall, with higher totals among women and those over age thirty. BMW and Mercedes-Benz, the number-two and -three finishers, were the first choice of men and, in BMW's case, the overwhelming under-thirty favorite. Lexus, Toyota's luxury line, finished fourth, followed by Honda. The highest-ranking American brand, Ford, finished sixth—despite the fact that 13 percent of respondents said they currently owned Fords. Nine percent of respondents drove Chevys and 5 percent had Dodges, two makes that registered barely a blip in this survey. When owners don't want the car they currently have, chances are slim to none that they will be buying the same make next time they are in the market, another bit of bad news for a domestic auto industry already drowning in it.

The numbers also tell us that GM's jingoistic This Is My Country ad campaign for the Chevy Silverado is the wrong message in the wrong decade to a shrinking demographic. By all accounts the Silverado is a very good pickup truck: a big seller (second only to the Ford F-150), highly praised by critics including auto reporter Christopher Jensen of *The New York Times,* and in a market that remains generally strong despite high gas prices. (Otherwise, Toyota wouldn't be going after an increased share of the full-size-pickup pie with its new ultra-muscle 5.7-liter V-8 Toyota Tundra model.) All that is for the good, and pickup truck drivers are almost certainly more prone than, say, Jaguar owners to snap off a salute when Old Glory is run up the flagpole. But selling a handsome, usable truck by appealing to patriotic values at a time when patriotism barely shows up on the radar screen of most car buyers—3 percent in our polling, to be exact—is ultimately a losing proposition, especially when those who do cite patriotism as a reason for making any purchase are the oldest segment of the American population and thus the least likely to be buying a pickup truck.

Rocket science, this is not. You don't have to be a Nobel Prize winner to understand why the Silverado's sales are slipping, while the halo effect of the Prius has spread so broadly across the entire lineup of Toyota makes and models that Toyota, not GM, is now the world's bestselling automaker. The auto- and truck-buying public has moved beyond appeals to patriotism because it cares more about quality and fuel efficiency than country of origin, because it understands that a made-in-Indiana-and-Texas Toyota Tundra has just as much domestic content and represents just as much domestic labor as a flag-waving Chevy Silverado, and because patriotism itself is a term undergoing dramatic migration in a newly globalized world. What constitutes patriotism? Buying a product that traces back to a company headquartered in the United States? Or buying a product that will help conserve limited resources and be kinder to the environment of the world at large? Auto consumers answer that question every day with their choices.

FROM TWO CARS TO FLEXCAR, MASS TRANSIT, AND MORE: GLOBAL WARMING DRIVES US BACK TO THE FUTURE

Sometimes, the future is so clear that when it finally does arrive it seems almost familiar. Netflix strikes me as such an example, a mode of delivery that fulfilled such an obvious consumer need that it appeared almost old when it first started. Other times, that vague spot on the horizon where the future waits doesn't look at all like you think it should once you get up close to it. Public transportation is one of those latter cases.

Public transit has a generally miserable reputation in the United States. Older subway and el systems such as those in Boston, New York City, Philadelphia, and Chicago often depend on creaky equipment. Even thoroughly modern subway lines such as the Washington, D.C., area's Metro system are chronically short of funds and constantly threatening to cancel service. Buses, both inter- and intra-city, are worse. Outside of the profitable Northeast rail corridor, passenger trains seem forever on the verge of extinction.

On the whole, not a pretty picture—but I look at the rising tide of concern for the environment, the new determination to do more with fewer resources, and the fact that so many younger Americans have been exposed to generally highly successful and convenient European mass transit systems, and I see a bright future for mass transit in the United States as well. And our polling backs me up.

This is not the 1970s redux where the resumption of lower gas prices and an end to long lines at the fuel pump will return Americans to their wasteful energy spending. The lessons have sunk in too deeply for that, both the economic and the geopolitical ones. The Middle East is a tinderbox; melting polar ice caps are drowning the polar bears. The polls show clearly that Americans do believe that global warming is at least partially driven by our behavior, especially by excessive carbon emissions. And polls show just as clearly that the mandate for change includes mass transit.

More than three in four (78 percent) in our May 2007 Interactive poll told us that mass transit is a "very" or "somewhat important" way to resolve "energy problems." Two in five said it is important to them "personally," including half of eighteen- to twenty-nine-year-olds and 35 percent of those who live in suburbs. Thirty-eight percent of respondents told us that mass transit is even important in their "selection of a place to live," including 47 percent of eighteen- to twenty-nine-year-olds and 35 percent of suburbanites.

Projected out, those are big numbers, precisely the sort of support that a "volume" business such as mass transit depends on. But I also think it's important to conceive of mass transit itself in broader terms. Flexcar, the Seattle-based auto time-share company that counts AOL cofounder Steve Case among its major investors, is not "mass transit" as we normally conceive of it. There's no bureaucracy underlying the business, no question of government subsidies, no set-in-concrete schedules to meet or stations to maintain. Yet Flexcar does expand the franchise of mass transit. By providing episodic car use for urbanites and suburbanites when they really need it—for large shopping trips, say—auto-sharing encourages participants to use buses and subways at other times. (A car in the driveway creates a virtual imperative to use it, even over walking a few blocks to a store.) In effect, Flexcar simultaneously breaks down two paradigms—the paradigm of car ownership itself and the paradigm of public transportation as it has historically been understood in this country.

All that alone would bode well for the future of the company, but there are three additional factors to add into the mix as well. In straitened economic times, spreading car ownership among multiple users provides financial protection against a "wasting asset." Sharing ownership also means that fewer of the earth's resources will be devoted to a transportation mode that has had much to do with destroying the earth's atmosphere. Just as important, the company's management is plain smart. Its Flexcar Goes to Campus program is already conditioning undergraduates at many colleges around the nation—from the University of Portland to Emory University in Atlanta—to time-share travel.

In our May 2007 surveying, only 1 percent of respondents told us they were part of a Flexcar-type arrangement, but 5 percent said they were very likely to consider becoming a member of a group that owns a flex vehicle the next time they were looking to purchase a vehicle, and another 12 percent said they were "somewhat likely" to do so. That's a growth curve with very pleasant prospects for Flexcar and other auto-share providers. Like the Toyota Prius, these providers are going to be waiting on the corner when the future comes chugging into town.

FROM HARVARD YARD TO PHOENIX ONLINE:
JUST-IN-TIME LEARNING AT A FRACTION OF THE COST

Like Flexcars, online higher education provides access—in this case, to knowledge—on demand and at a fraction of the financial burden of traditional learning. It breaks down the bricks-and-mortar model of the university and reduces the learning process to a stream of electronic impulses flowing from a professor's modem to a student's modem and back again. Infrastructure disappears—the classroom is a basement den or a corner of a bedroom. The student, not the school, provides heat and electricity. As that happens, the cost of education declines toward nothing. Class schedules become largely meaningless. These are courses that can be built around jobs, rather than building jobs around a course schedule. In a postindustrial age, when brains are rewarded in the workplace far more than brawn, online education represents the democratization of opportunity. And it's all done with less, not more. Essentially, consumers have used technology to respond to constraints on access to higher education—cost, geography, and otherwise—and in doing so have created an abundance of highly personalized choices.

To be sure, the old model of American higher education—the large state university centralized on a single campus—has been eroding for years. Under enrollment pressure and stuck with finite space for expansion, state universities have exploded outward in dramatic fashion over the last half century, adding satellite campuses and regional universities to alleviate pressure on the main campus and to satisfy state legislators who want their district's share of the higher-ed budget dollar.

The University of North Carolina system is typical. The oldest state university in the country, UNC was once confined to the pre–Civil War central campus at Chapel Hill. Now the system includes sixteen constituent institutions, ranging from East Carolina University in Greenville to Western Carolina University in Cullowhee, and including historically black campuses such as Winston-Salem State University and North Carolina Central University in Durham.

By contrast, consider the almost completely dematerialized model of the online University of Phoenix, a place that has an address implicit in its name but whose physical location is far less important than its URL. Like the ancient phoenix, this one is risen from the ashes of an old paradigm. While the campus-based model of higher education has seen basically stagnant enrollment in recent years, growth in the dematerialized online segment has been staggering. According to a study for the Alfred P. Sloan Foundation, 3.2 million students were taking at least one online higher-education course in 2005, up more than eight hundred thousand students from a year earlier and twice the growth rate seen in any previous year. The Boston-based market research firm Eduventures estimates 10 percent of all college students will be enrolled in online degree programs by 2008. In our own 2007 surveying of more than five thousand adults, 30 percent said they are "currently taking or have taken an online course," including 37 percent of all eighteen- to twenty-four-year-olds polled. And another 50 percent told us they would "consider taking an online course."

So, is Phoenix the future of higher education, and are UNC and its sister systems the past? No, for two very good reasons. One, the bricks-and-mortar model has been racing toward the online one, aware that cyberlearners generate revenues at a fraction of the physical costs of on-site students. And, two, online education suffers from and will continue to suffer from an "enthusiasm gap" so long as it lacks the imprimatur of the traditional standard-bearers of higher education.

In our 2007 polling, only 27 percent of respondents agreed that "online universities and colleges provide the same quality of education as traditional universities and colleges," while 62 percent disagreed. For those most likely to be taking online courses, students eighteen to twenty-four years old, the enthusiasm was even lower: Only 23 percent in that critical age group agreed that online courses were equal to on-site ones. Meanwhile, of those who have taken or are currently enrolled in an online course, just one in eight said "the overall quality of the course" was better than an on-site course, while 40 percent said it was worse. (Forty-four percent felt the quality was about the same.)

Perhaps even more important is the perceived gap between online and traditional education in the minds of both the professoriate and future employers. The figures below tell that story:

WHICH IS BETTER, ONLINE OR TRADITIONAL UNIVERSITIES AND COLLEGES, FOR . . .

	ONLINE	TRADITIONAL	BOTH EQUAL
Acceptance by academic professionals	2%	80	8
Acceptance by employers	2	65	19

Rather than either end of the higher-education continuum dominating the other, I'm convinced a new paradigm will emerge in the years immediately ahead. Large state universities and even the largest and most prestigious private higher-education institutions will aggressively pursue online students and thus will lend the prestige of their brands to off-campus learning and to the degrees awarded in the name of online education. That, in turn, will provide a learning opportunity at minimal cost for those who lack the means or perhaps the background for on-site education but who have ambition and understand that, in the modern world, knowledge is power. In fact, the two worlds are already coming together. In polling we did at the very end of 2007 for the online Excelsior College, based in Albany, New York, we found that 45 percent of 1,004 adults nationwide felt that "an online class carries the same value as a traditional classroom class" and 43 percent of 1,545 CEOs and small business owners nationwide agreed that a "degree earned through an online or distance-learning program is as credible as a degree earned through a traditional campus-based program."

In the end, everyone will win. The integrity of higher education and its products—that is, degrees—will have been preserved at the same time students are empowered to learn more with fewer resources.

FROM THE EVENING NEWS TO THE HUFFINGTON POST: WHY CBS BOUGHT THE WRONG MEDIA QUEEN

As with education, so with the media, and especially news gathering. The past is daily newspapers and the network news shows; the present, *The New York Times,* with one foot in an inkwell and the other in the blogosphere; and the future, something like Arianna Huffington's online Huffington Post or the ever-growing and popular RealClearPolitics.com—the news-gathering, commentary, and dissemination business literally atomized into pulses and blips. (Truth in packaging: I contribute a blog to the Huffington Post, and I submit data and occasional columns to RealClear Politics.com.)

Here, too, the top-down paradigm is melting away. Walter Cronkite, Chet Huntley, and David Brinkley—the news titans of the 1960s and '70s—had been virtually the voices of God. As recently as a decade ago, the day's ration of daily events was still being delivered from the major newsrooms and the studios of NBC, CBS, and ABC almost as received wisdom. The prophets of the news industry talked, the people listened, and the political script played itself out accordingly. No more.

If I had to pick a moment when the stranglehold of the old news industry hierarchy was broken, I would pinpoint the final week of January 1998. On January 21 of that year, and again on January 25, ABC News correspondent Sam Donaldson predicted that Bill Clinton would be forced out of the White House if he was shown to be lying about his relationship with Monica Lewinsky. "If he's not telling the truth, I think his presidency is numbered in days," Donaldson said on his January 25 Sunday morning show with Cokie Roberts. By then, NBC News Washington Bureau Chief Tim Russert was already beginning to fashion a postmortem on the Clinton presidency. Conventional wisdom had formed. Blood was in the water. The authoritative voices of the day had spoken authoritatively, and the consensus was overwhelming within the news business and inside the Beltway. The question wasn't whether Bill

Clinton could stay as president but whether Hillary would move out of the White House before he was forced to. But, of course, Donaldson and Russert had it wrong. Bill Clinton did fail to tell the whole truth, but he also survived and rode out his term in office, and in the years since has written a 957-page bestseller and made a fortune on the speaking circuit as well as raising hundreds of millions of dollars for humanitarian purposes.

Others can pick their own tipping points, separate moments when the public stopped believing in the leading news voices and institutions and started trusting itself and its own interest networks. But whatever moment one picks, it seems to me that out of this flight from authority, the new media was born. Already faced with a declining viewer market share, the big three television news organizations now found themselves challenged by emboldened cable news—more immediate, more available, and angrier. Soon, too, the Internet weighed in with modern-day muckrakers mostly on the political right, people such as Matt Drudge and Lucianne Goldberg. Almost inevitably, given the nature of the Internet, the slam-reporting of the Drudge Report and others yielded to blogs—journalism in multiple dimensions—and soon enough, blogs themselves became both reporting mechanisms and political tools, since blogs have the capacity to organize rallies and interrupt or even destroy political campaigns. (See George Allen and his famous "macaca" blunder in the 2006 Virginia senatorial race.) In effect, blogs provide a combined source of news and 1776-style "committees of correspondence" to their devotees, and the devotees are quickly becoming legion.

In our May 2007 Interactive poll, 55 percent of the more than five thousand respondents said blogs were a very or somewhat important source of "international news," 62 percent called them an important source for "national news," and 50 percent said the same for "local news." While 45 percent said they think newspapers provide "better quality on reporting" than blogs, 25 percent said blogs were better in quality of reporting and 15 percent said they were equal in quality. On the issue of "lack of bias," 38 percent trusted newspapers more, but 24 percent favored blogs, and another 20 percent said they trusted both equally.

Blogs were even more competitive against "traditional television news." While 37 percent felt old media TV was better in providing quality reporting, an almost equal amount—34 percent—felt blogs had the edge, and 12 percent said both were equal. The numbers were just as close on "trust more for lack of bias": 33 percent said TV, 30 percent voted for blogs, and 18 percent felt both were equally trustworthy (or untrustworthy).

When we asked what our respondents thought was the "main advantage of traditional news sources," about a third (36 percent) said "no advantage," while a quarter (25 percent) liked that traditional sources cover "only the most important aspects of the story." Who were more likely to see no advantage for old media? Conservatives (51 percent) and those who identified themselves as "very conservative" (56 percent).

How about the main advantage of blogs? Twenty-eight percent cited the "immediate source of news," and an almost equal number (24 percent, and 39 percent of self-described "very liberals") said "more detailed and in-depth coverage of news." Only 17 percent of respondents said there was no advantage.

Other surveying we have done has yielded strikingly similar results. In nationwide polling for the We Media conference at the University of Miami School of Communication, Zogby International found that only 16 percent of respondents considered newspapers their most trusted source of news and information, and just 21 percent said the same of TV. Radio scored even lower, at 14 percent, while the Internet ran ahead of every other media at 33 percent. In the breakdowns, 53 percent of "elites" favored newspapers, but my guess is that if two papers—*The New York Times* and *The Wall Street Journal*—were removed from consideration, that number would plummet into the teens or lower. Radio fared far better among "very conservatives," at 28 percent, than among any other group, while TV did well (27 percent) among those sixty-five and older. No surprises there—just look at the ads and listen to the shouting. What did surprise me, though, was how strongly online sources scored, not just with respondents age eighteen to twenty-nine (40 percent), but all across the age spectrum and with every political leaning. Even when the Internet did lose, as with those sixty-five and over, it trailed by only a very small margin.

Clearly, such numbers reflect grim realities for the old media, particularly that staple of past generations, the daily newspaper. According to the U.S. Census Bureau, in 1970 about sixty-two million of the nation's sixty-three million households received a daily newspaper. Today, fewer than one in two households do the same. Daily newspapers themselves have dwindled from 1,772 in 1950 to 1,437 in 2006. Some of the oldest and best papers to survive the contraction—stalwarts such as *The Philadelphia Inquirer,* the Baltimore *Sun,* the *Chicago Tribune,* and the *Los Angeles Times*—remain profitable, in some cases very profitable, but are being stripped of reporters and bureaus to meet the demands of new investors whose capital was supposed to rescue faltering operations.

The radical political and social thinker Ivan Illich has written about the two watershed moments in the development of an organization. The first comes when it is expending as much energy in sustaining itself as it is in delivering a service; the second is when it spends more energy in sustaining itself than in delivering a service. Newspapers such as the *Chicago Tribune* are adding a third watershed moment: when the organization is profitable but no longer meets the corporate plan. And that moment in turn is hastening the creation of the new paradigm of dematerialized news at the same time that it speeds the destruction of the old paradigm of print journalism.

But the grim numbers coming from the circulation department and the grim faces in so many newsrooms also explain why newspapers and television news reporting are joining instead of fighting the blogosphere. In newsrooms, they know that their new readership wants to pick and choose its own stories, interact with news reporters to get more details, communicate with others to obtain more meaning (or express more outrage), and ultimately make informed decisions. The media lords, at least some of them, are finally getting this, too. They and the investment community understand what is at stake in terms of ad channels and much more, which is why capital has been flowing into blogs in recent months. And therein, I think, lies a reversion to the mean that will prove to be a boon and salvation for both the old and new medias.

For newspapers especially, blogs change the playing field. Newspapers no longer have to fight the losing battle of immediacy that has defined their relation to network TV over the last several decades. They couldn't beat TV at it, and they certainly can't beat the Internet, but they—and TV news—can return to what both do so well: providing the deep texture of the unfolding story and capturing the sense and feel of the community they serve. In early October 2007, in an online, not a print, interview with *The Washington Post,* the humorist Garrison Keillor said in response to a question, "Newspapers are being killed off by bad writing and lousy editing. They became corporate, and they need to get back to the streets and talk about the things people actually talk about." How strange and meaningful that *Washington Post* readers would have to go online to learn that essential bit of wisdom.

For blogs, aligning with old media offers much the same benefit that online education gains through association with bricks-and-mortar schools. For all its problems, old media understands decency and fairness in reporting. Over the centuries it has learned what blogs have yet to even approach: how to filter the story from the hype. Blogs regularly turn noncombatants—innocent people leading innocent lives—into unwilling sensations. (Think of the California high school pole-vaulter Allison Stokke, who became a YouTube pinup girl.) In practical terms, too, new media generates little news of its own. The blog's role is mostly to recycle and enhance. Old media provides the ore for the new media's mills. Without that, there's nothing, or only gas.

The future of news gathering, in short, is running headlong toward the blogosphere: resourceless (no forests are felled); small, nimble, and irreverent (unlike, say, the lumbering giants of network news); virtually free (especially vis-à-vis print media); and thus with all the right values for new citizens of this new world of limited resources prominently on display. But the hard fact is that the media, new and old, still need each other. Together they can supplement their limitations; share their strengths; give us a new form of journalism notable for its immediacy, accuracy, and fairness; and turn the news business generally, in Dan Gilmor's wonderful phrasing, from a lecture into a conversation.

And in fact that's exactly what is happening, not just locally but globally. At the end of 2006 we polled 435 editors from around the world for Reuters and the World Editors Forum. Nearly half of those surveyed were editors in chief. Their newspapers were published in 143 different languages in eighty-one countries. Twenty-nine of the newspapers had circulations of more than one million; another eighty-nine had daily readership of between two hundred thousand and one million. Only 37 of the papers did not have a website; of the 398 that did, more than 60 had at least five hundred thousand unique visitors a day and another 159 had between fifty thousand and five hundred thousand. These are newspapers from Albania to Yemen, Zambia, and Zimbabwe. When the papers can afford a website, and not all of them can, it's crackling with readership and activity.

Eighty percent of the global editors we surveyed called online and new media journalism a "welcome addition." Seventy-four percent said interacting with readers online had a positive effect on quality journalism. Better than one in three said the first thing they would invest in to improve editorial quality would be training for journalists in new media—recruiting more journalists ran second, with 23 percent. Another two in five said that within ten years the most common way of reading the news in their community would be online, six percentage points more than chose the second-place finisher, print. Just as important, half the editors thought the quality of journalism would improve over the next ten years, and another 16 percent thought it would remain about the same.

That's not the portrait of an industry sinking into oblivion. Rather, it's a textbook case of a paradigm reinventing itself to do more with less. Strangely, the supposedly moribund newspaper business is in its own way a model for many industries to come.

In fact, much the same thing is happening to my own business, for the most part with fewer histrionics and less gnashing of teeth. Door-to-door polling is about as extinct as the passenger pigeon. As I noted earlier, telephone surveys become harder year by year. And so we pollsters—from Zogby Interactive to Greenfield Online, Harris Interactive, and others—migrate to cyberspace to find the answers to our questions. As we do, and as we hone our techniques, the corporate and university worlds are coming to accept the Internet as a medium for solid survey research. Now, at Zogby Interactive, we're testing face-to-face polling using webcams to recover the sense of intimacy that was lost years ago when we abandoned door-to-door surveying for the phone. Just as online journalism is freeing newspapers to go back to the immediacy of a breaking story, so online polling seems to be liberating us to return to where we started. Thus, one paradigm migrates into the next, and the material goods of the business—shoe leather, phone banks, and the manpower to operate them—dematerialize increasingly into tiny bursts of energy.

A QUICK GUIDE TO MARKETING IN A MORE PERSONAL AND PERSONALIZED WORLD

- Institutional authority is all but dead and gone. Self-reliance and self-determination are on the rise. To stay ahead of the curve, you need to stress individual choice, independence, and personalized service.
- "Green" is more than a good slogan; it's good business. The young especially have internalized sustainability as a life goal, and that's true across the planet, not just at home.
- The road to hell is paved with stereotypes. To cite one example, Christian conservatives, especially those under thirty, have moved far beyond their putative spokesmen on issues such as stem cell research, global warming, and health care. Meet people where they are, not where they used to be.
- American values remain strong, but Americans increasingly see themselves as part of a bigger picture. To connect with them, you need to wave the whole-earth flag, not just an American one.
- Don't forget the elderly. They're living longer, and they want more from retirement than a golf course, laxative ads, and a condo in the sun. They are, in fact, the greatest untapped market in America today.

4

Global, Networked, and Inclusive

A YOUTH MOVEMENT THAT IS RESHAPING ALL OF SOCIETY

Are the kids all right? Not if you listen to some of our leading social commentators. To hear people such as Juliet Schor and William Bennett tell it, today's youth have been virtually brainwashed by marketers, advertisers, and a mushy-headed professoriate. But if your measure of "all right" is a group that is not just tolerant of but welcomes diversity, if it is young adults who do not march in lockstep with any political ideology, who in the majority are willing to think through the subtleties of some of the most contentious issues of the time, if the measure is eighteen- to twenty-nine-year-olds who are open with one another to an astounding degree and take their cues globally, not just locally, then, yes, the kids are doing just fine.

Don't misunderstand. I don't make a claim of perfection for any age cohort, even one that includes my three great sons. Like young adults throughout history, these twentysomethings are prone to preen. Maybe more so than other generations, they also are conditioned to define themselves by the things they own. In researching her book *Born to Buy,* Schor found that by kindergarten, children can identify on average three hundred logos. By ten, they have memorized some four hundred brands.

We see the consequences of that endless marketing bombardment playing itself out in our surveying. In Zogby's May 2005 consumer profile poll, a third of eighteen- to twenty-nine-year-olds told us "owning things" was "very important" for their self-esteem, far higher than any other age group. One in eight said that "appearing wealthier" was very important, and one in five said the same about "feeling more complete as a person." Again, no other age cohort came close to those numbers. But it's also important to note that two in three of the young adults we surveyed *didn't* consider owning things to be very important to their self-esteem. To conclude, as Schor basically does, that today's youth are robotic buying machines, programmed from birth to consume, is to capture only one small and blurry dimension of a multifaceted group.

Likewise, I think Bill Bennett has half a point but not a whole one when he laments that relentless sensitivity training and political correctness have robbed students of their critical faculties and inquisitive spirits, instilling instead a kind of we're-all-equal liberalism. I remember particularly a 2002 news release put out by Bennett and the conservative pollster Frank Luntz, citing their survey that found a large majority of college students did not consider American values superior to those of other nations and cultures. I've done my own polling on the subject, with similar results. In our June 2007 Zogby Interactive poll, for example, we asked respondents to agree or disagree with the following statement: "I don't support the concept of 'My country, right or wrong.' " The results, broken down by age, follow.

DON'T SUPPORT "MY COUNTRY, RIGHT OR WRONG"

	18–27	28–41	42–61	62–80	80+
Strongly agree	44%	33	33	32	16
Somewhat agree	19	23	17	18	31
Total Agree	**63**	**56**	**50**	**50**	**47**

	18–27	28–41	42–61	62–80	80+
Somewhat disagree	13%	21	22	19	18
Strongly disagree	10	14	20	25	31
Total Disagree	**23**	**35**	**42**	**44**	**49**
Unsure	14	9	9	6	4

But although my numbers echo those of Bennett and Luntz, I don't read them the same way. To be sure, the youngest American adults are less inclined than their elders to defer to American values. The results are clear on that score, but the question is, Why? What's the underlying dynamic? I think the answer can be found in the high "unsure" percentage among the young. My belief is that it traces back to confusion over precisely what "my country" means in this day and age. Those in their sixties and beyond might be at odds on superpatriotic slogans, but they have no doubt about what country they live in. These late teens and twentysomethings are different. More so than any other generation of Americans in history, they see themselves as citizens of the planet, not of any nation in particular.

Today's youth have been exposed to clothing, games, and other products made all over the world. MTV and the Internet have brought Amnesty International, Human Rights Watch, and a variety of international rock concerts devoted to fighting global inequities right to their home screens. Their musical heroes are global and internationally involved: Sting, U2's Bono, the half-Colombian and half-Lebanese Shakira, and on and on. Even a relatively ancient relic such as Ireland's Bob Geldof, who launched the Live Aid concert in 1985, was able to attract millions of young concertgoers to the Live 8 performances staged on July 2, 2005, at ten venues around the world to focus attention on global poverty.

Thanks to Starbucks, First Globals know Ethiopian coffee beans from Bolivian ones. Thanks to Whole Foods, they know which beans are organic and which are chemically nurtured. And thanks to Oxfam, they know which coffees trace back to multinational corporations and which deliver profits to farmer-owned cooperatives. Indeed, if one single coffee importer could be said to catch the zeitgeist of an entire generation, it might be Higher Grounds Trading Company out of Traverse City, Michigan. As its web address—javaforjustice.com—suggests, you're not buying only beans; you are buying a global mind-set.

Many young adults live and think globally. In surveying we did for IBM in June 2007, 56 percent of respondents age eighteen to twenty-nine told us they had family or friends living outside the United States. No other age cohort approached that number. To drill down even more precisely, better than one in three eighteen- to twenty-four-year-olds has traveled outside the United States once or twice in the past five years. Better than one in four has done so three to five times—and remember, these are people not yet halfway through their twenties.

A few years back, during a panel discussion on the teaching of history in American universities and secondary schools, one of my fellow participants commented that young people are less knowledgeable about facts and events than ever before. My response was that, whatever their factual base of knowledge, members of this generation are more networked and globally engaged than members of any similar age cohort in American history. That's a sweeping statement, but I stand by it.

FROM GAY BASHING TO *QUEER EYE FOR THE STRAIGHT GUY* AND BEYOND: EMBRACING DIVERSITY

No group of Americans more appreciates the multiethnic, multiracial world in which we all live than today's teens and young adults, and none is anywhere near as accepting of the full range of the human experience. In a November 2005 poll for Hamilton College, two out of three high school seniors told us that "homosexual relations between consenting adults should be legal." Four out of five of all those surveyed supported a law "to protect gays against discrimination," and a majority (55 percent) said they were in favor of a "law that would allow same-sex couples to get married." Two out of three agreed that "same-sex couples should be allowed to adopt children," and almost three in four concurred that "gay people contribute in unique and positive ways to society." Less than half (44 percent) agreed that "it would be better if gay people kept their sexual orientation private and hidden," while a majority (54 percent) disagreed. Eighty-six percent said they "know someone who is gay," and 69 percent said they had "friends, relatives, or close acquaintances" who are gay.

To an extent, those numbers are only a reflection of the general loosening of attitudes toward gays and lesbians, and a reflection of the far more visible presence of both groups in American society than even twenty-five years ago. According to data gathered by the American Enterprise Institute, public acceptance of gays in the military grew from 51 percent to 80 percent between 1977 and 2003. Over the same period acceptance of gays as elementary school teachers grew from 27 percent to 61 percent. In our own surveying from May and June 2007, nearly half of all Americans (49 percent) said they had a close friend who was gay, 42 percent said they didn't, and the rest weren't sure.

But while the numbers on teen tolerance reflect societal drift, they also exaggerate it in powerful ways. No other U.S. age cohort comes anywhere close to the acceptance levels found among teenagers in our Hamilton College survey. In fact, they are much closer to the acceptance levels found in the most permissive western European societies. In polling for the European Union, only the Netherlands, Sweden, and Denmark were more supportive of gay marriages than our sampling of American high schoolers, and homosexual unions are already legal in the Netherlands and Sweden. On the issue of adoption rights, the Netherlands was the sole EU nation to record a higher level of support than U.S. teens, and that by only a few points.

The results of our Hamilton College survey weren't uniformly pro-gay or altogether consistent, either. These are, after all, high schoolers. While a majority of high school seniors did support gay marriages, they grew wary when faced with more detailed proposals. By a 52 to 44 margin, they opposed laws that would allow same-sex couples to form civil unions that would give them equal rights with dual-sex couples, and they supported by a slightly wider margin a Constitutional amendment that would ban same-sex marriages.

In a similar vein, they disagreed by a wide margin (61 percent to 38 percent) with the proposition that "gay lifestyles are morally wrong," while generally accepting the anti-gay premise that homosexuals choose to be what they are. Asked if homosexuality was (a) something one was born with, (b) a condition that develops because of the way people are raised, or (c) the way some people choose to live, 47 percent of the high school seniors chose c, 23 percent went with b, and 15 percent chose option a. Just about all the rest opted for a combination of the factors above. As a matter of interest, almost none of those surveyed were unsure or without an opinion on the subject.

Nor were the results the same across races and ethnicities. Because our sampling reflected the racial and ethnic composition of the nation at large, white opinions dominated the undifferentiated results. As the table below suggests, we would have had slightly less tolerant numbers had we surveyed African Americans only and slightly more tolerant ones had we stuck with Hispanic Americans.

		WHITE	BLACK	HISPANIC
Do you think homosexual relationships between consenting adults should be legal or illegal?	LEGAL	67%	52	71
	ILLEGAL	31	30	28
Would you support or oppose a law to protect gays against job discrimination?	SUPPORT	80	81	86
	OPPOSE	17	15	13
Lesbians are disgusting.	STRONGLY AGREE	8	9	5
	AGREE	18	25	18
	DISAGREE	40	39	38
	STRONGLY DISAGREE	33	26	35

		WHITE	BLACK	HISPANIC
Gay men are	STRONGLY AGREE	11%	19	7
disgusting.	AGREE	19	24	21
	DISAGREE	38	33	37
	STRONGLY DISAGREE	31	23	31
As far as you know,	YES	66	79	82
are any of your friends,	NO	34	20	18
relatives, or close				
acquaintances gay?				

These polling results were much on my mind early in 2007 when I read that then-chairman of the Joint Chiefs of Staff Peter Pace had told the *Chicago Tribune* editorial board that he found homosexual acts "immoral" and by extension criticized the tolerance of homosexuals in the armed forces. Pace's attitude is mainstream for someone born in 1945, but as is the case with other leaders isolated by age, he was out of step not only with the young Americans the military depends on to join the fight but also with the men and women then serving under him. The Williams Institute at UCLA has estimated at least sixty-five thousand gay and lesbian Americans are currently serving on active duty. Meanwhile, my own 2006 polling found that nearly three quarters of military members are comfortable serving with gays and lesbians and nearly 25 percent know that someone in their unit is gay. For them, "Don't ask, don't tell" is yesterday's battle. Time to move on.

FROM BLACK EXCEPTIONALISM TO JUST PLAIN BEIGE: WHAT OBAMA HAS THAT POWELL DIDN'T

On race, too, the nation's youth are leading the way into a far more accepting future. It's not that they have been significantly more exposed than the generations just above them to people of different races and ethnicities. Our June 2007 Interactive poll found that adults age eighteen to twenty-seven and those age twenty-eight to forty-one attended integrated grade schools in just about dead-equal proportions. The older group was slightly more likely (3 percentage points) to have gone to integrated middle schools and high schools, and two points more likely to have attended a dinner party within the past year where one of the guests was African American. (Those age forty-two to sixty-one were just as likely as the youngest adults to have done the same, although that might say more about the frequency of dinner parties as social events for the two age groups.) Among white respondents only, the older age cohorts were more likely than the youngest one to say they have a close friend who is African American, while the youngest cohort was far more likely than older ones to have a close friend who is Hispanic (8 points more than twenty-eight- to forty-one-year-olds) or Asian (16 points).

On two fronts, though, the experience of young white adults significantly outstrips that of older ones. They are twice as likely (23 percent to 11 percent) as those age twenty-eight to forty-one to have an African American supervisor at work, twice as likely also (14 percent to 7 percent) to have a supervisor who is Hispanic, and two and a half times as likely (15 percent to 6 percent) to have an Asian American supervisor, and for that matter, four points more likely (14 percent to 10 percent) to have a supervisor who is gay.

Part of that has to do with lower-level jobs, especially where African Americans are concerned. One in four Americans earning less than fifteen thousand dollars a year has a black supervisor, while only one in eight of those earning over fifty thousand dollars annually does. The chance of having a Hispanic supervisor increases as annual income grows, but only up to thirty-five thousand dollars annually. For Asians as for blacks, supervisory jobs are most common at the lower levels. Still, work relationships—even at the low end of the economy—teach lessons. They flatten the history of white dominance in American society. They inculcate that a work directive is a work directive, no matter from whom it originates. They are, in short, a start.

Interracial dating and marriage are more than starts. They are taboo-busters. Just four decades ago miscegenation was a crime punishable by jail time in, among other states, Virginia, just a hop, skip, and jump across the Potomac River from the White House, Capitol, and U.S. Supreme Court. Visit any semi-urban high school today and, while you aren't likely to find it more integrated than it was a generation ago, you are almost certain to find the dating scene far more so. What's more, the faces that pass by you are likely to represent a rainbow of races and ethnicities, powerful evidence that the figurative "melting pot" of American society has now literally entered the nation's gene pool.

Intermarriages more than doubled between 1990 and 2000, to an estimated 7 percent of all American marriages. Meanwhile, approval ratings of intermarriage grew from 70 percent of all adults in 1986 to 83 percent in 2003, according to a study by Roper Reports. Credit younger Americans with leading the way. In a 2002 Gallup poll, 86 percent of adults age eighteen to twenty-nine approved of marriages between blacks and whites, while only 30 percent of those over age sixty-five did the same.

A June 2007 Zogby Interactive poll asked respondents to rate their feelings, from very negative to very positive, "if a member of your family was dating someone of a different race." Twenty-one percent of all respondents said they would feel negative, 25 percent said positive, and the rest picked "neutral." Among those age seventy and older, the negative responses spiked to 40 percent. The self-described "very conservative" went even slightly higher than that. But among those age eighteen to twenty-nine, only 12 percent expressed negative feelings, while 38 percent were positive and 26 percent were very positive.

To a large extent, this flattening of old taboos is the result of years of exposure, especially for whites in their teens and twenties, that was simply unavailable to earlier generations. Will Smith was their TV buddy and Bill Cosby their TV dad. Michael Jordan was their marketing icon and athletic hero; Oprah, their confessor. Even a politically astute fourteen-year-old probably doesn't remember a time when America's secretary of state wasn't a person of color. And

then there's the case of the golfer Tiger Woods, interracially con-
ceived, and one of the most popular sports figures in America and
across the world.

A dozen years ago when Colin Powell was being courted as a
presidential candidate, the discussion almost always came down to
race. Powell had served with distinction at every stop along the way:
during two tours in Vietnam, as a military attaché to Defense Secretary Caspar Weinberger in the early years of the Reagan White
House, and as national security adviser in the final year. As chair-
man of the Joint Chiefs of Staff under George H.W. Bush, Powell led
the effort to assemble the international coalition force that would
drive Saddam Hussein's Republican Guard from Kuwait and send it
scurrying well within Iraq's own borders. Poll after poll showed
Powell to be among the most admired people in America as the
1996 presidential election drew near. And yet in the end, his skin
color was what people finally focused on.

Had he gotten where he was because the army and a succession
of Republican presidents had been looking to push African Americans forward? More to the point, would those who told pollsters
they would vote for Powell for president really vote for him in the
sanctity of the voting booth. In fact, that looked shaky at best. The
polling on Powell had him running best among white Southern
males, not the natural constituency for a black candidate even if
many of them were sympathetic to Powell's military background. In
the end, Alma Powell scotched the "campaign" for personal reasons, but by then it was evident that while her husband might do
well in a general election, he would have a brutal time securing the
Republican nomination.

Three presidential election cycles later, the old argument over
race and the presidency seems, for the most part, to be a relic of another era. Yes, the issue heats up on occasion, but in our June 2007
polling, a majority of every age group except those over age eighty
and of every self-identified political ideology except conservatives
(and they barely missed with a 49.5 percent approval rating) answered affirmatively when we asked if the nation was ready for an

African American president. To an extent, that's only the complicated new demographics of American society playing themselves
out in the electorate. Indeed, part of the strong appeal of Barack
Obama is that he *is* such an uncanny reflection of the new beige hue
of the voting public: a mixture of races and ethnicities, with a strong
dash of foreign exoticism thrown in for seasoning.

The same held true when we asked whether the country was
ready for a woman president, although this time conservatives
could muster only 45.5 percent, a reflection most likely of their
deep antipathy toward the most likely female candidate, Hillary
Clinton. Overall, three in four of the youngest voters and even
three in five of those age sixty-two to eighty either strongly or
somewhat agreed that the nation was ready for a female president. Compare this (for example) to 1949, when fewer than half
those polled by Gallup said they would vote for a woman president even if she seemed the best qualified candidate for the job,
and to 1969, when that number had barely crept over the middle
line to 53 percent.

Below, the results of our June 2007 poll are broken down by
age. As you'll see—and to belabor what by now has become a theme
song—the youngest voters are pushing the pluralities. (And this time
note that the "not sures" on race especially weight toward the older
end of the spectrum.)

THE AMERICAN PEOPLE ARE READY FOR AN AFRICAN AMERICAN PRESIDENT.

	18–27	28–41	42–61	62–80	81+
Strongly agree	41%	23	22	16	11
Somewhat agree	31	41	39	39	28
Total Agree	**72**	**64**	**61**	**55**	**39**
Somewhat disagree	13	16	17	19	22
Strongly disagree	6	8	11	14	17
Total Disagree	**19**	**24**	**28**	**33**	**39**
Not sure	9	11	11	13	22

THE AMERICAN PEOPLE ARE READY FOR A WOMAN PRESIDENT.

	18–27	28–41	42–61	62–80	81+
Strongly agree	41%	26	26	25	16
Somewhat agree	35	38	36	35	27
Total Agree	**76**	**64**	**62**	**60**	**43**
Somewhat disagree	9	18	16	15	20
Strongly disagree	6	8	13	18	27
Total Disagree	**15**	**26**	**29**	**33**	**47**
Not sure	8	9	9	8	9

FROM THE LIBERAL AGENDA TO A LIBERAL MIND-SET:
LEANING LEFT BUT NOT FALLING THAT WAY

In what will come as no surprise, self-identified liberals are more ready for a female president or a president of color than any other political cohort. By an 82 to 13 percent margin, liberals felt the country was ready for a woman president. By a 77 to 17 margin liberals felt that way about an African American president, too. Both positions are far closer to eighteen- to twenty-seven-year-old voters than to any other age group, but as I've tried to stress throughout this report, a distinction has to be made between "liberalism" as a collection of modern political beliefs and objectives and "liberalism" in the dictionary sense of "broad-minded" and "not bound by authority, orthodox tenets, or established forms in political or religious philosophy." (Both the latter definitions are taken from the 1937 unabridged second edition of *Webster's New International Dictionary of the English Language*.)

Are the kids politically "liberal"? That depends on whose "liberal agenda" you're talking about. Are they liberal in a dictionary sense—that is, are they broad-minded, free of orthodoxy, willing to think things through on their own, resistant to imposed answers? Absolutely.

Abortion is another one of those polling questions that stick a finger into all sorts of issues: religion, politics, morality, gender (is it the woman's right, or does society get a say?), law, history (the bad old days of back-alley abortionists), language ("late-term," "partial-birth"), and much more. The issue is packed as well with news stories and images: The sniper shooting of a prominent obstetrician-gynecologist in western New York state and the subsequent bombing during the 2000 Olympics in Atlanta by a militant and deranged pro-life advocate are two of the most horrific. I mentioned in the last chapter that, as amazing as it seems, we appear to be arriving at what amounts to a national conversation on such a divisive subject. Our 2005 survey for Hamilton College of high school seniors suggests to me that the youngest adults— and those frankly with the greatest personal stake in the debate— are at the forefront of this still inchoate effort to find a middle ground.

At a time when a shrinking majority of all Americans identified itself as "pro-choice"—56 percent, about ten to twelve points lower than the figure a few years earlier—high school seniors in late 2005 were evenly split, with 47 percent pro-life and 48 percent pro-choice. While a slight majority of high school seniors (53 percent) said abortion should be "legal in all or most cases," 46 percent felt it should be "illegal in all or most cases." However, only 36 percent thought that Roe v. Wade should be overturned, while 62 percent said it should stand. Maybe this is nothing more than another example of youthful inconsistency. Those of us who have lived through the teen years with our kids know that high school students tend to be all over the place on many issues. But I look at the results above and at other results from the same survey, shown on page 104, and I begin to see a distinct nuance emerging, an appreciation of the real complexity of the issue, and a willingness to judge each element of the debate on its own merits, rather than providing a pro-life or pro-choice answer to every question.

HIGH SCHOOL SENIORS AND ABORTION

Whether you think that abortion should be legal or not, how do you feel about the morality of abortion?

Always morally wrong	23%
Usually morally wrong	44
Usually acceptable	28
Always acceptable	4

If the pregnancy seriously threatens the woman's health, should a woman . . .

Have a legal right to an abortion	89
Not have a legal right	10

If the woman is under eighteen and unmarried, should she . . .

Have a legal right to an abortion	48
Not have a legal right to an abortion	50

If the woman is married and does not want more children, should she . . .

Have a legal right to an abortion	27
Not have a legal right to an abortion	71

If the pregnancy is the result of rape, should she . . .

Have a legal right to an abortion	82
Not have a legal right to an abortion	18

If the baby will have a serious birth defect, should a woman . . .

Have a legal right to an abortion	46
Not have a legal right to an abortion	54

If the family is poor and cannot afford another child, should a woman . . .

Have a legal right to an abortion	38
Not have a legal right to an abortion	60

Suppose a student in her senior year of high school becomes pregnant. Generally, what do you think would be the best thing for her to do?

Keep the child	26
Have an abortion	13
Give up the baby for adoption	54

In your opinion, should a woman under eighteen be required by law to get the permission of a parent before she can have an abortion?

Yes	66
No	32

Collectively, are those survey results the expression of a liberal political bent among high schoolers or the expression of a broader liberal mind-set? I think the answer is the latter, and I think that's clear. For decades the abortion debate has skewed policy and politics without offering any hope of a solution. Now along comes a generation that is unwilling to impose a simple "always right" or "always wrong" template on questions that are terrifyingly complex. That's hopeful, and it's not lockstep anything—liberalism or conservatism, Democratic or Republican.

Below is another example of the way in which young Americans are feeling their way toward a middle ground on complex issues, this from an unlikely source: two "mad scientist" questions taken from an August 2006 Zogby Interactive survey.

Do you strongly support, somewhat support, somewhat oppose, or strongly oppose scientists producing woolly mammoths in the modern era?

If scientists were able to bring back extinct dinosaurs, would you strongly favor, somewhat favor, somewhat oppose, or strongly oppose their doing so?

The table below shows the response of eighteen- to twenty-nine-year-olds to both questions, but before consulting it, take a moment to predict whether their answers will correlate most closely with liberals, moderates, conservatives, or independents. Here are the results:

SHOULD SCIENTISTS RE-CREATE WOOLLY MAMMOTHS?

	18–29	LIBERALS	MODERATES	CONSERVATIVES	INDEPENDENTS
Strongly support	13%	12	10	7	10
Somewhat support	22	26	20	15	23
Total Support	**35**	**38**	**30**	**22**	**33**
Somewhat oppose	22	25	23	20	22
Strongly oppose	32	23	34	47	33
Total Oppose	**54**	**48**	**57**	**67**	**55**

SHOULD SCIENTISTS BRING BACK EXTINCT DINOSAURS?

	18–29	LIBERALS	MODERATES	CONSERVATIVES	INDEPENDENTS
Strongly support	8%	6	6	5	7
Somewhat support	16	17	13	8	15
Total Support	**24**	**23**	**19**	**13**	**22**
Somewhat oppose	20	23	18	17	18
Strongly oppose	50	46	55	63	53
Total Oppose	**70**	**69**	**73**	**80**	**71**

While the eighteen- to twenty-nine-year-olds much more nearly echo liberals than conservatives, they also run almost in tandem with moderates and political independents, and on the opposition side are slightly closer to both groups than to liberals. On the issue of woolly mammoths, eighteen- to twenty-nine-year-olds and independents agreed almost totally: 35 percent of young adults supported re-creating the prehistoric elephants, as did 33 percent of independents, while 54 percent of the former and 55 percent of the latter were in opposition.

The dinosaur question brought more fervent opposition from all quarters—who hasn't seen at least one of the *Jurassic Park* movies?—but brought a very similar correlation among young adults, the ideologically moderate, and political independents. The eighteen- to twenty-nine-year-olds opposed bringing dinosaurs back by a 70 to 24 margin, moderates were against doing so by 73 to 19, and independents weighed in at 71 to 22 opposed. Here and on the mammoth question, as well as on a broad variety of political-issue questions, the numbers run so closely together that one has to wonder if we're not seeing the birth of a new political union that will finally break the Democratic-Republican stalemate across a broad range of issues, or perhaps the birth of a third party that will spell the end of two-party hegemony in American politics—a coalition not of the willing, but of those willing to listen. Given the state of politics over the past decade, that would be little short of revolutionary.

FROM PRIVATE LIVES TO PUBLIC DOMAIN: HOW MYSPACE, FACEBOOK, YOUTUBE, AND OTHER VIRTUAL COMMUNITIES ARE CHANGING THE WORLD FOR US ALL

One reason that First Globals are so willing to listen is that they are so practiced at it. This is a group in almost continuous conversation—using cell phones, e-mail, text-messaging, instant messaging, chat rooms, or what have you. Much of that conversation, inevitably, is idle chatter, but it's also a form of conditioning with inevitable results. First Globals want borders pushed back because in their own minds they exist in the largely borderless world of the Internet. This is a group that looks for access and information everywhere, a group that cybershops around the world, and puts itself out in the ether for all the world to see.

In our May 2006 Interactive poll, 42 percent of respondents age eighteen to twenty-nine said that they have a page on MySpace.com, three times as many as the nearest demographic group, those age thirty to forty-nine. A quarter of them visit their MySpace page more than once a day; another 23 percent do so once a day; 72 percent are using the page to keep in touch with friends. In the summer of 2007 we polled nearly one thousand New Hampshire residents, evenly divided politically between the two major parties. Fourteen percent of eighteen- to twenty-nine-year-old Democrats told us they visited Facebook.com every single day. No other age group came anywhere near that. (Of the 53 Republicans age eighteen to twenty-nine included in the survey, not one visited Facebook.com even rarely.) The Internet is where First Globals congregate to socialize, to exchange information, and often to be entertained, as witness the roaring success of YouTube.com.

Such deep familiarity with cyberspace inevitably breeds a certain amount of wariness. Young adults are only marginally more excited than other age groups about being able to cast ballots online: 43 percent are for it, while half say no, they prefer to go to a polling place. More than any other age group, they are facile with Internet technology, which also makes them more acutely aware of its limitations and the capacity for abuse. Like other age groups, and in roughly equal numbers, they would like to see sexually explicit websites tagged with a distinct suffix—something such as .xxx instead of .com. Seventy-five percent agree or strongly agree with that proposition, as opposed to 81 percent of thirty- to forty-nine-year-olds, 83 percent of fifty- to sixty-five-year-olds, and 86 percent of those over age sixty-five. To the vast bulk of young adults, though, the Internet is pure public domain, and they are part of its public spectacle. When we asked a series of questions to gauge what various age groups considered an Internet invasion of privacy—from having someone post their photo in a swimsuit to having their own dating profile and GPS coordinates available online—every other age group answered in the affirmative on all counts. Among eighteen- to twenty-nine-year-olds, only GPS coordinates were considered a privacy invasion, and that by a bare majority.

As to what such a high level of openness portends for society at large, I think I had a glimpse of that future in a chance encounter my wife and I had with a twenty-year-old waitress in Utica during the summer of 2007. In the course of a conversation about YouTube and public access, I asked our waitress about her own limits on what she would reveal. "My boobs," she answered, not terribly demurely, "but only on Halloween, and only for my friends."

"Well," I said, "I'm your friend today, but tomorrow I might not be. Can you stop me from sharing your, um, breasts with the rest of the world, or with the company you're hoping will hire you?"

"No," she said, after some serious thought, "but so many of us do this in one form or another that employers are just going to have to adjust or they won't have anyone left to hire."

And thus, I remember thinking as she wandered off to the next table, what's bad for beauty queens and teenage ingénues today becomes business as usual the day after tomorrow.

Not surprisingly, a group so ready to embrace multiculturalism and so willing to share even intimate details with a global community is multilateralist in its worldview, too. The Kyoto accords, the International Criminal Court, an activist role for the United Nations—

these aren't necessarily settled questions for any age cohort, but First Globals have staked out a position on all of them sharply at odds with the generations just ahead of them. By a 48–35 plurality, eighteen- to twenty-nine-year-olds favor ratifying the Kyoto accords even if that grants a temporary advantage to China and India. On the same question, thirty- to forty-nine-year-olds go in almost exactly the opposite direction, opposing ratification by a 49–34 plurality.

The extra-border perspective of young adults is equally evident when we move the borders much closer to home. By a vast spread—91 percent to 67 percent—young adults are considerably more likely than those over age sixty-five to see Mexicans as "hardworking." By almost identical numbers, they believe that Mexicans are discriminated against in the United States. Three in five young adults think we should make our relationship with Mexico a "high priority." Not only do they support NAFTA, they think free trade agreements should be expanded throughout the Americas. On all those scores, they differ dramatically with every age cohort above them. (The bottom two items are from a January 2006 poll of 1,191 adults we conducted with the Mexico City think tank CIDAC.)

		18–29	30–45	46–65	OVER 65
Do you believe that NAFTA has been a good thing or a bad thing for the U.S.?	GOOD THING	51%	41	35	31
	BAD THING	21	26	39	36
The government is considering expanding NAFTA to include not just Mexico but some other Latin American nations.	FAVOR	53	34	30	21
	OPPOSE	38	44	53	57
Would you agree or disagree [with] a U.S. plan to help Mexico's development in exchange for control on illegal migrants?	AGREE	71	52	55	51
	DISAGREE	28	32	35	33

(table continued)		18–29	30–45	46–65	OVER 65
Would you agree or disagree [with] a U.S. financial aid program for Mexico in exchange for allowing more U.S. investment in Mexican oil and gas operations now reserved to the Mexican government?	AGREE	64%	45	43	43
	DISAGREE	32	44	47	45

First Globals want a foreign policy as inclusive and embracive as they are. They expect impediments to trade to be removed so they can shop anywhere, and they want developing countries and their peoples protected from predatory multinational corporations and fiscal policies that hold the world's poorest people ransom. For First Globals, the American Century is already over, and the Whole Earth Century has begun.

Many polling experiences have driven home for me the vast chasm between these global-minded young adults and the leaders who govern the nation and determine its stance toward the world, but one in particular stands out. In a survey we did back in late 2004 for the Committee of 100, a group of prominent Chinese Americans, eighteen- to twenty-nine-year-olds led the way in expressing favorable views of China and Chinese-made products, but solid majorities of Americans joined them, even including Americans who find themselves in jobs paying less than their previous one. Of all the many subsets we broke our results into, the only genuinely negative responses we found to both China and its products came from members of Congress and their staffs. That's cultural disconnect in stark relief.

FROM STAY-AT-HOME TO GLOBAL ROAMING: THE POSITIVE POWER OF A PASSPORT

The Internet is one of the great discriminators between then and now. It reconfigures geography and creates a mind-set that looks beyond physical borders for answers and inspiration. The other great discriminator—and I think an even more powerful one—is travel. Travel exposes people to other cultures, alternative ways of doing things, new products and brands, and sometimes competing worldviews. For the young especially, travel is the physical completion of the global connection that begins on a computer screen. And no Americans in history have traveled abroad in greater numbers than the Americans of today.

In 1976, the U.S. Department of State issued 2.8 million passports. By 1985, that number had climbed to five million, a figure it wouldn't top again until 1995. Since then, the passport numbers have all but exploded. An impressive 7.3 million passports were issued in 2000, 10.1 million in 2005, and 12.1 million in 2006. Over the past thirty years, the U.S. population has grown by about 40 percent, while the number of passports issued has jumped more than 400 percent.

Why such explosive growth? More air carriers and discount fares, more relatively inexpensive cruises, greater curiosity about the larger world, more college and university exchange programs and organized high school programs, maybe more legal immigrants returning to visit the families they left behind—the reasons are myriad, and the age spread is broad. About one in five passports gets issued to those age twenty to twenty-nine, another one in five to those age forty to forty-nine, and still another 20 percent to those age sixty to sixty-nine, with lower shares going to those in their thirties and fifties—the years when people are starting families and saving for college.

What we do know is that the attitudinal and opinion gap between those who have a passport and those who do not is wide enough, particularly among the young, to suggest that foreign travel might be among the experiences that most separate Americans. We also know from our polling that while the young get passports in about equal proportion to other age groups, they use them more than any other generation of Americans. The table on page 112 is from our June 2007 Interactive survey.

HOW OFTEN HAVE YOU TRAVELED ABROAD IN THE PAST FIVE YEARS?

	18–24	25–34	35–54	55–69	70+
1–2 times	37%	35	30	25	24
3–5 times	27	16	13	13	16
5+ times	6	10	7	8	6

When we asked all adults in the same Interactive survey if the United States should sign the Kyoto global warming treaty, 46 percent of those with passports strongly or somewhat agreed, compared to only 36 of those without a passport. When we put the question to those age eighteen to twenty-seven, the spread between passports and non-passports was 54–45. The spread was even wider when we compared those of all ages who expected to travel abroad five or more times over the next five years with those who had no intention of traveling abroad. Forty-eight percent of prospective non-travelers strongly disagreed with signing the Kyoto accords, while only 16 percent strongly supported doing so. Prospective frequent travelers went in the opposite direction: 38 percent strongly supported the treaty, while 32 percent strongly opposed it.

On the issue of whether the United States should be a participant in the International Criminal Court, 30 percent of all adult passport holders strongly agreed, compared to 23 percent of those without passports. The more times people of all ages had traveled abroad over the past five years, the higher the rate of strong agreement climbed, from 28 percent of those who had been abroad once or twice to 36 percent of those who had traveled abroad more than five times. Among eighteen- to twenty-seven-year-olds, the "strongly agrees" among passport holders (37 percent) outstripped the same among those who were not passport holders, by 20 points.

In still other polling, this in December 2006, we asked a series of questions meant to gauge the effect of travel on the perception of other cultures. Was American culture and civilization superior to that of China? Twenty-five percent of eighteen- to twenty-nine-year-olds with passports said yes, compared to 44 percent of those without passports. The split was virtually identical when we asked the same question about Latin America. What about Africa? Thirty-five percent of young adult passport holders said America was superior; just shy of half of those without passports (49 percent) agreed. And how about the U.S. compared to Arab culture and civilization, a question loaded with overtones, given the world situation? Thirty-four percent of eighteen- to twenty-nine-year-old passport holders said yes, America was superior, as compared with 51 percent of those without passports. When we asked how important it was for a company to have all its operations within the United States, better than one in five of those without passports answered "very important," while one in thirteen passport holders said the same.

I don't want to draw too many conclusions from figures like these. Family resources can play a big role in whether young people get to travel outside the country. Other sociological factors intervene. But I don't want to downplay the significance, either. Travel alters perspective; it breaks up prejudices and preconceived notions. The table below is from a June 2007 survey in which we asked over eight thousand respondents to identify their residency from three choices, then broke the results down by age and by those who had traveled abroad in the past five years and those who hadn't. As you look at the results, ask yourself which group is more likely to fit into and prosper in a world without boundaries: those who think of home as a small dot on the globe, as a continental chunk of that globe, or as the whole globe?

WHAT IS YOUR RESIDENCY?

	MY CITY OR TOWN	AMERICA	THE PLANET EARTH
Age 18–27			
Travel	28%	43	29
No travel	31	48	21

WHAT IS YOUR RESIDENCY? *(continued)*

	MY CITY OR TOWN	AMERICA	THE PLANET EARTH
Age 28–41			
Travel	25%	46	29
No travel	23	52	25
Age 42–61			
Travel	20	52	29
No travel	22	55	23
Age 62–80			
Travel	17	59	24
No travel	18	60	22
Age 81+			
Travel	22	60	18
No travel	29	58	12

FROM ONE-ON-ONE TO RAINBOW MARKETING: SELLING IN THE GLOBAL SOUK

How do you sell to a generation that takes globalism as a given, one that has embraced diversity so thoroughly that distinctions of race, gender, and sexual orientation have faded into a faint background music? How do you even communicate with a group that picks "friendly Labrador" and "powerful rottweiler" when we ask eighteen-to twenty-nine-year-olds which type of dog they most resemble, and "elegant magnolia" when we ask them to choose a tree?

Okay, some of our questions *are* a little wacky, but to me those metaphorical selections suggest a generation of young people who feel strong, decisive, and smart (the rottweiler in them); attractive and self-confident (that elegant magnolia); and very much at ease with themselves (friendly Labrador)—people, that is, who are ready to take on the world on their own terms and who have the personal and social skills to succeed. More than any other age group, this one has been exposed to the world, not just to family and friends.

The marketing implications of this epic generational embrace of diversity seem obvious enough. Benetton, Tommy Hilfiger, and Versace are the jumping-off point, not the end destination. Benetton's United Colors campaign—begun in the late 1980s with such powerful images as a black woman breast-feeding a white baby and two male hands, one black and one white, joined by handcuffs—was brilliance itself. More so than any other campaign I can think of, it might have actually pushed the world toward being a better place. But United Colors is no longer the next new thing; it's the world these First Globals live in. It's the given of their lives, not the aspiration of them.

In its June 4, 2007, edition *Advertising Age* ran a front-page story under the headline "Ditch the Flags; Kids Don't Care Where You Come From." As Ted Morris, a senior vice president at Brand-Intel, put it in the article, "They don't care about country of origin because of the way their world has been defined. Being online transcends geography. . . . Point of origin is becoming irrelevant." By way of evidence the article cites an Anderson Analytics survey of American college students that suggests an almost colossal indifference to what brands come from where. Fewer than one in twenty students knew that Nokia was Finnish; more than half thought it was Japanese. Fewer than one in ten were aware that LEGO originated in Denmark, that Samsung was Korean, or that Adidas was German. Even IKEA left more than two thirds of the students in the dark, despite the fact that many of the students' dorm rooms and apartments were furnished straight from the Swedish retailer's showrooms.

To be sure, the United States still leads the world in brands, brand value, and brand recognition. In its 2006 annual ranking of top brands for *BusinessWeek,* the research group Interbrand included thirteen American companies among the top twenty brands, including the top five: Coca-Cola, Microsoft, IBM, GE, and Intel, in that order. Only two other nations managed as many as two brands: Japan (Toyota at number 7 and Honda at 19) and Germany, with Mercedes-

Benz (10) and BMW (15). But according to Interbrand's calculations, three of the top five U.S. brands—Coca-Cola, Microsoft, and Intel—had all lost brand value during the previous twelve months, while four non–U.S. brands—Nokia (6), Toyota, BMW, and Louis Vuitton (17)—had seen double-digit growth in their value. Indeed, the only top-twenty U.S. brand to gain double-digit value was Gillette, which pulled in at number 16. Even more ominous for U.S. brand hegemony, in the Anderson Analytics survey of college students cited in the previous paragraph, respondents who mistakenly thought Lexus was a U.S. brand rated the Toyota luxury product 13 points lower than students who knew it traced back to Japan.

In our own surveying for IBM in December 2006, just one in seven eighteen- to twenty-seven-year-olds (14 percent) told us it was very important "that a company have all its operations within the United States," as opposed to 23 percent of forty-two- to sixty-one-year-olds. Only one in eleven of the youngest age cohort said that the country where a product was produced was more important than the quality of the product, while one in seven of those age forty-two to sixty-one chose point of origin first. How can anyone be surprised that better than one in four young adults think of themselves as citizens of planet Earth? Next time we ask the question, perhaps in another year or so, I expect that number to crowd 50 percent.

So many of the First Globals' elders are constantly amazed by the flattened (to borrow from Thomas Friedman) world we live in. I'm sometimes among them. I marveled along with most sports commentators and columnists that the 2007 NBA championship San Antonio Spurs were built around a center from the Virgin Islands, Tim Duncan; the Argentine Manu Ginobili, the league's best sixth man; and the French-born scoring machine Tony Parker, who draped himself in his country's flag as he accepted the championship series MVP award. Then again, I date back to a time when America's international dominance in basketball was unchallenged—the days of the first Olympic "dream team" and forty-point trouncings of the competition. That's not the world of the youngest First Globals. They've seen our

Olympic "dream teams" become dysfunctional agglomerations of one-dimensional multimillionaires. First Globals load their fantasy-league NBA teams with French guards, Croatian forwards, and if they can land him, the seven-foot six-inch Chinese center Yao Ming.

A week after the Spurs finished off the Cleveland Cavaliers to claim the NBA title, I had a similar moment of amazement as I watched another Argentine, the journeyman golfer Angel Cabrera, become the third international player in a row to win the U.S. Open title. Then I remembered that the man who failed to catch Cabrera down the stretch, the barely-out-of-his-twenties Tiger Woods, was himself the product of a Thai mother and a black American father, and I thought that what I had just been watching wasn't a U.S. competition at all but rather a stretch duel, by happenstance on American soil, between the products of three continents—another borderless encounter, in short, along an ever-shrinking horizon.

Even a flattened world isn't immune to the normal effects of passing time. Today's First Globals will have kids of their own, want a house, a second car; eventually, if they aren't already, they'll become the quiet Investors Next Door, worrying about whether they will have enough resources to retire on. Such is the progression of life, but we are not going back to the world of our fathers or even the world many of us grew up in. With the globalized economy and corporations less loyal to employees and communities, young people have no reason to even suspect that they will be in the same job for the next half decade, much less for years to come, and they know for certain they won't be handed a pension when they finally say goodbye.

It can't be stressed enough. Today's young adults are wired differently. To get them to listen to whatever you're selling, you have to get down to where they are. You have to make yourself equally a citizen of planet Earth, and you need to recognize that, for them, embracing diversity isn't a matter of political correctness but a habit of mind. To return briefly to the NBA, I am convinced that's why Commissioner David Stern exiled former star Tim Hardaway from the 2007 all-star game after Hardaway's homophobic rant about an-

other ex-player's out-of-the-closet memoir. Stern is a master sales-
man for his sport, and he knows how quickly intolerance can alien-
ate his youth demographic.

Another example: NASCAR's fan base is probably as conservative as that of any sport going. When we asked whether people approved of the policies of Bill and Hillary Clinton, only 37 percent of
NASCAR fans said yes, while 57 percent said no, and the rest were
not sure. That's a pure red state spread. Yet in successive tours
through the NASCAR.com website, I've found a home-page feature
on the sport's thirteen women drivers, from Carolyn Carrier to Patti
Wheeler, right below a pull-down menu for the sport's fifty greatest
personalities, and an article by website reporter David Caraviello on
that rarest of commodities, a black driver named Lewis Hamilton
who at the tender age of twenty-two is already competing successfully on the Formula One circuit.

That's how you make contact with First Globals—by opening
doors, not closing them; by stretching your borders (the National
Football League, for example, trying to make inroads in Europe);
and by remembering as NASCAR clearly does that while its present
fan base might be solidly red state, those Wal-Mart shopping GOP-
voting race-car enthusiasts have children who are growing up in a
globally based online world where distinctions such as red state–
blue state are increasingly meaningless.

If you don't keep all that in mind, the kids are going to leave you
in the dust whether you're pushing a sport, a product, or a presidential candidacy. They know who has the upper hand. They know
time is on their side. Like twentysomethings everywhere of just
about every generation, they're mostly convinced that they are in
the right. But don't worry about them. They know their weaknesses
as well as their strengths. When we asked First Globals if "high
school programs in the United States are adequately preparing our
young people to understand current international affairs," a staggering 93 percent said *no*.

A QUICK GUIDE TO MARKETING TO FIRST GLOBALS

- Surprise: Eighteen- to twenty-nine-year-olds actually care about more than just themselves.
- Not only do young adults live in a world dominated by diversity, they celebrate it, and they expect marketers and politicians to realize that.
- The entire world excites them, not just their community or nation of birth. The young think and buy globally, and they are sensitized to global issues from human rights to AIDS and poverty, even though they might not always command the facts.
- While First Globals poll "liberal" on many issues, they're more devoted than any other age group to finding common ground on tough social issues.
- For them, just about everything is in the public domain, up to and including intimate details of their lives.
- Maybe best of all, young adults have defined "their space" on the Internet and by using cell phones and text-messaging, and are easy to reach as influencers and individuals.

5

The New American Dream

WHO I AM, NOT WHAT I OWN

On a cold February day in 1843, Frederick Tudor paused on the edge of a pond, watching his reflection in the near-frozen water. Although the pond sat in the midst of a heavily farmed area only twenty miles west of Boston, the water was as pristine as the forest that surrounded it. Standing there, Tudor began to calculate the economic opportunity the pond represented. Tudor was a leading ice manufacturer of his day. In his business, water was money.

At the same time, unknown to Tudor, another man approached the pond from the other side, intent on contemplating the setting's broader meaning. To Henry David Thoreau, a philosopher and the leading social critic of his age, Walden Pond symbolized all that gave this country meaning: individualism, liberty, and man's relationship with nature. Two years later, in March 1845, Thoreau would begin to build a one-room house beside the pond—an experiment in simple living that produced one of the classics of American literature.

To both Tudor and Thoreau, Walden Pond was America in all its greatness. Both men dreamed. Both spoke for the era in which they lived. Men such as Tudor helped to usher in the industrial age, with its production of great wealth and its open door to immigrants from foreign shores. Thinkers such as Thoreau bore the conscience of this nation, providing the intellectual rationale for the abolition of slavery, for women's rights, for the right of workers to organize, and for the preservation of the natural environment.

In the tension between these two strains—the entrepreneur and the moral citizen—a balance was struck. Wealth was created, and the human spirit and mankind's capabilities were enhanced. Both dreams were and still are essential to the vitality of our nation.

■ ■ ■

I first heard that parable from a favorite professor, a mentor back when I was a graduate history student. Later, when I taught history, I often used the story to illustrate the American dream and its various meanings. Although my days in the classroom are long behind me, Tudor and Thoreau appear frequently in the commencement addresses I am more and more asked to deliver, and I'm still pursuing the American dream and the public's attitudes toward it. For a decade now, beginning in 1998, I've been posing the same simple question and tabulating the results. Here it is. You might take a moment to estimate what percentage of respondents choose each answer.

WHICH OF THE FOLLOWING STATEMENTS BEST REPRESENTS YOUR GOALS IN LIFE?

Statement A: I believe the American dream means material success. It is possible for my family and me and for most middle-class Americans to achieve.

Statement B: I believe you can achieve the American dream through spiritual fulfillment rather than material success.

Statement C: I believe the American dream means material success. It exists but is more likely to be attained by my children and not me.

Statement D: I believe I cannot achieve the American dream, whether material or spiritual, nor can most middle-class Americans.

The two answers that consistently draw the fewest responses are, not surprisingly, C and D—the ones I think of as the Deferred Dreamers and the Dreamless Dead. The Deferred Dreamers, those who choose statement C, haven't given up on material success, nor have they stopped defining the dream in terms of material goods and riches, even if they think their children are more likely to get there than they are. In many ways they are the heirs of so many of the families who entered America through Ellis Island, determined to make a better life for the generations to follow.

For the Dreamless Dead, the ones who pick statement D, the American dream however it is defined has simply stopped being germane to their lives. These are not necessarily people who live in grinding poverty. Some do, of course, and the one in eight Americans who live below the official poverty line are very heavily represented among the Dreamless Dead. But as a 2005 U.S. Census Bureau study found, to be poor in America is not the same as being poor in Haiti or Bangladesh or much of Africa. As of 2002, 99 percent of those living below the poverty line had refrigerators; 98 percent had stoves and color televisions; 93 percent had microwave ovens; 88 percent had VCRs; 86 percent owned a car, a truck, or a van; 80 percent had a washer and 77 percent a dryer; 73 percent had a stereo system; 59 percent had a computer; and 58 percent had a dishwasher. To be sure, many of the Dreamless Dead might lack health insurance or enough money to properly take care of their children, but the real poverty from which many of them suffer is a poverty of optimism and expectations, not possessions. For them, the famous refrain of Reverend Jesse Jackson's 1984 and 1988 presidential campaigns—"Keep Hope Alive"—falls on deaf ears.

The numbers for the Deferred Dreamers and Dreamless Dead migrate slightly back and forth, depending on the state of the economy, natural disasters such as Hurricane Katrina, man-made ones such as 9/11, and other events; but collectively, the two have composed anywhere from 15 to 21 percent of American adults over the decade I have been doing this. (Those numbers, I should add, are probably underrepresentative since the poor are more likely to have out-of-service phones or no computers and thus be harder to reach and include in our tabulations.) When we posed the question in a June 2007 Zogby Interactive survey, both groups together totaled 15 percent of all respondents, at the historic low end but with a troubling twist: The Dreamless Dead outnumbered Deferred Dreamers by better than three to one. In 2005, the two groups had been evenly matched, and the year before that, Deferred Dreamers had exceeded Dreamless Dead by roughly four to three. More worrisome still in our 2007 survey was the high representation of women among those who have given up hope. About one in seven women chose statement D, compared to one in eleven males on the same survey and compared to one in fourteen females when we asked the question in April 2004. Single women, widows, and those in failed marriages and civil unions were particularly vulnerable to despair, as were those who never attend church.

How about Frederick Tudor's heirs—the ones who choose statement A, who believe that the American dream means material success and that such success is well within the grasp of most of the middle class? In truth, this is the group that I expected to dominate the question when I first started asking it. What was America about if it wasn't consumption? As frequently happens when I make such presuppositions, I was wrong. These Traditional Materialists do constitute a large bloc, 36 percent of all respondents in our June 2007 poll, but their numbers are almost identical to those who chose statement B—the ones I call Secular Spiritualists, those who believe that the American dream is measured in spiritual, not material, fulfillment. (In our 2007 poll, Materialists outpaced Spiritualists by a scant .5 percent, well within the margin of error of 1.6 percentage points.)

Given that Americans have so long been defined by the desire to acquire and a willingness to uproot self and families in search of better financial opportunities, I find this remarkable. To live in the United States is to be bombarded with advertising messages. Marketers sometimes seem to be living inside our televisions and computers. In theory, we should be obsessed with consumption, with getting and spending. In practice, 36 percent of all of us—and nearly half of those who believe that the American dream is attainable in any form in our lifetime—now view it in nonmaterial terms.

We see this playing out in ways big and small. Every November since the start of the new century, Zogby has been asking people if they are going to spend on holiday giving less than, more than, or the same as they did in the previous year. And every year, through rising stock markets or falling house prices, the answer is basically the same: Significantly more people tell us they intend to spend less on gifts in the upcoming holiday season than they did in the last one. Sixty-four percent more people told us this in 2001, 166 percent more in 2004, and almost 70 percent more in 2006. Our Christmas 2007 polling for Reuters once again correctly predicted a holiday spending downturn.

Of course, people tend to overspend when they actually get down to shopping, and Christmas shopping is always subject to a mass of variables, including weather, energy prices, the day of the week Christmas falls on, and much more. But, in fact, total household Christmas holiday spending has been in sharp decline ever since the mid-1990s, according to the Department of Labor's Bureau of Labor Statistics, down by $200 billion between 1996 and 2003 alone. Numbers like that can't be ignored. They speak to a larger movement in society. To the Secular Spiritualists, what we own and buy and give isn't the test. The test is how fulfilled we are personally and spiritually. Their quest isn't for bigger houses and more cars; it's an inner search, a quest for spiritual meaning.

FROM TUDOR TO THOREAU: ENOUGH ALREADY

Like the Investors Next Door, Secular Spiritualists are largely invisible to the naked eye. They have few distinguishing demographic characteristics, a dearth of signifiers to mark them in a crowd. Compare them to Traditional Materialists, though, and a zigzag pattern does begin to emerge. The table on page 125—based on a June 2007 Interactive survey of four thousand adults—shows only those demographic categories with the greatest distinction between Secular Spiritualists and Traditional Materialists, and it omits percentages for Deferred Dreamers, the Dreamless Dead, and "not sures" (12 percent of all those responding). When we break the results down by where people live (big city, small city, suburbs, or rural), whether they have a passport or not or serve in the armed forces, or by region of the country, the split between materialists and spiritualists is nearly dead equal.

TRADITIONAL MATERIALISTS COMPARED TO SECULAR SPIRITUALISTS

	% ANSWERING TRADITIONAL MATERIALISTS	% ANSWERING SECULAR SPIRITUALISTS
Male	44	33
Female	29	38
Parent with child at home	34	42
No child at home	37	34
Age 18–27	31	40
28–41	33	40
42–61	36	36
62–80	44	30
80+	48	27
Liberal	22	35
Moderate	36	34
Conservative	47	39
Libertarian	50	31
$15,000 a year or less	26	36
$15K–$25K	11	36
$25K–$35K	25	46
$35K–$50K	25	41
$50K–$75K	36	35
$50K–$75K	36	35
$75K+	45	36

TRADITIONAL MATERIALISTS COMPARED TO
SECULAR SPIRITUALISTS   *(continued)*

	% ANSWERING TRADITIONAL MATERIALISTS	% ANSWERING SECULAR SPIRITUALISTS
In a job that pays less	26	38
Gone without food	11	44
NASCAR fan	45	33
Democrat	27	34
Republican	48	38
Independent	36	35
Voted for Bush in 2004	47	38
Voted for Kerry in 2004	26	33
Investor	49	35
Non-Investor	38	37
White	37	36
Hispanic	35	36
African American	33	33
Asian	48	32
Catholic	41	36
Protestant	36	41
Jewish	38	18
Born-again	30	49
Not born-again	41	33
Attend church more than once a week	24	59
Attend church weekly	36	43
Attend church once or twice a month	40	40
Attend church on holidays only	39	35
Attend church rarely	42	27
Attend church never	33	22

Can a profile be teased out of all that? Yes, absolutely. Secular Spiritualists are much more likely than Materialists to be age forty-one or younger. They are less likely to be male and, perhaps not surprisingly, members of the investor class, more likely to be female parents with a job at home and make fifty thousand dollars a year or less. Secular Spiritualists know better than Materialists what it is like to lose a job and go hungry. They attend church far more regularly than Materialists and are far more likely to be born-again. And yet they are also more likely than Materialists to identify themselves as liberal and to have voted for John Kerry in the 2004 presidential election. That's in large part why I think of them as "Secular" Spiritualists. Yes, they are more prone to be religiously inclined, but when you look at this group collectively, politics and religion virtually cancel each other out. Their personal relationship to God or any particular faith or creed, or their lack of same, might be a key issue in their own lives, but it's not a salient issue in defining their relationship one to the other. Rather, what pulls them together and gives them definition is the need to move beyond professional and financial ambition, the acquisition of things, and the quest for a luxurious lifestyle.

More than a third of Secular Spiritualists told us in our polling that they have willingly given up a raise or promotion. Two thirds had moved to a smaller community. Nearly all (96 percent) said they had purposely cut down on the amounts they purchased. In other polling we have done, fully 86 percent of all groups questioned said that "There is a higher meaning to life than accumulating goods." That doesn't make them Secular Spiritualists—it's the rare philosophy or religion that *doesn't* posit a higher meaning than possessions—but it does get to the kinship of Secular Spiritualists with the broader American population.

Another example of this new spiritualism's wide appeal and great growth potential: In our June 2007 Interactive poll, we first asked people if their expectations for their career and possessions had increased, decreased, or stayed about the same over the past few years. We then took the 22 percent who said their expectations had decreased—as opposed to 31 percent who said expectations had increased and 43 percent who said their expectations were unchanged—and asked them to choose from among three possible reasons why: (a) They realized they couldn't attain their goals, (b) They were working at a job that paid less than their previous job and never expected to be so well off again, or (c) They just wanted a simpler life. Twenty-six percent chose a and 28 percent b, but the greatest number by a good margin (36 percent) opted for c: "I just want a simpler life," and as the table below shows, they came from all across the demographic spectrum. This, too, is the raw material out of which Secular Spiritualism is growing.

"I JUST WANT A SIMPLER LIFE."

GROUPS CHOOSING THIS RESPONSE 40% OF THE TIME OR MORE	GROUPS CHOOSING THIS RESPONSE 30% OF THE TIME OR LESS
Rural (41%)	Age 81+ (8%)
Union (41)	Moderate (27)
18–27 (46)	Single (29)
Libertarian (50)	Less than $15K (22)
Civil union (44)	$25K–$35K (18)
$50K–$75K (40)	Lost job (30)
Gone w/o food (42)	Fear losing job (30)
West Coast (42)	South (30)
Hispanic (50)	Nader 2004 (9)
Asian (45)	

(Note that 81+ and Nader were both very small samplings.)

Like the political center now forming—and inseparable from it—Secular Spiritualists are not a voting bloc or any other kind of bloc. Instead, they are a broadly based group coalescing around a nexus of values that sometimes mimics religion (and indeed might be the "Democratic religion" that the Center for American Progress seeks) but in fact has only a single doctrine: that the old American materialism has far too many empty calories. These are people who are moving beyond defining success by possessions and position and the bottom line of their brokerage accounts. These people look inside for motivation, not across the street or at the next office over. Success to them isn't climbing the corporate ladder; it's finding peace within. Just as Thoreau looked out at the landscape of industrial age America and decried its dehumanizing effects, so these Secular Spiritualists have looked out at the landscape of an America obsessed with consumption and have decided that isn't working for them.

FROM MORAL MAJORITIES TO MORAL BEHAVIOR:
THE *REAL* STEALTH FORCE IN AMERICAN SOCIETY

As noted earlier, Secular Spiritualists don't fit any easy stereotype. They are born-again Kerry voters, rural liberals, walking contradictions at least when you look at their surface demographics. Such counterintuitiveness is their protective coloration, but their numbers are already large and their potential growth curve is off the charts. That's why I think of them as the stealth force in American society today. Just as with the B-1 bomber, Secular Spiritualists are built to confuse the usual radar configurations, but their impact is already significant and is sure to expand. Indeed, my polling strongly suggests that what Secular Spiritualists are really doing, in an inchoate way, is establishing a lifestyle for our future, a new set of expectations of what our humanity and our "American-ness" are all about.

In the spring of 2005, in polling undertaken in four Florida counties, we asked participants to rate a variety of topics on a five-point scale, ranging from "not important" to "highly important." The results are shown below, in descending order.

PERCENT ANSWERING "HIGHLY IMPORTANT":

Family: 94

Job security: 79

Marriage: 76

Quality of work: 72

Religion: 55

Leisure time: 50

Political issues in the United States: 40

Political issues in the world: 35

That's what I think of as the "agenda" of the Secular Spiritualists, but it's not an agenda at all. Family outranks everything for
everyone, even those without children at home. Women are only
marginally more devoted to families than men—four points in our
polling. Spanish speakers and English speakers and bilinguals finish
within .6 points of each other. Those earning less than fifteen thousand dollars and those making more than seventy-five thousand dollars are less than two points apart. Democrats, Republicans, and
independents are within three points of one another. The agreement
on the importance of family is virtually universal.

The comity breaks down somewhat when the subject is religion.
Republicans outpace Democrats by 11 points and independents by
19 points. Females run almost 18 points ahead of males. Protestants
are 22 points up on Catholics, in large part because 83 percent of
born-agains rated "religion" as simply "very important." But even
that high number—83 percent—speaks volumes when the polling
subcategory is born-agains. Religion is outranked not only by the
quality of relationships and of work but by paycheck security, one
of the grim realities for many workers in an increasingly global
economy. Even leisure time is only slightly less important than the
practice of whatever faith one might subscribe to.

In fact, if you expand the results just a bit, religion finds itself ri-
valed by political issues in the world. Only 35 percent gave global
political issues a rating of highest importance, but another 25 percent ranked them at the second highest tier of importance, while
only a combined 11 percent gave them the lowest two rankings. Religion fared better on the upside—71 percent called it either very or
somewhat important—but slightly worse on the downside: 12 percent said it had little or no importance in their lives.

None of that is to say that religion is unimportant in American
life or in the lives of Secular Spiritualists. Obviously it is important.
To some, religion is of prime importance. But on the whole, even the
lives of born-agains—people who have been specifically touched by
the hand of God—are more balanced than commonly portrayed. In
our Florida polling, almost a third of respondents described their re-

ligious practice as "very active," and another 45 percent said that they were "somewhat active." Collectively, that's more than three in four who take religious practice seriously. But 70 percent of all respondents also said they were very or somewhat active in charity work. Nearly as many (67 percent) said the same about cultural activities, 57 percent described themselves as very or somewhat active at sports, and almost half said they were active in politics and current events. These are people who care about relationships, who are engaged with the world. They worry about their jobs more than they worry about their possessions. They are devoted to family. They are not one-dimensional.

Below is another example from the 2005 Florida surveying. In addition to asking people what was important in their own lives, we asked them to assess, again on a five-part scale, the level of importance of teaching various qualities to children. Again, only those who ranked the quality of "highest importance" are shown in the table below, but this time we'll break the results down by gender, by youngest and oldest respondents, and by ideology.

HOW IMPORTANT IS IT THAT THESE BE TAUGHT TO CHILDREN? (PERCENT ANSWERING "HIGHLY IMPORTANT")

	OVERALL	MALE	FEMALE	18–29	65+	LIBERAL	CONSERVATIVE
Good health and hygiene	92	89	94	91	91	92	93
Self-respect	92	91	93	92	92	94	97
Responsibility	90	88	92	86	92	93	93
Respect for elders	89	85	93	81	92	86	94
To achieve a better life	87	86	89	89	88	84	90
Respect for authority	85	83	87	78	91	78	91
Self-reliance	84	82	86	77	87	86	90
Obedience	76	72	81	72	86	63	83
Serious work habits	76	72	79	59	85	70	80
Creativity	70	70	69	68	69	65	68
Tolerance of others' views	66	60	73	67	75	67	66
Religious faith	59	50	68	43	67	44	76

I hear lots of old disputes lurking in those statistics: wives telling husbands that it's high time they took the kids to Sunday school; gray-hairs lecturing the young about slovenly work habits and the young telling the gray-hairs to just chill out; conservatives shouting "godless" at liberals and liberals shouting "authoritarians" right back at them. Some things don't change. But I also see numerous points of agreement that cut through the usual screaming of public discourse: males and females on the importance of teaching children to achieve a better life; the young and the old on the same subject; liberals and conservatives in a dead heat on teaching responsibility; everyone on teaching good hygiene, creativity, and self-respect.

Beyond that, I see an order of importance that reflects the real concerns of real lives. They want children to be healthy, to respect themselves, and to be responsible. They care less about creativity—perhaps because they think it's hard to teach or because the rampant standardized testing in public schools today has already leached creativity out of most curricula. Teaching tolerance is even lower on their list, maybe for the very simple reason that we already are a far more tolerant society than we were four decades ago, especially the young. Teaching religion is at the bottom of the list—especially among males, eighteen- to twenty-nine-year-olds, and liberals—but that doesn't necessarily mean the respondents don't want a religious dimension to children's lives. They just don't want to see it rammed down anyone's throats.

To me, this is the yeast with which Secular Spiritualism is rising. People are hungry to address the nonmaterial side of their lives. They're worn out with getting and spending; in some cases, they are broken by it. They want an America that looks to the spirit as well as to the pocketbook, and they want to move beyond specifically religious nostrums to get there, including specifically Christian nostrums.

In our May 2007 Interactive poll, we gave more than four thousand participants two statements about God and asked them to choose which one best represented their view. The actual statements and the results follow. ("Not sures" are not shown.)

| Statement A: | God is an all-powerful, all-knowing God who monitors the earth, rewards good, and punishes evil. |
| Statement B: | God is a loving God who created humans and, like the watchmaker, sets us in motion and lets us live our own lives and lets others live theirs. |

OVERALL RESULTS

Statement A	24%
Statement B	49
Neither/other	20

RESULTS BY AGE	18–27	28–41	42–61	62–80	81+
Omniscient God	23	27	25	19	26
Watchmaker God	40	46	50	57	48
Neither/other	26	22	19	17	16

RESULTS BY INCOME	LESS THAN $15K	$15K–$25K	$25K–$35K	$35K–$50K	$50K–$75K	$75K+
Omniscient God	33	23	30	22	25	23
Watchmaker God	35	49	44	50	48	52
Neither/other	26	19	22	24	22	19

RESULTS BY 2004 ELECTION VOTES	VOTED FOR BUSH	VOTED FOR KERRY
Omniscient God	36	12
Watchmaker God	48	51
Neither/other	10	31

Yes, in 2004, John Kerry was preferred by three times as many agnostics and atheists as George Bush, and Bush was preferred by three times as many of those who believe in what is largely an Old Testament God, but about half of the support for both men came from Americans whose view of religion is very much akin to the deism of many of our founding fathers, including Benjamin Franklin, George Washington, and Thomas Jefferson.

Later in the May 2007 survey, we asked the same four thousand-plus participants to choose which of three statements best describes the difference between someone with a good moral personal life and someone with good Christian values. The choices follow. You might try to estimate what percentage of respondents would fall into each class. (Again, "not sures" are omitted.)

Statement A:	Christian values are more moral [than other values].
Statement B:	Christian values are not necessarily more moral.
Statement C:	Religious affiliation is not a factor in values/morals.

OVERALL RESULTS

Statement A	19%
Statement B	29
Statement C	49

BY GENDER	MALE	FEMALE
More moral	24	15
Not necessarily more moral	27	30
Not a factor	46	51

BY REGION	EAST	SOUTH	CENTRAL/GREAT LAKES	WEST
More moral	13	20	23	19
Not necessarily more moral	26	33	28	26
Not a factor	54	40	49	54

BY RACE	WHITE	HISPANIC	AFRICAN AMERICAN	ASIAN
More moral	20	15	16	7
Not necessarily more moral	27	28	39	46
Not a factor	49	55	40	43

As always, fluctuations and anomalies abound, but to me the bottom line is clear. However you crunch the data, whatever groups we isolate, with the exception of born-agains and those who attend church more than once weekly, it's not the moral teaching that matters but the moral behavior itself. Even among the most religious, that's true. Forty-five percent of born-agains and 43 percent of the most regular churchgoers did say that Christian values are more moral, but 50 percent of the former group and 42 percent of the latter told us either that Christian values were not morally superior or that religious affiliation wasn't a factor.

FROM "MONEY, HONEY" TO "CAN'T BUY ME LOVE": SORRY, ELVIS, THE BEATLES WERE RIGHT

For those at the lowest income levels, embracing the paradigm of Secular Spiritualism dovetails with the loss of any hope of growing rich or even comfortably middle-class. I recall so well a survey I conducted in my local county in central upstate New York in 1987— a simultaneous countywide telephone poll and door-to-door survey in high poverty census tracts. The focus was to determine the prevalence of hunger. We asked if anyone in the household had "not eaten any food in any twenty-four-hour period during the past year because of a lack of money or food." The results pleased me greatly professionally: The House Select Committee on Hunger would eventually adopt our survey as a model for community polling. But the results also surprised and sometimes startled me, especially the instances of hunger among those living in households earning between $50,000 and $75,000 per year. (And remember, this was two decades ago.)

My wife, Kathy, did some detailed follow-up interviews with people in this middle-income range who said they had gone hungry, and we found fully credible cases of people who were earning less than they once had but refused to give up their house, car, or other amenities of their former lifestyle. The one variable in their monthly budget, and the one least visible to others, was their monthly expense for food, and so that's where they bit the bullet. Unable to come to grips with a more modest lifestyle, they still hoped to get their old life back. For them, to give up the trappings of middle-class life was simply to give up altogether.

That was years ago, and since then the percentage of people in this country who earn less than they once did has almost doubled— from approximately one in seven of all adults in 1990 to more than one in four today. Indeed, many Americans today are in their second or third generations of jobs that earn less than the one they had before⟨Among these downwardly mobile, millions have come to the realization that they will never return to where they were before. In fact, one sees many of these people moving through the same stages of grief that Elisabeth Kübler-Ross first identified: from shock, anger, despair, and resignation, to acceptance and finally adjustment to diminished circumstances.

For many in this group, Secular Spiritualism is an accommodation by default. Materialism didn't work for them; maybe introspection and a search for deeper meaning will. But what continues to amaze me is how thoroughly these individuals have adjusted to that reality, not just in their spending habits—over the long term, that's hard to avoid—but in their attitudes toward wealth⟩

The media constantly throws out stories about misbehaving heiresses and brokerage house partners with end-of-the-year bonuses equal to the annual payroll of a medium-size factory. We know by now that economic disparity is growing in America by leaps and bounds. Yet rather than boil with resentment that some have so much when others have so little, most Americans seem to accept the billionaires among us and even empathize with the problems that come with having too much of everything. We know the tragic stories of the Kennedys. We've read in the supermarket tabloids about the drug habits, alcoholism, marital problems, and sheer unhappiness of stars such as Kurt Cobain, Lindsay Lohan, Britney Spears, and Jessica Simpson. As inclined as many might be to whisper "good riddance" when Paris Hilton reports for jail, we also can't help but think that like the rest of us, she has parents, and they must be ashamed.

When we asked respondents in our 2005 consumer profile poll to react to various descriptions of the word "billionaire," this is what we found. (Respondents could choose as many terms as they wanted.)

TERMS THAT BEST DESCRIBE BILLIONAIRES

Fortunate	65%
Shrewd	52
Leadership	50
Blessed	47

Ruthless	34%
Greedy	31
Selfish	25
Genius	24
Role model	20

Note that only one in four respondents was ready to characterize billionaires as selfish and only roughly one in three as greedy or ruthless. The very, very rich might be leaders, and shrewd ones at that, but what they mostly were was fortunate or, for those with a religious bent, blessed. And what they decidedly were not were geniuses or, at the bottom of the heap, role models. Why the latter? In part because attaining billionaire status is so hard for most Americans to even wrap their minds around but also because the ground is shifting beneath us and more and more people are seeking role models that will lead to greater spiritual fulfillment, not greater mounds of goods and possessions. As we'll see in the next chapter, the new heroes of the American public are authenticity-based, not constructed out of artifice. The billionaires and gilded royalty that do connect with us—the new and generous Bill and Melinda Gates; Warren Buffett; even the late Diana, the "People's Princess"—do so not because of their wealth but because of their humanity, something that a Donald Trump could never understand.

Higher up the income ladder the pull toward spiritualism shifts from accommodating to the grim facts on the ground to accommodating to shifting needs in life. Money might have bought them a house, several cars, European vacations, even a second home at the beach or in the country, but it hasn't brought them inner peace. These are the Americans that Gregg Easterbrook writes about in *The Progress Paradox*—the ones who are living in the midst of a "revolution of satisfied expectations" and dealing with "the uneasy feeling that accompanies actually receiving the things that they dreamed of."

According to University of Pennsylvania psychologist Martin Seligman, whom Easterbrook cites, our consumption-driven passion for "shopping, sports cars, expensive chocolates, and the like are 'shortcuts to well-being,' " and to clinical depression as well. "Acquiring material things may produce a momentary feeling of gratification, but the feeling rarely lasts. . . . Spending as a shortcut to well-being is crippling owing to debt, or by locking a person as a head of a household into the soul-draining existence of always maximized income."

In his 2000 bestseller *Bowling Alone,* Harvard sociologist Robert D. Putnam painted an America in which the social contract is in tatters. Voting is down disastrously; civic organizations such as the Boy Scouts, the League of Women Voters, and the national PTA beg for members and volunteers. Between 1980 and 1993, total U.S. bowlers grew by 10 percent, while the number of league bowlers declined by 40 percent. (Hence the title: We're bowling alone.) That, too, I'm convinced, is part of what underlies the Secular Spiritualism. Materialism gave us ever-larger houses with imitation wraparound Victorian porches where almost no one ever sits or visits. It filled our garages with cars that take us to workplaces where we stay longer and longer to earn the salary that meets the bills. It even gave us disco bowling lanes where keglers can sip martinis, chow down on gourmet-level munchies, and watch MTV videos while their scores are automatically calculated, but where they don't know the people bowling on either side of them.

In a January 2007 Interactive poll, we asked nearly ten thousand adult Americans to tell us what they were most hoping to get out of their jobs in the immediate future. Pay and advancement were important, to be sure. Getting a promotion was a top goal for 11 percent of American workers, while 10 percent said they wanted to make a job or career change this year. Predictably, these goals jumped to the top of the list for those on the bottom of the income ladder. Participants with household incomes of less than $25,000 said they most wanted a promotion (19 percent) and a new job or career (15 percent).

But as you scale up the income ladder, specific rewards such as titles and pay wane, and abstract ones ("happiness," most notably) wax. One in six (17 percent) American workers told us he or she hopes to get more personal fulfillment from his or her work this year. Among those with household incomes of $100,000 or more, that figure jumped to 20 percent—the highest segment in our poll. Another 12 percent said they wanted to make a difference this year, on the local level or the world stage.

I try to ask questions on a regular basis that get at the ultimate meaning of life, because I think you can explain much of what happens day to day by reading backward from how people view the big picture. Sometimes we'll throw out clichés and see what happens. We tried that with Traditional Materialists and Secular Spiritualists, asking which of a series of broad adages most applied to the respondents' lives. The results are shown below, broken down by age as well as by Traditional Materialists and Secular Spiritualists.

WHICH OF THE FOLLOWING PHRASES BEST DESCRIBES YOU?

To live a life that helps others and leaves the world a better place, even if it means you will not achieve many of your own dreams.

18–29	57%
30–45	62
46–65	68
65+	65
Traditional materialists	52
Secular spiritualists	79

To live a life that is more happy than sad, even if it means that you are sometimes selfish.

18–29	32%
30–45	26
46–65	19
65+	21
Traditional materialists	30
Secular spiritualists	15

WHICH OF THE FOLLOWING PHRASES BEST DESCRIBES YOU? *(continued)*

To live a life that is comfortable and materially successful, even if it means that you are sometimes not spiritually or emotionally fulfilled.

18–29	3%
30–45	5
46–65	5
65+	7
Traditional materialists	10
Secular spiritualists	1

What do the figures on such questions ultimately say? That those of us in our late middle years are looking outward, away from the daily struggle and beyond any dreams we might once have had for our own well-being; that even the youngest among us can see that money can't buy you love; and that the old promise of materialism is falling on deaf ears everywhere. There's a huge gap between having things and having the happiness that Secular Spiritualism seeks to provide.

FROM TIKI BARS AND CLUB MEDS TO ELDERHOSTELS, LIFELONG LEARNING, AND ADVENTURE TRAVEL: DRINKING THE WORLD IN, NOT DRINKING IT UP

Age factors into the equation as well. For historian Robert Fogel, the new emphasis on spiritual growth and well-being has deep roots in a recent structural demographic change: People are living longer, in some cases much longer. In the not very distant future, America will be home to more than a million centenarians—more than have ever existed collectively in the history of the planet. The Census Bureau projects that by the early 2030s, the number of Americans over age eighty-five could total as high as nine million. Many of us have seen our own parents age. We've witnessed up close the dehumanizing effects of the often well-intentioned warehousing of the aged, whether it's the relatively golden handcuffs of an upscale assisted-living center or the tighter handcuffs of a nursing home. We've depleted the financial resources of the ones we love, the ones who brought us into this world, so they will qualify, under Medicaid, for facilities that tend of necessity to the body and not the spirit. And we don't want that paradigm any longer, for our parents if they are still alive, and especially for ourselves. Money didn't work—even when there was enough of it. Quality of life is about more than linen tablecloths and real silver on the nursing home dining tables.

As the baby boom spills into the golden-years boom over the next decade and a half, tens of millions of Americans are going to be facing the prospect of twenty, thirty, or even forty years of life after retirement, much of that time in generally fine health. For many of them—I think for most—golf, TV reruns, and staring at the rising ocean from the porch of a Florida condo isn't going to fill the bill. Nor, for that matter, are the vast majority of the soon-to-be elderly looking for a retirement defined by trappings and possessions.

In our May 2007 Interactive poll, we asked respondents to strongly agree, somewhat agree, somewhat disagree, or strongly disagree with the following statement: "My goal is a retirement that is comfortable and modest." Fifty-one percent strongly agreed and another 38 percent somewhat agreed, and the agreement was across the board. Eighty-three percent of eighteen- to twenty-seven-year-olds signed on, as did 90 percent of forty-two- to sixty-one-year-olds. Liberals and conservatives came within two points of one another, union members and nonunion workers within five points. NASCAR fans and non-fans matched one another exactly. Among income groups, the highest levels of disagreement were found in the wealthiest two categories: those with incomes between $50,000 and $75,000 and those who earn more than $75,000 annually, but the numbers were relatively minuscule. Even among those who presumably have a chance to shoot for something grander in their retirement years, 90 percent in both categories agreed that "comfortable and modest" will do them just fine. In other polling, only about one in seven participants said they wanted to "do nothing" in retirement, while three in four chose "I want to fill my life with things I didn't get a chance to do."

What the soon-to-be retired and many of those already there are looking for are activities to enrich their minds and souls, and connect them not just with one another but with the generations rising behind them. Robert Fogel estimates that "vol-work" (as opposed to "earn-work") will generate millions of hours annually that older Americans can give back to the community and through which they will come to define the meaning and success of their lives.

Elderhostels will flourish, as will travel opportunities that engage the intellect and arouse curiosity, rather than simply herding pensioners from famous site to famous site. Continuing education and lifelong learning programs will be reaching out in earnest to people in their eighties and even their nineties because the numbers and the economic opportunity will be there along with a compelling demand. Better than three hundred universities already offer such programs. Within two decades, every university that wants to survive will have joined in. The market is too big, the need too great to ignore. Most of all, there will be—because there has to be—a revolution in the care of the infirm elderly and those who are simply too old to continue living on their own or without round-the-clock care.

All that, too, is part of the Secular Spiritualism, part of a new definition of what our humanness is all about: a longer and healthier life; retirement years rich with experience, not just things; and an old age filled with meaning, not emptiness.

Whatever is inspiring the movement—whether it's age or necessity or a simple feeling of emptiness—Secular Spiritualism's impact is indisputable: Even those with the resources to spend more are often choosing to spend less, and they're readjusting the motives for their spending. Traditional Materialists are significantly more likely than Secular Spiritualists to derive great pleasure from "an exotic trip to a tropical island" or "an elegant evening at a pricey restaurant." Even when the tab begins to top a thousand dollars, they don't feel the pain if they're celebrating a big event. Secular Spiritualists prefer "a week in the mountains," even when they can afford a month in Anguilla. They are also more likely to say they have "deprived themselves of something they wanted because they would feel guilty," and they have a low guilt threshold: Nearly half of Secular Spiritualists start to feel pangs of conscience around one hundred dollars.

The two groups are almost equally likely to have someone in their household who works a second job or a third job, but the motives for these jobs are quite different. Secular Spiritualists are substantially more likely to work an added job "in order to pay the bills and survive," while Traditional Materialists say their second or third job allows them "to live a little more comfortably without worry."

In our consumer profile poll of 2005, half of all adults (48 percent) told us they had never bought something they didn't need and couldn't afford. Seven in ten (70 percent) said that they had never found themselves short of money for essentials after buying something they didn't need. Two in three had never responded to an unsolicited ad for a credit card, and more than nine in ten said they don't buy at all through the QVC television network—a place that sells almost nothing anyone needs.

A plurality of almost sixteen thousand respondents told us they have only one or two business suits; just 3 percent have eleven or more. Only one in three has more than ten pairs of pants, trousers, or jeans. Just one in ten has more than five watches, while 58 percent have only one or two. Only one in twenty has more than ten items of jewelry with a precious gem, and just one in eight owns a fur-trimmed garment.

To be sure, some of that is out of necessity—people earning less tend to spend less. But it's also out of conviction. We asked respondents what in an ideal world they would most like people to say about them, and then we gave them eight superlatives to chose from. Here are the results:

WHAT OTHERS ARE SAYING ABOUT ME IN MY FANTASY.

Fill in the blank: "I am the __ person they know."

Happiest	27%
Nicest	21
Smartest	14
Luckiest	7
Thinnest	7
Funniest	5
Richest	2
Prettiest	1

Rather than being symptomatic of a sick society, those results strike me as the profile of a very healthy one that we seldom read about. Prettiest counts almost not at all, bad news for the future of plastic surgeons outside of greater Hollywood. Richest matters only slightly more. When we asked Americans just how much money they need to be happy, four out of five (83 percent) responded with the lowest figure we presented: "less than one million dollars." How much do they need each year to live comfortably? Seven out of ten said they could do it on less than $100,000, including the 43 percent who said they could live on $50,000 to $100,000 and the 27 percent who said between $21,000 and $50,000. Many Americans might play Powerball and watch "millionaire" TV shows in large numbers, but in their privates lives, they are learning to be minimalists, and they are aligning their emerging values with their long-term needs. Money matters, no doubt, to just about all of us to one degree or another, but to many of us, it matters less than we once thought it would.

**FROM GETTING TO GIVING: A FRESH
GENEROSITY OF CASH AND SPIRIT**

At the top of the economic heap, Bill and Melinda Gates have heeded Andrew Carnegie's advice that the wealthy should spend the first half of their lives making money and the second half giving it away. As of March 2007, the Gates foundation had given nearly eight billion dollars in grants to promote global health—a king's ransom. But people are hearing that call up and down the food chain. Americans who feel guilty spending a hundred dollars on themselves, who constantly (not just frequently) deprive themselves of something they want because they can't afford it, and who work second and third jobs "in order to pay bills and survive" make up almost half of those who have "given to a charity a larger portion of their income than usual" in recent years, according to our surveys. There's nothing like being one paycheck away from calamity yourself to feel the pain of others.

In fact, in an age of grinding political meanness, I see a fresh spirit of generosity blooming everywhere—a generosity in giving, a generosity of spirit toward others and toward the world at large. Our survey data bank is full of examples. Let me offer a few here.

In our June 2007 Interactive survey, we asked participants to strongly agree, somewhat agree, somewhat disagree, or strongly disagree with the following statement: "Most people are poor because they make bad decisions in life." In all, 41 percent agreed or strongly agreed, while 55 percent came down on the opposite side. Among those age eighteen to twenty-seven, 60 percent disagreed. Almost nine in ten liberals and six in ten moderates disagreed. Among the lowest income group—those most directly tied to the question—30 percent agreed or strongly agreed, while 65 percent disagreed. In the highest income group, those earning above $75,000, the agreement rate was higher—45 percent—but 51 percent refused to blame the poor for their troubles.

We followed that question up moments later with another, related statement: "Most people are poor because their jobs don't pay enough, they lack good health care and education, and things cost too much for them to save and move ahead." Not surprisingly, the numbers this time turned on their heads from the previous question. Only among self-identified conservatives and Republicans (both 58 percent), libertarians (51 percent), and 2004 Bush supporters (55 percent) did a majority disagree. That stance put them at odds with born-agains (42 percent disagreement) and those who attend church more than once a week (41 percent), and might suggest another rupture point in what has been until recently a winning GOP constituency.)

We posited yet another statement in the same survey: "Regardless of my position on the war in Iraq, American veterans must receive better treatment when they return to the United States." This time, the agreement rate was both high (84 percent strongly agreed, and 13 percent somewhat agreed) and broadly spread. No income bracket had a disagreement rate of higher than 3 percent. Those in the armed forces and those out of them agreed equally and highly. True to their respective ideologies, liberals were more inclined to strongly agree (92 percent) than conservatives (76 percent)—"better treatment" is likely to entail more federal expenditure and the growth of more government programs—but it is perhaps telling that moderates (90 percent) were far closer to the liberal position than the conservative one, while independents split the gap between Democrats and Republicans almost exactly.

I find the same sense of generosity and fairness at play when we survey Americans on complicated international issues. In August 2004, for instance, we asked participants to choose which of the following two statements they most agreed with.

Position A:	The U.S. should try to mold the new democracies of other countries into our image and likeness.
Position B:	The U.S. should foster democracy within the context of each country's culture, mores, and traditions.

Here the response was almost universal. Ninety-four percent chose position B, while fewer than 5 percent opted for position A. What's the moral of that, other perhaps than to wish that L. Paul Bremer and the neoconservatives who tried to remake Iraq in our image had been paying attention when the results were first published? I think it's this: Just as the First Globals are helping to break down traditional American isolationism, so the Secular Spiritualists are broadening the ways we connect to one another and with the world at large. They are leading us to look beyond *things* to the humanity behind them, and when you do that your perspective of necessity changes—whether the subject of your attention is Iraqis or the American poor or only yourself.)

A GUIDE TO MARKETING TO SECULAR SPIRITUALISTS

- For at least one in three Americans, spiritual fulfillment is a higher priority than acquisition, ownership, and consumption.
- That doesn't mean they don't buy—they do, of course—but they buy in accordance with their re-prioritized lives. Cut the frills, mute the whistles, give good value. It's back-to-basics for this new stealth force of American society.
- Secular Spiritualists are not big spenders, even when they can afford to be. Once the tab tops a hundred dollars, they start to feel guilty.
- God matters to many of them, but they aren't building their lives around specifically religious values. They're looking for more meaning, not more doctrines and isms to live by.
- Appeal to their giving side. Rich or poor, these are the most generous Americans with their time and treasure.
- And don't forget the one in four Americans who are working at jobs that pay less than their previous work. They're also looking for more meaning, their numbers are huge, and they have wants and needs just like everyone else.

6

One True Thing

**SEARCHING FOR AUTHENTICITY
IN A MAKE-BELIEVE WORLD**

Here's a reality show you won't see on TV. In January 1923, my father set sail from Lebanon via Marseilles to New York City, hoping to join his brother, who had come to America in 1910 and settled in my hometown of Utica. At Ellis Island, Dad was rejected under the terms of the Emergency Quota Act of 1921, the first law ever to set limits on the number of immigrants allowed into the United States. The act capped total annual immigration at 357,000 foreigners and limited immigrants from specific countries to 3 percent of that nationality's total in the 1910 U.S. Census. In the case of Lebanon, which was formed in 1920 out of the postwar remnants of the Turkish Ottoman Empire—and in the case of Turks generally—that amounted to 3 percent of virtually nothing.

Undeterred, Dad sailed back to Marseilles, found work on the docks there as a stevedore, and a year later returned to the United States and once again presented himself at Ellis Island.

This time, he was rejected under the terms of the newly enacted Immigration Act of 1924, which cut the annual quota to 165,000 immigrants, less than half of what it had been the year before and less than a fifth of the average annual immigration in the years prior to World War I. Targeted generally at southern and eastern Europeans and specifically at Italians, the new "permanent" bill limited immigrants from any specific country to 2 percent of people of that nationality recorded in the Census of 1890. Thus, for example, more than 51,000 Germans were allowed into the United States in 1924, while Italians, who had poured into the country at a rate of some 200,000 a year in the first decade of the twentieth century, were limited to fewer than 4,000 immigrants. Since the number of people from the Ottoman Empire living in the United States in 1890 was even fewer than the number living here in 1910, and since the allowable percentage of that tiny number had been cut from 3 to 2, Dad missed out on his second try at immigration.

What happened next is unclear. One version of the story—a version Dad never bothered to entirely discredit—has him jumping off a ship at night into New York harbor, swimming ashore in the dark, and using his broken English to find his way upstate to Utica. I don't necessarily buy that version, though. Dad was from a tiny mountain village, not from coastal Lebanon, where people were more comfortable with water and swimming. My guess is that even as desperate as he undoubtedly felt and notwithstanding his experience working on the docks, the thought of jumping into that black water and thrashing his way ashore would have paralyzed him with fright. I think he sailed back to Marseilles once again, then returned to North America a third time by boat, but on this go-round to Canada, from which he stole illegally into the United States.

What's known for certain is that Dad arrived in Utica late in 1924 and worked four months in a factory before he and his brothers started a grocery business that they called, predictably, Zogby Brothers. What's also known is that Dad lived the next five years in the United States as an illegal alien and that he was frequently threatened with exposure by those who knew his status and wanted to get the upper hand somehow in dealing with him. Finally, in the early 1930s, through my uncle, who was an attorney, and with the help of a very favorable judge who himself was the son of Irish immigrants, Dad's status was made legal, and he began the road to citizenship.

As is the case with so many second-generation Americans whose parents had to endure such hardship to get here, the story of my father's struggle to become an American is never far from his children. Certainly, it colors my own views on immigration reform—or what often masks as "reform." Dad's experience, I'm sure, explains why I go out of my way to accumulate polling data on immigration and why Zogby International does polling in the Arab world, where my father was born, and has partnerships with other polling organizations in places such as Cairo, Abu Dhabi, and Beirut. My brother, Jim, has felt the effects just as strongly. After helping to launch and lead the Palestine Human Rights Campaign and the American-Arab Anti-Discrimination Committee, Jim founded and remains president of the Arab American Institute, based in Washington, D.C.

I think of Dad's story sometimes when I'm grazing the TV channels in the evening and hit upon one of the "reality shows" that are about anything but reality: staged endurance contests in parts of the world so "remote" that they seem to be swarming with camera crews; "talent" shows that are short on talent and long on what seems almost like sadism on the part of the judges; shows featuring "actual" bosses such as Donald Trump, who hardly seems to be human at all. In a TV world full of phony events, Joseph Rachid Zogby's story is real. It's authentic. For his family, it is—in the words of the wonderful title of Anna Quindlen's novel—one true thing.

Oddly, Dad's story also came back to me powerfully a few years ago when I was first reviewing the results of a detailed, comprehensive survey that Zogby International undertook in 2005 of the spending habits of a broad cross section of Americans. My expectation was that the survey would provide an important opportunity to study the infamous faults of American consumers: greed, overspending, obsession with luxury and brands, living beyond our means, failing to save for the future—the pursuit, in short, of an unreal reality.

Authenticity, truth, the *real* reality—these weren't the last things on my mind, but they were at best a faint blip on the radar screen. Yet the demand for them kept echoing back from our findings, and they have been reverberating ever since in polling we have done on a broad array of subjects. If there is a single element driving the operating manual of our lives more than any other, it is the demand after so many years of falsity—in products, claims, and promises— that things finally get back to being honest and actual. Americans have overdosed on baloney, and we've long ago choked on spam. To borrow from the memorable refrain of the movie *Network:* We're mad as hell and not going to take it anymore. But more than anger is at work here: There's a longing, too, a deep-felt need to reconnect with the truth of our lives and to disconnect from the illusions that everyone from advertisers to politicians tries to make us believe are real.

FROM KEN LAY, DUKE CUNNINGHAM, AND BARRY BONDS TO ETHICS 101: LIAR, LIAR, PANTS ON FIRE

What's behind this push for authenticity? Part of it is the onslaught of lying and half-truths that have plagued American public life over the last decade. Democrats seem to have forgiven Bill Clinton for looking the nation in the eye in January 1998 and vowing, "I did not have sexual relations with that woman, Miss Lewinsky." Indeed, my polling (and my gut) suggests that if Clinton were able to seek the presidency in 2000 (and perhaps 2004), his party members likely would renominate him. But while Clinton's failings were far from the impeachable offenses congressional Republicans tried to hang on him, his dissembling about what had taken place with Monica Lewinsky—about what is "sex" and what is, well, something else—became a symbol of a larger disgust with efforts to wriggle out of accountability for misdeeds. In that sense if in no other, figures as diverse as Kenneth Lay, Randy "Duke" Cunningham, Floyd Landis, Jack Abramoff, Mel Gibson, Barry Bonds, and others all can be said to be Bill Clinton's rightful heirs.

Meanwhile, the Bush administration was justifying domestic

measures through an almost Orwellian use of language. (Thus, for example, "tax relief" for hedge fund billionaires, and the 2003 forestry act that the Natural Resources Defense Council called a giveaway to the timber industry but that the president and his aides insisted on calling the "Healthy Forest Initiative.") As a kind of coda to it all, Bush in July 2007 commuted the prison sentence of former Dick Cheney number-two Lewis "Scooter" Libby despite (a) the president's coming to office with the promise to restore respect for the law, (b) Libby's lying to a grand jury to protect his boss and showing no regret for his actions, and (c) the president's own history with commutations. In fifty-seven opportunities as governor of Texas to commute death sentences—some of them meted out to the mentally retarded, others to juveniles and to those grossly misrepresented in court—George W. Bush refused to sign a single one.

Is it any wonder that cynicism on all sides of public life and from every ideological camp is as deep-seated as it is? What's truly remarkable, though, is how quickly trust in government and other large institutions has eroded. In the months immediately after 9/11, our polling consistently showed the American public bonding with leadership and authority to a remarkable degree. As a people, we needed comforting, and for it, we turned to the familiar: government, the church, even corporations, which seemed a rock of stability in a world suddenly drastically altered.

At the top of the pyramid, trust in George Bush soared. His autumn 2001 approval ratings (85 percent in my polls, over 90 percent in some others) were the highest ever achieved by an American president. Then the wheels began to come off. Within months of 9/11, former Enron CEO Ken Lay was invoking the Fifth Amendment rather than testifying before a congressional subcommittee. Soon, Enron CFO Andrew Fastow would be charged with securities, wire, and mail fraud; money laundering; and conspiring to inflate the company's profits. WorldCom, the Catholic priest scandals, the growing controversy over the administration's cherry-picking of intelligence to justify going to war against Saddam Hussein all would follow. Hurricane Katrina gave this growing distrust a distinctly human face—those miserable families all but abandoned by their government remain unforgettable—but mostly what Katrina did was catch a trend and set it in concrete.

In a spring 2006 Zogby Interactive poll commissioned by author and ethicist Jim Lichtman, three in four respondents said they trusted government less than they had five years earlier, only one in four felt that the reporting in the newspapers they read and on network news broadcasts they watched was fair and accurate, and just one in twenty—a strikingly low 5 percent—said that corporations do right by consumers. When we asked participants to select from a lengthy list the "two or three specific changes [that] would have to take place in order to improve your trust in government today," the top three finishers in order were: "personnel changes/impeachment proceedings," "curtail/eliminate lobbying, minimize cronyism," and "campaign finance reform." To me it was intriguing—and a sign of the public's despair—that the most draconian solutions were the top choices.

We also asked participants to rate the trustworthiness of various groups on a scale of one to five, with five being the most trustworthy. Those results are shown below, with one and two grouped into a "low" category and four and five into "high."

HOW AMERICANS RATE THE TRUSTWORTHINESS OF SELECT GROUPS, BY PERCENT

	HIGH	MEDIUM	LOW
Corporate leaders	7	23	69
The media	11	31	58
The president	24	7	69
The courts	29	33	38
Congress	3	20	76

A year later, in a July 2007 Interactive survey, we asked the same basic question again, this time focusing in on government and military leaders. Those results follow, broken down by age.

DO YOU THINK HIGH-RANKING OFFICIALS IN THE GOVERNMENT AND THE MILITARY CAN BE TRUSTED TO TELL THE TRUTH ALL THE TIME, MOST OF THE TIME, SOME OF THE TIME, RARELY, OR NEVER?

	OVERALL	18–29	30–49	50–64	64+
All of the time	1%	0	1	1	2
Most of the time	22	20	22	21	25
Some of the time	45	48	44	43	45
Rarely	25	27	24	28	23
Never	4	2	6	5	4

Those numbers are perilously low, across the board. How effective can even highly ethical and well-meaning congresspeople be when only three of every one hundred adult Americans have a high opinion of the trustworthiness of the institution in which they serve? Indeed, how effective can government itself be when one quarter of all adult Americans say that civilian and military leaders rarely tell the truth? There has to be some basis of belief for democratic government to even function. But while we were asking the trustworthiness question back in our spring 2006 polling, we added another group to the equation, one not often found in queries of this sort. That result is given here.

HOW AMERICANS RATE THE TRUSTWORTHINESS OF SELECT GROUPS, BY PERCENT

	HIGH	MEDIUM	LOW
Friends and coworkers	75	21	4

That response, in turn, was enforced by other results in the same polling. Not only did three in four respondents consider their colleagues trustworthy; virtually everyone (97 percent) said they consider themselves trustworthy, and 85 percent said they think their personal goals in life are less important than acting with honesty and integrity.

What's going on here? Is the vast bulk of the public simply delusional about its honesty level? I don't believe so. Rather, I think that in this as in so many other regards, the public is simply disentangling itself from its putative leaders. On the street, they have seen where the moral compasses of presidents and senators and generals and talking heads and sports heroes are pointing, and they want nothing to do with it. The public wants a higher standard, and since no one above them seems inclined to point the way, they are doing it in their own lives. This is not so much a grassroots movement as a ground-up sensibility—a fundamental shift in public attitude that like the old wildcat labor strikes is all the more volatile because no one specific is leading it.

FROM SPIN DOCTOR HEROES TO REAL ONES:
AT LONG LAST, CYNICISM BOTTOMS OUT

As much as it is being driven by epidemic dissembling at the highest levels, the push toward authenticity is also fueled by the near ubiquity of non-events and overblown ones: candidate "debates" that are debates in name only, political "town" meetings where only partisans are allowed in and any dissenters that happen to crash the party are whisked out the door by security guards, Super Bowls where the competition on the field is obscured by the surrounding advertising frenzy and halftime shows that would be fitting for a Roman emperor if only they were entertaining.

With Hollywood's help, the image-makers in Washington have become wonderfully adept at creating stage sets to mark our grand and sad moments—the beautifully lit Jackson Square in New Orleans where President Bush spoke several nights after Hurricane Katrina had all but destroyed the city, for example, or the deck of the USS *Abraham Lincoln* with its by now infamous MISSION ACCOMPLISHED banner. To unite Americans behind the Iraq war effort, the Pentagon heavily promoted a grainy five-minute videotape showing the midnight rescue of army private Jessica Lynch, who had been captured and wounded early in the fighting when her ordnance maintenance company took a wrong turn and got caught in an ambush near Nassiriya. Unmentioned in the Pentagon's version was the fact that the hospital where Lynch was found was virtually undefended when the U.S. special forces team and its film crew arrived, or the fact that, the day before her rescue, Lynch's Iraqi doctor had tried to deliver her to U.S. forces using an ambulance that had to turn back when it came under fire from an American checkpoint. In the same name of uniting the nation, the Pentagon let stand for five weeks the story that Pat Tillman had been killed by the enemy in Afghanistan in 2004, when officers well up the chain of command knew he had died from friendly fire. It was as if central casting had sent Tillman, and Hollywood had supplied the script. The hero was chisel-faced perfect—the football star who had turned his back on the NFL to avenge 9/11—and the story line was way too good to let the facts intervene.

Authenticity demands a different approach, if only for practical reasons. The world is too connected, the outlets are too many, dissembling spreads too quickly. In July 2007, we surveyed more than seventy-five hundred adult Americans in an effort to gauge the impact of various "truth-challenging" events over the past decade, on both the general populace and specific subsets of it. Here's what we found.

FOR EACH OF THE FOLLOWING EVENTS OVER THE LAST DECADE, PLEASE INDICATE IN EACH INSTANCE WHETHER THE EVENT SHOOK YOUR FAITH IN THE CAPACITY OF GOVERNMENT AND MILITARY OFFICIALS TO BE HONEST WITH THE AMERICAN PEOPLE A GREAT DEAL, SOMEWHAT, A LITTLE BIT, OR NOT AT ALL.

Bill Clinton's assurance on nationwide TV that "I did not have sexual relations with that woman, Miss Lewinsky."

	OVERALL	MALE	FEMALE
Great deal/Somewhat	48%	52	44
A little bit/Not at all	52	48	54

Colin Powell's appearance before the United Nations justifying the U.S.-led invasion of Iraq

	OVERALL	WHITE	HISPANIC	AFRICAN AMERICAN	ASIAN
Great deal/Somewhat	49%	48	55	56	43
A little bit/Not at all	48	49	44	42	52

George W. Bush's assurance just after Hurricane Katrina that FEMA director Michael Brown was doing a heck of a job

	OVERALL	WHITE	HISPANIC	AFRICAN AMERICAN	ASIAN
Great deal/Somewhat	59%	58	69	70	52
A little bit/Not at all	37	40	30	28	47

The military's claims of the dangers faced by Jessica Lynch and the supposed torture inflicted on her in an Iraqi hospital

	OVERALL	ARMED FORCES	NON-MILITARY
Great deal/Somewhat	52%	50	56
A little bit/Not at all	40	44	37

The military's contention that Pat Tillman had been killed by the enemy in Afghanistan when high-ranking officers knew he died of friendly fire

	OVERALL	DEMOCRAT	REPUBLICAN	INDEPENDENT
Great deal/Somewhat	66%	84	48	68
A little bit/Not at all	29	14	47	26

President Bush's commutation of the sentence handed down to Scooter Libby

		—RESIDENCY—		
	OVERALL	MY CITY/TOWN	AMERICA	PLANET EARTH
Great deal/Somewhat	50%	52	35	84
A little bit/Not at all	46	42	62	15

As is almost always the case with large quantities of data such as this, a certain amount of solace can be found for just about everyone. Women can't help but forgive Bill Clinton. Colin Powell's U.N. speech shook the faith of fewer than half of white adults. Scooter Libby's sentence commutation was a disaster with "planet Earth" residents, but it went down okay with those who consider "America" their address. But look at what's hiding—often in plain sight—in the numbers. Whether Powell was set up by bad intelligence or not, his U.N. speech most shook the faith of those who most need minority representation in the high councils of government: blacks and Hispanics. President Bush's all but pathetic initial response to Hurricane Katrina broke trust most strongly with the same groups. Forty-four percent of military respondents weren't particularly bothered by the Jessica Lynch charade, but 50 percent were, and nearly one in four (23 percent) were bothered a great deal. Two in three Democrats and two in five independents felt the same about the dishonesty regarding Pat Tillman's death, and while only one in five Republicans agreed, nearly half of all Republicans (48 percent) had their faith shaken at least somewhat. Even almost a decade later, nearly half of all Americans (48 percent) also say their faith in government was hurt by Bill Clinton's confabulations about his "relations" with Monica Lewinsky.

This is what the public is pushing back against—the unreality of so much of what is presented as real, the inauthenticity of "authentic" events, the raw dishonesty that gets confidently peddled as truth, and the sheer cynicism that underlies so many such efforts. There would be cause for deep despair in that if the people themselves didn't know better, but as Jessica Lynch herself told a congressional committee four years after the fact, "The American people are capable of determining their own ideas of heroes, and they don't need to be told elaborate tales."

FROM OUTPERFORMING TO OUTBEHAVING:
NOW *EVERYONE* HAS A BULLSHIT DETECTOR

The Internet has played an important and growing part in this grassroots drive toward authenticity. Almost of necessity, the Internet has broken down old walls of privacy and made all our lives more transparent. The older we are, the more likely we are to worry about or resent that new reality, but many younger Americans are already conditioned to their lives being, in essence, public property. And why not? Facebook entries are only the beginning. Any teenager with a webcam can launch his or her own reality show, and many do. Just see YouTube. For that matter, fifteen-year-olds can become porn stars in the privacy of their own bedrooms, while Mom and Dad molder in front of the TV downstairs. Some do that, too.

Is this exhibitionism or part of the push toward greater authenticity? In truth, probably some of both, but in an important way, that's the point. Privacy is out; the open book is in. To be considered truly authentic today, especially among the youngest adults and their still younger siblings, you have to be willing to share even intimate details about yourself. In January 2007 polling we did for 463 Communications, a consulting firm based in Washington, D.C., more than nine in ten respondents told us that the Internet and other technologies had changed their expectations of privacy. When we probed further to find where they drew the lines between acceptable transparency and invasions of privacy, the generational fault lines began to split wide open, as you can see in the table below:

WHICH OF THE FOLLOWING WOULD YOU CONSIDER TO BE AN INVASION OF PRIVACY?

	18–29	30–49	50–64	65+
Someone you know posts a picture of you in a swimsuit	47%	66	68	63
A video of you talking with friends shows up online	31	54	61	56
Your dating profile can be seen online	24	55	63	56
Your geo-location was available to others (such as through GPS)	51	71	68	62

Inevitably, all this transparency has pushed back the frontier of authenticity. Whether it's by using a blog or a webcam, you have to put yourself out there, warts and all, and indeed, you might as well, because so much of your history is already available to whoever wants to Google it. Like it or not, everyone lives in glass houses these days. Virtually all of us—and every organization, every corporation, every elected official—has a shadow record sitting somewhere out there, waiting to be discovered. Meanwhile, bloggers, citizen video makers, cell phone paparazzi, and others stand ready to spread the good and the bad news about us (and the good and bad images of us) with the speed of a summer prairie-grass fire. In a very real sense, today's young adults are Holden Caulfield's grandchildren; like J. D. Salinger's great fictional creation, if there's one thing they can't stand, it's a phony.

As terrifying as all this can be, it is also in a strange way liberating and a powerful push toward living your life and conducting your business as if others were watching, because chances are, they are doing just that. This is the thesis behind the book *How,* written by Dov Seidman, the CEO and founder of LRN, which monitors and promotes business ethics. Seidman argues, I think convincingly, that when there are no secrets, when everyone can essentially copy everyone else's products and services and inculcate the latest business paradigms into their corporate structure, the greatest point of competitive distinction becomes not what you make or offer but simply how you behave—toward your customers, your suppliers, your employees, and everyone else with a stake in the business.

Are you honest with them? Are you respectful of them? Are you authentic in your concern? Are your responses real, not staged? Seidman tells the story of a Michigan hospital that had the novel idea of teaching its doctors to say they were sorry when they screwed up. The result? They cut malpractice claims significantly. Seidman tells another story about a New York City street vendor who built loyalty and saved time by letting customers make their own change. Neither the vendor nor the hospital necessarily outperformed the competition, but they did outbehave them, and it didn't take the world long to find out. According to Seidman, the vendor's business boomed. Virtue, it turns out, really is its own reward, and the Internet is one of the forces pushing us there—pushing us toward more moral and thoughtful behavior if only for self-preservation or an improved bottom line.

FROM TIFFANY TO WAL-MART AND COSTCO: IT'S WHAT'S INSIDE THAT COUNTS

Inevitably, there's a certain amount of stumbling through the dark when it comes to authenticity. People know they want it, but they are far from certain what "it" is. In a July 2007 Interactive poll, 35 percent of respondents said that personality was the greatest factor in making others "authentic" to them. No other single trait came anywhere close to that—"political/social views" was second at 8 percent—but the real winning answer, with 38 percent, was "other." In the same poll, we asked the more than seventy-five hundred adults participating to pick the best definition of "authentic" from a list of eight adjectives. This time, the winner was unambiguous: 61 percent of all participants went with "genuine," while 19 percent chose "real." The other qualifiers—"true," "legitimate," "factual," "original," "bonafide," and "uncorrupted"—each scored less than 5 percent, while "other" and "not sure" together barely topped 1 percent. But that still doesn't tell us what "genuine" and "real" mean in practical terms, a more challenging task.

In polling we did for MSN in early 2007, 32 percent of the nearly ten thousand American adults surveyed said they favored allowing couples to pick the traits they would like to see in their children before they conceive, but only so long as they were culling traits for medical reasons. Another 30 percent (and 39 percent of those with minor children living at home) said the practice is immoral. Eight percent wanted a government ban on trait selection, and 15 percent thought the government should stay out of it altogether. That's a battle tied to religion and science, a clash between the Luddites and technophiles, but at heart it's also a battle about authenticity, about what is real and what is artificial. Indeed when *The New York Times Magazine* ran a cover story on this subject on July 15, 2007, under the headline "So Many Fertile Thoughts," the subhead concluded, "What, in the end, is an authentic motherhood?" As our poll numbers suggest, the public collectively is split just about down the middle on that answer.

To some people, "authentic" is what the eye can see. I saw survey data not long ago suggesting that 80 percent of Americans—up from 50 percent in only a year—would be more likely to purchase electronic devices such as cell phones and laptops if they were finished off with "authentic" materials. According to the survey, these consumers would pay an additional $62 for cell phones and nearly $170 more for laptops that used actual wood or real metal on the exterior instead of plastic finishes painted with a metallic look. The survey, it should be noted, was commissioned by a company that manufactures "innovative enclosure technologies," but I have no doubt that there are people out there, and maybe more than a few, for whom authenticity is all on the outside. One person's "real" is another person's designer touch.

To others—many more, fortunately—authenticity is on the inside, not always out in plain view. Here is one small example from the reams of data we have collected on this front. In June 2007, we asked a large national sampling the following question (actually, two questions since we used both Wal-Mart and Costco): "There are two articles almost exactly alike. Article A costs $500 at Tiffany's and comes in a blue box. Article B costs $250 at Wal-Mart [or Costco]. Which are you most likely to buy?" No doubt, if we had asked the same question of shoppers on the Upper East Side of Manhattan, we would have gotten different results, but we were trying to find the price line among no-frills shoppers at which the status of a Tiffany's box would lose out to the basic authenticity of the object itself. Since regular Costco shoppers are more left-leaning than Wal-Mart regulars, we were also trying to capture a broader demographic sampling by including both stores. Overall in the Wal-Mart pairing, only one in seven respondents (14 percent) thought the wrapper was what mattered. Eighteen percent were unsure, while two in three (68 percent) valued what was inside the box over the famous Tiffany blue on the outside. Costco trumped Tiffany by an even larger margin, with 83 percent of all respondents favoring the lower-cost alternative, 6 percent opting for Tiffany, and 11 percent unsure. A breakdown of the results follows:

WHICH ARE YOU MOST LIKELY TO BUY?

	TIFFANY	WAL-MART	TIFFANY	COSTCO
Male	13%	72	6	84
Female	15	64	6	82
Married	12	73	5	86
Single	22	55	10	76
Divorced/Widowed/Separated	12	70	6	81
Less than $15K	11	66	1	81
$15K–$25K	13	62	11	72
$25K–$35K	14	70	6	80
$35K–$50K	11	68	4	82
$50K–$75K	11	72	3	88
$75K +	17	66	7	84

Clearly, Costco shoppers are less likely to fall for a pretty box than Wal-Mart ones, but the larger point is that none of the demographic segments broken out above is very likely to want to spend double for a wrapper that doesn't alter the article itself. They've moved beyond the package to what's inside—a shift toward authenticity that is as applicable to discount- and bulk-store shoppers as it is to voters considering candidates for the House, Senate, and presidency. Retailers and marketers aren't going to abandon fantasy appeals entirely, and they shouldn't—sex will always sell to someone. But the more marketers rely on packaging alone to move a product in an authenticity-driven marketplace, the more they will be punished by consumers. Keep it true. Keep it real. Cut the b.s.—that's the new mantra of sales.

FROM WHITE TO BLACK AND BEYOND: BROADENING THE BASE OF WHAT IS FOR REAL

Collectively, we Americans might not know exactly what "authentic" is, but for the most part we know what it is not, and we know that we want whatever "authentic" might be. When we asked respondents what single quality they looked for in a lifetime companion, the overwhelming answer was "authentic" with 58 percent, followed by intelligent (22 percent), witty (4 percent), and dead last and almost negligible: good-looking (1 percent). As the table below (from our July 2007 surveying) shows, we also know where to find "authentic" on a daily basis, although that changes generation by generation as the self-absorption of the young gives way to the broader interests of family.

WHAT IS THE MOST AUTHENTIC ASPECT OF YOUR LIFE?

	OVERALL	18–24	25–34	35–54	55–69	70+
Family	39%	35	33	38	43	50
Myself	29	40	28	31	27	23
Religion/Spirituality	17	13	19	16	18	16
Work	2	2	2	3	2	1
Friends	2	2	3	2	2	1
Leisure activities	2	2	5	2	1	0

We also seem to know "authentic" when we see it in someone else. Nearly a decade ago, in 1999, we were commissioned by *Forbes* to conduct a poll on the subject. Among other lines of questioning, respondents were asked to consider celebrities from the worlds of entertainment, sports, politics, and religion, and tell us which figures struck them as the most genuine. The results yielded a layer of meaning that I had never expected. The people perceived as the most genuine in almost every category were men and women of color: Oprah Winfrey was picked as the most authentic entertainer, Colin Powell (prior to his debacle at the U.N.) as the most authentic politician, and Tiger Woods as the most authentic sports figure. Even when we turned the question slightly to explore the connection between public and private authenticity, the same pattern held. Asked to choose from among seven well-known personalities which one was in private most like he or she was in public, respondents picked Bill Cosby over, among others, Jimmy Carter and Bill Gates.

The sole exception in the 1999 polling came with religious leaders, where Mother Teresa triumphed over Pope John Paul II. Even there, though, I couldn't help but note that as a Macedonian-born Albanian, Mother Teresa would have had as much difficulty migrating to the United States in the years after World War I as my father had. In a nation that once enslaved Africans, slaughtered our indigenous population, dominated Latinos, and excluded Asians, our most authentic heroes had begun to emerge from the ranks of those we most oppressed.

We repeated the same questions again in our July 2007 Interactive polling, adding new names and omitting all those who had died or passed from public view in the interim, with one exception. We kept Mother Teresa in the mix of religious leaders since her influence seems undiminished by her death. The results follow. In each instance, we have included relevant demographic breakdowns.

**I AM GOING TO READ YOU A LIST OF PEOPLE.
PLEASE TELL ME, WHO AMONG THE LIST DO YOU THINK
IS THE MOST AUTHENTIC?**

ENTERTAINERS	OVERALL	DEMOCRAT	REPUBLICAN	INDEPENDENT
Denzel Washington	15%	15	14	15
Oprah Winfrey	14	20	7	14
Bruce Willis	9	3	16	10
Rosie O'Donnell	8	15	1	7
Don Imus	5	3	7	6
Garth Brooks	5	2	7	5
Julia Roberts	4	5	4	4
Leonardo DiCaprio	2	5	0	2
Clay Aiken	1	1	2	1
Eddie Murphy	1	0	1	2
Madonna	1	1	0	1
Jennifer Lopez	0	1	0	0

I AM GOING TO READ YOU A LIST OF PEOPLE.
PLEASE TELL ME, WHO AMONG THE LIST DO YOU THINK
IS THE MOST AUTHENTIC? *(continued)*

POLITICIANS	OVERALL	18–24	25–34	35–54	55–69	70+
George W. Bush	20%	9	14	20	24	29
Jimmy Carter	18	14	18	21	18	13
Colin Powell	15	19	13	16	13	13
Al Gore	13	20	18	12	10	8
George H.W. Bush	5	5	4	4	7	7
John McCain	4	5	5	5	4	5
Bill Clinton	4	8	4	4	4	5
Hillary Clinton	2	3	2	2	2	2

| RELIGIOUS LEADERS | OVERALL | —ATTEND RELIGIOUS SERVICES— | | | | |
		WEEKLY+	WEEKLY	1–2/MONTH	HOLIDAYS	NEVER
Mother Teresa	42%	28	41	44	49	33
The Dalai Lama	18	4	9	15	20	35
Pope Benedict XVI	11	14	18	14	8	3
Rev. James Dobson	9	32	14	8	2	1
Rev. Rick Warren	3	7	5	2	1	1
Rev. Jesse Jackson	1	0	1	2	1	1

SPORTS FIGURES	OVERALL	MALE	FEMALE
Tiger Woods	28%	29	37
Peyton Manning	15	16	13
Tim Duncan	6	9	4
Shaquille O'Neal	6	6	5
Venus Williams	5	3	7
Derek Jeter	4	5	3
Annika Sorenstam	2	2	1
Roger Clemens	1	2	1

We also once again asked whose public and private lives were most congruent. This time we offered up the same names as a mea-

sure of what the intervening eight years had done to the public's per-
ceptions of authenticity among the rich and famous.

**WHICH ONE OF THE FOLLOWING PEOPLE DO YOU THINK IN THEIR
PRIVATE LIFE IS MOST LIKE THEY ARE IN THEIR PUBLIC LIFE?**

	OVERALL (2007)	OVERALL (1999)
Jimmy Carter	22%	24
Bill Gates	19	11
Bill Cosby	13	26
Rush Limbaugh	12	11
Queen Elizabeth II	5	5
Howard Stern	3	8
Katie Couric	2	10

What to make of it all, other than the obvious? Republicans and
independents are dying harder with Bruce Willis than Democrats.
George W. Bush's authenticity improves with the age of those being
surveyed, while Hillary Clinton's seems to be flatlined across the
generations. The Dalai Lama is the favorite religious leader of those
least inclined to organized religion. Tiger Woods looks real to both
sexes. Bill Cosby's outspoken campaign for more responsible par-
enting in the black community has given him a sharpness he didn't
have in 1999, at the same time that Bill Gates's foundation work has
softened his image. Jimmy Carter meanwhile ages like a fine wine,
and Katie Couric can't seem to buy good news anywhere. The public's perception is always a moving target, and those who thrust
themselves into it rise and fall accordingly.

What I take away from all this data ultimately is that the longing
for a more real reality that we began to see surfacing in our polling
back in 1999 is today stronger than ever. We see it in the Secular Spiritualists who are digging down deeper into their own lives and uncovering new wants and needs, in the way so many young adults are
embracing their membership in and responsibilities to a global community, in the adjustments large and small that so many of us are

making to help restore this fragile planet to health. Americans want more out of their lives—not more possessions, not more power, not more artificiality or engulfing lies, but more meaning and purpose, more truth, more authenticity. At some level, most Americans are coming to understand and even accept the fact that the Internet *has* changed the game: Everyone is on display; everyone's triumphs and failures are a matter of public record. And in ways big and small they—we—are beginning to fashion lives and make choices that will help us find the one true thing for ourselves and for and in others.

FROM IMPLANTS AND AB SIX-PACKS TO AU NATUREL AND EMERIL LIVE: WHAT MEN AND WOMEN WANT IN EACH OTHER

Study the tabloids or the ads in many of the glossy city and regional magazines and it's easy to imagine that half the adult American population—and 90 percent of the most glamorous among us—are slaves to enhancement, whether it's by BOTOX, through slave-driving personal trainers, or through the tender mercies of plastic surgeons and their medical kin. In a culture obsessed with youth, the desire to look better, to have fewer wrinkles, to show off a six-pack of abs at an age when a real six-pack would mean a headache the next morning, is almost inevitable. To combine an old saying with some new ones, we can never be too rich, too thin, or too buff (not to mention a few other things). And yet we see a trend moving exactly in the opposite direction.

As part of a December 2005 survey of nearly three thousand adult males for CNBC's *The Big Idea with Donny Deutsch,* we asked men what they wanted—*really* wanted—in a woman and women what they wanted (again, *really*) in men. The results don't necessarily bode poorly for plastic surgeons or for the glamour-and-enhancement industry generally. Their core market is hard to shake. But in this broad survey of the American public, participants spoke resoundingly in favor of authenticity and sticking with the hand you were dealt. On page 169 is a sampling of the results:

TO WOMEN: WHAT DO YOU WANT IN A MAN?

A majority (52 percent) said that a man "fixing a meal" was sexier than a man "fixing his car."

Only 12 percent told us that "money plays into sexiness a lot."

Fifty-five percent said money did not affect sexiness at all.

And forget about male pec implants: Only 2 percent of women saw those as sexy, while 90 percent did not.

TO MEN: WHAT DO YOU WANT IN A WOMAN?

One third of male respondents found a size-two woman sexy (33 percent), but just as many men said a size-ten woman was sexy. The remaining third (34 percent) chose "other."

Nearly three in four men polled (72 percent) preferred a "few wrinkles" over a "woman with BOTOX" (6 percent).

Seven out of ten men (69 percent) said that female breast implants were "not sexy" on a woman, while only 17% said they were.

Half of all men (49 percent) told us that a woman wearing no makeup was sexier than one with makeup. Fewer than one out of three (30 percent) thought makeup was sexier.

Three out of five men (62 percent) preferred "a great personality" to "great looks" (23 percent) in a woman—a spread, by the way, that diminished only slightly (to 58–24) when we sectioned out men age eighteen to twenty-nine, and diminished not at all when we broke out such other subsets as NASCAR fans and active members of the military.

We also asked men in the same survey to rate the attributes and body parts of a perfect woman on a five-point scale, with five being "very important" and one "not important at all." Those results follow.

ATTRIBUTES OF A PERFECT WOMAN (5 = VERY IMPORTANT)

Kindness	4.56
Sense of humor	4.44
Intelligence	4.32
Weight	3.51
Beauty	3.43
Ambition	3.36
Breast size	2.53
Earning power	2.27
Height shorter than own	2.05
Age younger than own	1.95

BODY PARTS OF A PERFECT WOMAN (5 = VERY IMPORTANT)

Heart	4.35
Brain	4.22
Face	4.02
Weight	3.72
Teeth	3.69
Legs	3.62
Eyes	3.52
Buttocks	3.52
Hair	3.32
Breasts	3.21
Feet	2.38

Maybe we men never were quite the pigs we are made out to be. Maybe a male population that's aging along with the rest of the population is edging toward a greater appreciation of the deeper qualities of the opposite sex. Or maybe in a society as open and permissive as ours is today, we're so satiated with everyday over-the-counter available-online pornography that we've started looking for something else in our wives and girlfriends. But I think something more profound is changing, something that the fashion industry has been slow to catch on to.

My belief is that many of these males who tell us that heart and brain are far more important in women than purely visual traits are part of the massive core group that Paul H. Ray and Sherry Ruth Anderson describe in their book *The Cultural Creatives: How 50 Million People Are Changing the World.* This is the emerging centrist majority—a group that wants a more ethical business world; is ready to move beyond simply talking about the environment to making changes in their own lives, worldview, and expectations that can lead to real ecological sustainability; and in Ray and Anderson's words, demands "authenticity at home, in the stores, at work, and in politics." Ray and Anderson saw it in their research as surely as I see it in my polling: an emergent new value system of which sex and its turn-ons are only one small part.

FROM TRUTH SQUADS TO PLAIN TRUTH: SAY GOODBYE TO SMEAR-AND-SMASH

My organization has run thousands of surveys focusing on political campaigns and has parsed the electorate in every way imaginable, but I don't know who the next president of the United States will be, or the next one after that, or who will control Congress going into the next decade. I do know, though, with a conviction approaching absolute certainty that the days of divide-and-conquer and smear-and-smash campaigning are just about gone. The "truth squads" of typical campaigns have never really been about truth—most often, they were pushing shades of its opposite—but they seem to have created a great appetite for that which they mocked.

To echo a subhead from earlier in this chapter, everyone today owns a bullshit detector, and an inordinate number of them are aimed at politicians in general and at the Clintons in particular. When the coordinates of your real self are so well known and so easily accessible—and can be so easily checked against, say, Carl Bernstein's biography of the New York senator—there's really nothing to do but be the real self anyone can find. Otherwise, you will find the person that you try to present to the world as yourself mocked in a

New York second by the amateurs on YouTube and by profession-
als such as Jon Stewart and Stephen Colbert.

FROM LOW PRICES TO GOOD CITIZENSHIP:
THE NEW CONSUMER CHOICE

I look on with awe at how well tens of millions of Americans have responded to the cataclysmic events of recent decades. Instead of cav-
ing to the devastation caused by economic dislocation, corporate and
job (and tax base) flight from our communities, war, and political
scandal, they've weathered the bad and matured mightily in the
course of adjusting to new and sometimes harsh conditions. On their
own they have figured out what is false and real, what is ephemeral
and what deeply matters, and now they are starting to demand that
same authenticity in the products they buy, the companies they buy
from, the institutions they frequent, and the people they vote for.

In our surveying, we see evidence of this everywhere, but it often
comes into its sharpest focus when we ask about corporate and personal ethics. People want and expect the stores they shop at and the
businesses they buy stakes in not to just provide them with good
product value and good share value but good moral value as well. Is
that across the board? No, not really. Those who identify themselves
as conservatives and libertarians, for example, are much less likely
to worry about fair wages than to worry about healthy profits.
Males are more profit-oriented than females, but as the table below
suggests, by most measures Americans want companies to do good
and do well, in that order.

**"I PREFER NOT TO INVEST IN A COMPANY THAT DOES NOT PAY
A FAIR WAGE, EVEN THOUGH IT MAKES A HEALTHY PROFIT
FOR ITS STOCKHOLDERS."**

	STRONGLY/SOMEWHAT AGREE	SOMEWHAT/STRONGLY DISAGREE
Male	49%	42
Female	69	20

	STRONGLY/SOMEWHAT AGREE	SOMEWHAT/STRONGLY DISAGREE
Union	69%	24
Nonunion	57	32
18–27	53	31
28–41	59	31
42–61	62	28
62–80	58	34
81+	58	35
Liberal	87	7
Moderate	69	21
Conservative	36	53
Libertarian	33	56
Less than $15K	64	22
$15K–$25K	64	20
$25K–$35K	65	28
$35K–$50K	66	25
$50K–$75K	62	28
$75K+	54	36

The extensive polling we did for a union-originated group called WakeUp Wal-Mart in late 2005 and early 2006 was equally revealing in this regard. While it was clear that respondents shopped more often at Wal-Mart than at any other store we tested, significant numbers of consumers felt that the retail giant's public image had been tarnished over the past few years by media reports of questionable labor practices and rock-bottom wages. Here are the results of several questions we asked.

HOW IMPORTANT IS IT FOR YOU PERSONALLY THAT A STORE YOU SPEND YOUR MONEY AT ALSO REFLECTS YOUR OWN MORAL AND ETHICAL VALUES?

Extremely important	18%
Very important	35
Somewhat important	34
Not very important	9
Not important at all	5

IN GENERAL, BEFORE YOU SHOP AT A PARTICULAR STORE, HOW MUCH THOUGHT DO YOU GIVE TO WHETHER OR NOT THAT STORE TREATS ITS WORKERS FAIRLY OR ETHICALLY?

Great deal	32%
Some	37
Very little	19
None at all	12

HOW IMPORTANT IS IT TO YOU PERSONALLY THAT A STORE YOU SHOP AT PAYS A LIVING WAGE AND PROVIDES HEALTH CARE FOR ALL OF ITS EMPLOYEES?

Extremely important	26%
Very important	33
Somewhat important	26
Not at all important	7

WOULD YOU PERSONALLY BE . . . TO SHOP AT A STORE THAT YOU BELIEVED SAVED YOUR FAMILY MONEY EVERY MONTH BUT DID NOT PROVIDE AFFORDABLE HEALTH CARE OR PAY A LIVING WAGE TO ALL OF ITS EMPLOYEES?

Much more likely	8%
Somewhat more likely	14
Somewhat less likely	26
Much less likely	26
No difference	24
Not sure	2

WOULD YOU PERSONALLY BE . . . TO SHOP AT A PARTICULAR STORE THAT YOU BELIEVED SAVED YOUR FAMILY MONEY EVERY MONTH BUT DISCRIMINATED AGAINST ITS FEMALE WORKERS?

Much more likely	8%
Somewhat more likely	5
Somewhat less likely	26
Much less likely	46
No difference/not sure	14

Does all this matter? Or are the responses above a collective example of high-sounding rhetoric that has little or no application in the real world of the marketplace? In fact, there's compelling evidence that shoppers today are ready to put their pocketbook where their beliefs are. In our 2005 surveying, we gave respondents a long list of retailers and asked them which store they would pick if they could shop at only one for the rest of their lives. The winner, no surprise, was Wal-Mart, the jumbo retailer with the largest market penetration in America.

In June 2007, we repeated the same question, this time with different results. The table below shows stores that received greater than four percent of the vote. Boscov's, Bloomingdale's, Filene's, Marshalls, Neiman Marcus, and Dollar Store did not reach that threshold.

IF YOU COULD SHOP AT ONLY ONE OF THE FOLLOWING STORES FOR THE REST OF YOUR LIFE, WHICH WOULD YOU CHOOSE?

Target	24.5%
Wal-Mart	20.9
Costco	11.3
Macy's	5.6
Sears	4.5
JCPenney	4.5

When Target, with a customer base roughly two thirds that of Wal-Mart's, overtakes Sam Walton's brainchild as the one store people would choose, I suggest values are in play at least as much as Target's more upscale presentation and merchandise. And when Costco, a company widely acknowledged to treat its employees well, breaks into double digits despite significantly lower market penetration than either Target or Wal-Mart, values and value seem the only feasible explanation. Take a look at the head-to-head comparison below between Wal-Mart and Costco, again from our June 2007 Interactive survey.

WHAT IS THE MAIN REASON YOU SHOP AT . . . ?

	WAL-MART	COSTCO
Prices	41%	19
Quality of goods	1	6
Good value	11	16
Store philosophy	1	5
Customer service	0	0
Convenience	15	2
Other/Not sure	31	53

Clearly, the great discriminators between the two discounters are price and convenience. Wal-Mart undercuts everybody but the dollar and big-lot stores, while Costco is simply harder to get to for most people because the chain has many fewer outlets. Yet if I were part of Wal-Mart's top management, the discriminators I would most worry about in the table above are "quality of goods" and "store philosophy." Just one in roughly seventeen respondents cited the quality of goods as the main reason for shopping at Costco, and only one in twenty said the same about the store's philosophy, but only one in one hundred Wal-Mart shoppers said the same about the quality and philosophy of that retail colossus. To be sure, Wal-Mart has to feed its customer base low prices, but at a time when authenticity is selling at a premium and the public is looking for good citizenship in retailers and manufacturers alike, stressing low cost over quality and philosophy is moving in the opposite direction from a public that is choosing values over value. As we'll see at the end of this chapter, that message finally seems to be sinking in at corporate headquarters in Bentonville, Arkansas.

This same drive toward good citizenship is being expressed at the individual level. The public isn't demanding that businesses act one way while the public acts the other way. Instead, it's demanding that its business and government leaders act the way the public has been trending all along. For years now, Zogby International has been taking the ethical pulse of the nation. What comes back to me time and again when I go over the results is just how solid Americans' values are. Below are some representative questions and answers from our ongoing research.

Your employer has incorrectly credited you with more vacation time than you have earned. Your spouse and family are sure to be overjoyed with the extra time. What do you do?

Almost seven in eight respondents (86 percent) answered: "Report the error and plan a vacation based on the time I actually have earned."

■ ■ ■

The next question upped the stakes on the earlier one:

You are out of work and strapped with a mortgage, and you have kids in school. Now you are updating your résumé because you've learned of an opening for a job exactly like your last one at which you excelled. One problem: This new position requires a college degree for anyone interviewed, and you don't have one. Do you fake it, or honestly describe your education?

Four percent answered fake it; 92 percent said they would honestly describe their education.

■ ■ ■

How about the young? Are they ready to cheat the system in ways their elders won't consider? There's certainly no lack of polling results to argue that they are. In the December 2006 Teen Ethics Poll conducted by Deloitte & Touche for Junior Achievement, 69 percent of the thirteen- to seventeen-year-olds surveyed said they had lied in the previous year, 34 percent admitted to downloading a song without paying, and 22 percent said they had cheated on tests. The 2006 version of the Report Card on the Ethics of American Youth, issued biennially by the Josephson Institute of Ethics, contained even more alarming data: Three in five students said they had cheated on a school test within the previous twelve months, 28 percent said they had stolen something from a store in the past year, and 23 percent said they had done the same from a parent or relative.

Those numbers have to be taken seriously—lying, cheating, and stealing are bad habits to fall into. But in the Deloitte & Touche poll, 59 percent of teens said they would not act unethically to get ahead or make more money even if they were certain not to get caught. That number, the authors, noted, was up 40 percent from just three years earlier. In the Josephson Institute survey, 83 percent of students agreed that "It's not worth it to lie and cheat because it hurts your character," and 94 percent felt that trust and honesty were essential in business and in the workplace.

Our polling has yielded similar results. We asked teens to agree or disagree with the following statement: "I believe doing the right thing is more important than getting ahead in my career." The results: 92 percent took the high road. When we asked the same group if it was okay in sports to bend the rules because that's what others do, or if it was never okay no matter what others do, 26 percent said, sure, bend the rules, while almost three times as many, 73 percent, said cheating the rules is never right. That, I'm convinced, is the real world of most kids today, a place where "Do the right thing" has deep and serious meaning.

FROM HEART TUGS TO HEAD TUGS: THE ZOGBY CHAMPS AND CHUMPS

Marketing guru Sergio Zyman once said that the working principle that governed his ad campaigns for Coca-Cola was a simple one: "Grab their hearts and their wallets will follow." In broad terms, I wouldn't argue with that for a second: Over the years, no one has advertised more successfully than Coke. But I would issue one caveat going forward: There have been too many tugs at the heart in recent times—in advertising, in politics, and elsewhere—and too many of them have proven to be too blatantly manipulative. Even 9/11, that worst day in American history, finds itself reduced to a marketing opportunity for everything from pushing trucks to selling the war in Iraq.

Appeal to the heart, of course, but if you want to be truly authentic, appeal to the head, too. Market to the many key values that unite tens of millions of Americans rather than trying to exploit the divisions among us. Talk to who we are, instead of trying to make us long to be something we are not. In our June 2007 Interactive polling, we asked respondents to agree or disagree with the following statement: "I can relate better to ads that show people just like me than ones that feature supermodels and other perfect physical specimens." Thirty-five percent of all respondents and 44 percent of women strongly agreed; another 35 percent overall and 35 percent of women somewhat agreed. Only 21 percent strongly disagreed, including just six percent of women.

Businesses need to keep those figures in mind. They need to remember that consumers today are about more than consuming— that how you make a product, how you dispose of your waste, and how you exercise your citizenship all matter, too. And they need to trust in our decency and good sense as well. We're big people. Our values are intact, and we have every right to expect the marketers and advertisers to respect that in us.

Who gets it and who doesn't? Herewith my own Hall of Fame and Shame from recent years: The Zogby Champs and Chumps.

- **CHAMP:** Wal-Mart. Yes, this retailer has image problems, but management is moving aggressively to counter them, not with smoke and mirrors but with on-the-ground commitments. In late 2006, the company shook the competition by announcing that it would provide generic substitutes for more than three hundred prescription drugs for four dollars or less. How better to secure loyalty when so many Americans are feeling the pain of their own economic contractions? Couple that with the company's decision to go green by reducing energy use in its stores by 30 percent, increasing the fuel efficiency of its vehicles by 25 percent, and reducing waste from its stores also by 25 percent, all over a short three-year period, and you have the makings of a very good retailing citizen.

- **CHUMP:** Wal-Mart again, this time for its blog site Wal-Marting Across America. See Jim and Laura driving cross-country in their RV, visiting Wal-Mart stores; hear them conducting interviews with happy Wal-Mart employees; learn that Laura's brother works for Edelman, the PR company that created the blog; watch honesty and authenticity fly out the window. No wonder WSJ .com named this one of the three worst ads of 2006.

- **CHAMP:** Ford Motor Company. Another counterintuitive choice, perhaps, but I really like the "Bold Moves" advertisement for Ford's Freestyle SUV that features a divorced father. Do you remember it? With Mom at the wheel, a family drives five hundred miles across picturesque countryside and pulls up at a housing complex, where Dad climbs out with his luggage and hugs the kids goodbye. "Thanks for inviting me this weekend," he says to his ex before she drives off again. The happy world of Leave It to Beaver this is not, but it is the world we live in and the world that shapes our values today. To me, this is what reality advertising should be all about.

- **CHUMP:** "What Happens in Vegas Stays in Vegas." So, it's okay to lie, cheat, steal, carouse; get stinking drunk; marry a total stranger one night and divorce the same stranger the next night; and gamble away the kid's college money because in good old tight-lipped Las Vegas no one ever whispers a word? Give me a break. What planet are these people living on?

- **CHAMP:** Madrid, Spain. By contrast, consider what happened in the city of Madrid in September 2006. Madrid Fashion Week is Spain's top fashion show, one of those places where models want to be seen, but in 2006, Fashion Week decreed that no model could participate who had a body mass index of 18.5 or less. (The index is calculated by dividing weight in pounds by height in inches squared and multiplying the result by 703. The "normal" range is considered to be 18.5 to 24.9. To meet the Spanish requirements, a 5′9″ model would have needed to weigh at least 125 pounds.) Sure, a third of the invited models failed, and the model agency heads complained about discrimination and compromising the freedom of designers, but talk about striking a blow for real bodies in the real world.

- **CHAMP:** Dove and particularly its Dove Campaign for Real Beauty. Launched in June 2005 with a massive print, billboard, and bus-shelter promotion featuring unretouched photos of six models in their underwear, all with real bodies and real curves, the Dove ad blitz, like Madrid's stance on models, meets women where they live. I admire that, and I admire the related efforts: Dove's Self-Esteem Fund to "raise awareness of the link between beauty and body-related self-esteem," as the company's website puts it, and its partnership with the Girl Scouts of the USA aimed at building self-confidence in girls age eight to fourteen. To my mind, there's no need for a primer on good corporate citizenship. Dove has already written it.

- **CHUMP:** Hummer. Poor sales and smart consumers have already sent this ugly gas-guzzler to the scrap heap, but just for instructional purposes, let's review some of the ad campaigns that heralded its demise:

  Ad #1: A mini-Hummer crosses shallow rivers, climbs rocky terrain, and leaves the other minis in the dust while the Who's Roger Daltrey croons "Oh, they couldn't stop Jack."

Ad #2: Mom and her little girl are enjoying innocent fun at the playground until another mom allows her child to skip ahead in the jungle gym line. That gives the now enraged first mom a great idea—Buy a Hummer!

What's the message? To me, it's this: Whether you just want to chew up the landscape and won't let anyone tell you not to or you're tired of getting pushed around on the playground in an unfair world, Hummer is *the car* for crushing the competition, not for those who want the world to be a kinder, gentler place.

- **CHAMP:** The United Colors of Benetton. The grandfather of socially responsible advertising and the godfather and godmother of the First Globals. If the Nobel Peace Prize were ever opened up to advertisers, my nomination would go to the agency that created the 1985 Benetton ad that shows two little black boys kissing each other, one with a little U.S. flag in his hair and the other with a USSR flag.

- **CHAMP:** Cisco's The Human Network—an ad campaign and a website and a marketing tool and a kind of global kiosk that perfectly captures the spirit and the potential of a world without borders. (Truth in packaging: Cisco is a major client of Zogby International.)

- **CHUMP:** Just about every political campaign ever produced. Okay, so I'm exaggerating, but not by a whole lot. It's true—negative campaigning can work. Back in the 2004 presidential campaign, I would ask focus group after focus group what was the first thing that came to mind when I mentioned John Kerry or George Bush. The answers were almost always nearly direct quotes from the virulently nasty ad campaigns then sweeping the nation. As troubling as that is, what bothers me far more is the sheer cynicism of the whole enterprise: unkeepable promises, even absurd ones; the bland assumption that it doesn't matter how many voters you cause to turn off and tune out so long as you win 50.1 percent of the voters who remain. Abraham Lincoln, Franklin D. Roosevelt, and John F. Kennedy didn't come to power by appealing to the lowest common denominator. They offered broad visions and empowering promises; they appealed to the best in the electorate, not the worst. And they left lasting legacies. It's way past time to get back to that high ground again.

• **AND ONE LAST CHAMP:** Kellogg's, the cereal maker. Ten years after proclaiming in its ads that the empty sugar-drenched calories found in a bowl of Froot Loops or Corn Pops could actually be good for children, the company has reversed field and is now setting nutritional guidelines that its own products need to meet. What an idea! And what perfect congruency with the spirit of the times.

A GUIDE TO MARKETING AUTHENTICITY

- Reality doesn't bite. It's real, and people are demanding it.
- People are demanding truth, too. Don't lie, make ridiculous boasts, or dissemble. Remember: Everyone today has a bullshit detector.
- It's as much about what you sell as who's selling it. Consumers want to be respected.
- If you screw up, apologize. Humility is good.
- Except on Rodeo Drive and in South Beach, men and women want the same things in each other: natural over silicon, good personality over great boobs, real over make-believe.
- *First* treat your employees well; *then* tell everyone the story.
- In a world dominated by sizzle, it's all about the steak. Sell the steak.

7

The Way We'll Be

Perhaps geology or our ever-expanding universe is the ultimate destiny. Maybe it's something more immediate, even perhaps preventable: melting polar ice caps, the semi-toxic air that hangs over so many of our biggest cities around the world, the rarity of drinking water in so much of India and Africa, or the global over-abundance of nuclear weapons. The end of the cold war was supposed to stand down the threat of nuclear extinction. Instead, the rise of rogue leaders and the spread of fissile materials into radicalized hands has stood it right back up again, almost as tall as ever and even less predictable. Perhaps the future to end all futures will be defined by submicroscopic particles for which we humans have no defense, or by a colossal meteorite that does to our species what an earlier meteorite collision is thought to have done to the dinosaurs, another animal that once walked the planet with impunity. The Bible says our last days will be capped by the Second Coming of the Messiah, but the first coming of alien life forms might be just as efficient for extinction. Having tasted of desire, Robert Frost held "with those who favor fire," but as Frost famously concluded, "for destruction ice / Is also great / And would suffice."

I'm a pollster, not a poet. My professional horizons are more limited. Strictly speaking, according to most statisticians, I'm not even allowed to look around the bend of my last question. All I know for sure is what the polls and surveys tell me, and all they can tell me is what people are thinking and intending at the moment the questions are asked.

Certainly, that is true in politics. In a supersaturated media environment, things change too quickly to make any hard judgments about tomorrow. Candidates and candidacies blow up before the evening news, get sliced and diced overnight by bloggers, and are gone by the time newspapers hit the street the next morning. That's why those of us in the business poll constantly as Election Day approaches. Every snapshot we get from our surveying is in danger of being superseded by the time the numbers have been crunched and sorted. (Happily, of course, this instant obsolescence is also good for the polling business. If we could do one survey in early March of an election year that would tell us what the results would be eight months later, on the first Tuesday after the first Monday in November, our reason for being would largely disappear, at least in the political arena.)

But the fact is that trends do exist. Change builds up within societies. Seismic shifts start rumbling beneath us. As I wrote at the beginning of this book, nothing reveals the future to us, but polling does point the way. It shows the vectors as they rise up out of the here and now and begin to bend toward what lies ahead. I think that's especially true of generational shifts in attitudes and preferences and even core beliefs. For my money, those are as good and complete a guide to the future as anyone is likely to find. That's why for more than a decade now I've been studying the shifting momentum among the four dominant and highly definitive adult age cohorts of our time.

Each of the four cohorts reached maturity in the midst of a major defining event, or a series of related events, and each is, in a very real sense, still working its way through the experience. The senior cohort, the one I call the Private Generation, was born in the time span 1926 to 1945. They're old enough to remember some of the Great Depression, but they mostly came of age during World War II and the hot years of the cold war. This isn't the "Greatest Generation," but the one that followed it: quiet (hence "private"), loath to protest, inclined to go along to get along. Woodstockers, the generation that followed the Privates, remember the cold war at its peak, but they came of age in a time of civil unrest and in the midst of the explosion of sex, drugs, and rock 'n' roll that found its culmination at Woodstock, the event for which the generation is named. Born between 1965 and 1978, Nikes are the first generation of latchkey kids, self-raised in many cases, the after-echo of single parents and the dual-working couples that fueled the prosperity of the mid- and late 1980s. First Globals, the youngest of the cohorts, had their own defining events: Bill Clinton's impeachment hearing, the Internet bubble bust, and 9/11. But maybe the most defining element of their still-evolving experience has been the rise of worldwide marketing. Unlike perhaps any other generation in American history, this one transcends national boundaries.

Below, a more detailed look at each of the age cohorts:

THE PRIVATE GENERATION (1926–45). This is the generation most likely to defer gratification, to oppose equal rights for gays and women, to favor shutting America's doors to new immigrants, and to vote for cutting school budgets. Part of that is age: People get stuck in their ways as they get older. But part is experience, too. The Private Generation grew to adulthood mostly without questioning received American values. They did their jobs mostly without complaining, and now they're moving into and through retirement as silently as they have lived the rest of their lives.

Perhaps because they were born before or during a war in which America intervened decisively for the good, Privates are the age cohort that most favors a go-it-alone foreign policy. Having lived virtually all their adult years during the American Century, Privates also are the least apt to want to share power on the global stage or to compromise America's interests in favor of global goals. On question after question about America's relation with the larger world, the same chasm shows up between these oldest adults and the young adults of the First Globals generation. Some examples:

"I SUPPORT WHAT IS GOOD FOR THE PEOPLE OF THE WORLD AND OUR ENVIRONMENT EVEN IF IT IS NOT IN THE BEST INTERESTS OF THE U.S."

	PRIVATE GENERATION	FIRST GLOBALS
Strongly agree	21%	29
Strongly disagree	31	17

THE U.S. NEEDS STRONGER EFFORTS AT PUBLIC DIPLOMACY TO REDUCE TENSIONS AND HATRED FOR THE UNITED STATES AMONG SOME PEOPLE.

	PRIVATE GENERATION	FIRST GLOBALS
Strongly agree	44%	64
Strongly disagree	19	12

U.S. MILITARY INVOLVEMENT IN THE WORLD ACTUALLY THREATENS U.S. SECURITY AND MUST BE LIMITED.

	PRIVATE GENERATION	FIRST GLOBALS
Strongly agree	29%	44
Strongly disagree	39	25

AMERICA'S IMAGE OVERSEAS IS SEVERELY DAMAGED AND MUST BE IMPROVED BECAUSE IT IS DANGEROUS FOR U.S. SECURITY.

	PRIVATE GENERATION	FIRST GLOBALS
Strongly agree	44%	57
Strongly disagree	20	8

Don't take away too crabby a picture of the Private Generation, though. In some ways, they are surprisingly optimistic. Having made it into their sixties and beyond, they tend to see themselves, like the Energizer Bunny, going on and on and on. When we asked a sampling of more than ten thousand adults how long they expected to live, Privates were the most likely of any age cohort to expect to live into their eighties and nineties. About one in twenty-five of them expects to hit the century mark, and one in three expects to at least reach their nineties. Those numbers follow:

UNTIL WHAT AGE DO YOU EXPECT TO LIVE?

	18–29	30–49	50–64	PRIVATES
Under sixty	3%	2	2	—
Sixties	7	6	5	2
Seventies	15	20	20	14
Eighties	40	38	41	35
Nineties	19	19	21	28
100+	6	6	5	4

When we asked Privates to pick the dog and tree most like themselves from a lengthy list, they chose "loyal collie" and "down-to-earth maple." (Compare those choices to the First Globals' favorites: "powerful rottweiler" and "elegant magnolia.") Yes, this is more wackiness from the wacky question askers at Zogby International, but we're doing more than parroting Barbara Walters with this kind of query. To me, in fact, that dog and tree say a good deal. Privates *are* loyal and faithful. They *have* gone along with authority. Flamboyance has never been their thing; they would never call themselves elegant and powerful in the collective. Instead, this group is practical and down to earth in the extreme. Maybe Privates have set the bar low for themselves as a generation, but they seem to have gotten pretty much what they wanted.

THE WOODSTOCK GENERATION (1946–64). Woodstockers— and I'm one—stopped a war. We marched for civil rights. We redefined student life, shut down universities, and helped usher in a drastically new set of values regarding gender equality, sexual orientation, premarital sex, and the environment. Along the way to changing the world and harmonizing the planet, we also invented hundreds of neuroses for ourselves and our entire generation.

We are the baby boom, the "pig in the python" as demographers like to describe it. The sheer force of our numbers demanded attention and made society turn toward us, but maybe we were deferred to too much. Raised to high expectations, we endured what often turned out to be high disappointments and became a generation of complainers. Our watershed moment—the 1969 lovefest concert at Woodstock, New York, that was going to usher in the age of Aquarius—ended up being mostly just a stoned romp in the mud.

I was there, a doctrinaire radical devoted to disciplining myself for the revolution. My hope was to find some kind of uncompromising commitment to social change in the lyrics of Stephen Stills, Neil Young, Joni Mitchell, and Richie Havens. Instead, it was all about drugs, flight from responsibility, adolescent hedonism . . . and that's only what is worth describing. In some ways, none of that has really changed. The closer we Woodstockers get to our golden years, the more we want to look like kids. This is the generational cohort, after all, that created the market for Just for Men hair coloring, L'Oréal's line of wrinkle-fighting face creams, and BOTOX injections. The more we age, the more we sometimes want to act like kids, too—witness the astronomic sales of Viagra and related products—and the more we want our children and grandchildren to accept us as peers. This is the "Call me Trish, not Mom, or Grandma" generation. No wonder our offspring are mostly baffled by us.

The Woodstock Generation's old roots in activist politics haven't withered entirely. This is still the age cohort most likely to say that the products it purchases must be environmentally friendly, but Woodstockers have mellowed with time and drifted to the right politically. By their thirties, Woodstockers were solidly in the Reagan camp; in their forties, they barely gave Bill Clinton the nod in his first run for the presidency. In 2000 and again in 2004, they voted in the majority for George Bush. Even back in 1972 when their radicalism was supposedly at its peak, Woodstockers voted for Richard Nixon by a 52–46 percent margin over George McGovern—the generation's dark secret!

More than half of Woodstockers (53 percent) say they disagree with the political, economic, and social values of Bill and Hillary Clinton, while only two in five say they agree. Just 31 percent describe themselves as "liberal" or "very liberal," compared to 50 percent of First Globals. Slightly more than half of the non-Catholic Christians in this age cohort (51 percent) also describe themselves as "born-again" or "evangelical." In the 2004 presidential election, Woodstockers gave George W. Bush a 5-point edge over John Kerry even though Kerry's opposition to the Vietnam War had once made him a hero to the generation.

One thing the generation hasn't lost is its penchant for complaint. When we polled baby boomers in early 2006 for MetLife, 25 percent told us that they expected to be working beyond age seventy, far longer than they had envisioned when we'd asked the same question only a few years earlier. Why? Three in ten of them said that their "current lifestyle" is either "a little worse" or "much worse" than they thought it would be a decade ago. Unlike Privates, Woodstockers don't remember a time when just about everyone's "lifestyle" was much worse than it is today.

THE NIKE GENERATION (1965–78). Born into a world of political assassinations, presidential scandals, oil embargoes, military loss (America's first), and record-high divorce rates—and raised in the middle of a raging debate over abortion—this cohort learned early in life that no institution is permanent, that all relationships are fleeting, and that some are very dangerous. Many of the Nikes reached sexual maturity just as AIDS was emerging and STDs in general were exploding. For them, there are no "good old days." Left home alone as kids, they mostly watched television, parented themselves, and inherited few values from the generation that preceded them. These are the slackers of Gen X, or so we're told, but the story is more complicated than that.

Not surprising for a cohort that came of age under Ronald Reagan, this is the most libertarian generation in America, the least likely to believe in government as a problem solver, the least loyal indeed to any major organization, including the colleges they attended. For them, the sexual abuse scandals that have rocked Roman Catholicism over the past decade have been little more than confirmation of the obvious: Even the Church lets you down in the end.

The Nikes' generational distrust doesn't stop at America's borders. As the table below shows, they are less likely than other cohorts to identify putative friends of the United States as allies. France, especially, has earned their enmity.

COUNTRIES RATED AS ALLIES

		GLOBAL	NIKE	WOODSTOCK	PRIVATE
France					
	Good ally	25%	21	21	21
	So-so ally	51	29	36	37
	Not an ally	24	48	42	39
Israel					
	Good ally	58	45	59	65
	So-so ally	29	27	29	19
	Not an ally	10	23	11	10
Saudi Arabia					
	Good ally	11	8	9	7
	So-so ally	43	34	44	39
	Not an ally	40	52	44	48
Germany					
	Good ally	37	28	33	32
	So-so ally	49	45	47	42
	Not an ally	13	21	18	24

COUNTRIES RATED AS ALLIES *(continued)*

	GLOBAL	NIKE	WOODSTOCK	PRIVATE
South Korea				
Good ally	37%	34	48	57
So-so ally	16	18	29	26
Not an ally	41	43	21	12

Cut off from lasting institutional attachments and loyalties, Nikes live for the moment. More so than any other generation, they enjoy shopping for big-ticket items, whatever the budget consequences. In our polling, more than half (53 percent) said they had bought something they didn't need and couldn't afford. Only First Globals came close with 51 percent, but they have the excuse of youth. The youngest Nikes are thirty; the oldest, almost forty-five—an age range of supposed responsibility.

First Globals also get a youth pass for their answers to a question we asked the generations about the ultimate meaning of life. Was it to "Live happily and selfishly" or to "Do as much as you can for others and leave this earth a better place"? As you'll see, Nikes come uncomfortably close to not having escaped the self-absorption of their early years.

PERCENT AGREEING THAT THE ULTIMATE MEANING OF LIFE IS TO "LIVE HAPPILY AND SELFISHLY"

GLOBAL	NIKE	WOODSTOCK	PRIVATE
32	26	19	21

Indeed, these thirty- to forty-five-year-olds are a near-perfect embodiment of one of the great commercial slogans of the era— "Just Do It!"—which is why I refer to them as the Nike Generation.

FIRST GLOBALS (1979–90). We met this group in the Introduction, but with First Globals, there's always more to be said. This is a group with two distinct souls—one highly materialistic and self-absorbed, as might be expected of those not yet in their thirties, and the other caring, tolerant, and possessed of a wisdom well beyond its years. When we break our survey results down by age, First Globals often appear to be sui generis, a world unto themselves, but in fact, they are the clear and direct inheritors of the age cohorts stacked above them.

On most geopolitical issues, First Globals and Privates might as well be from different planets, but on social issues, they often share a strange affinity. In May 2007 we asked for a response to a simple statement on abortion—"It is in everyone's interest to reduce the number of abortions." Among First Globals, 54 percent strongly agreed, while only 7 percent strongly disagreed. When we broke the results down for other groups, the ones that aligned most closely with the youngest adults were the very elderly, libertarians, and conservatives.

Just as Woodstockers were in their youth, this group is hell-bent on change, but for First Globals tolerance and an expansive worldview are second nature, not learned—a part of the rhythm of their lives, not a statement they need to make at every turn. Their parents and grandparents might marvel at the range of First Globals' living arrangements and deep attachments—black with white, woman with woman, man with man, as well as more standard hook-ups, many of them unblessed by the church or civil authorities—but to First Globals this is the starting line of commitment, not the finish tape. And if their elders don't get it, well, too bad.

The causes of cynicism among their elders haven't been lost on them, either. Like Nikes, they are intimately familiar with the education debt that so many young people have to assume even to get to the front door of the global intelligence-and-skill-driven economy. From Woodstockers, First Globals also have learned how perilous a career journey can be, but because job insecurity is all most of them have known, they aren't as threatened by it. For them, the stories their grandparents tell about a lifetime job or career or even address are little removed from fairy tales—something that happened in a faraway place, in a time long ago. And yet, they resist despair almost to a remarkable degree. When we ask if their quality of life is better than, worse than, or the same as their parents, more than half say better, fewer than one in seven say worse, and somewhere between one in three and one in four say the same. Oddly, since they are the youngest of the adult cohorts, First Globals are also the most cosmopolitan age group in America, the most international, and the one most concerned about the environment and human rights.

■ ■ ■

Each of these generations is helping to shape the future. At a time when institutions are breaking down and old paradigms are melting away, Privates will continue to teach us about loyalty and sticking to jobs and family. The inheritors of the amazing advances in longevity made in recent decades, Privates will soon constitute a larger pool of octogenarians, nonagenarians, and centenarians than ever before existed collectively in the history of the world. From them, Americans will learn how (and how not) to age with dignity and how to make the postretirement years useful. Privates will be the foot soldiers of a new army of volunteerism that will benefit schools, private and public social agencies, libraries, hospitals, and untold other not-for-profits.

The presence of so many very elderly among us also represents a growing consumer market that has yet to be seriously tapped other than for medications, rest homes, and cemeteries. Some niches are obvious: lifelong learning and educational travel. Some are less so: transportation services, for example, for an expanding population segment that will be on the go long after many of its members can safely drive a car. The sheer numbers of this group will equally create an imperative to come up with better services and more humane long-term care for the frail and forgetful, and this group will revitalize gerontology, a branch of medicine that is now being all but closed down by shortsighted HMO policies.

Woodstockers know the power of protest, and as they slide into their sixties, they're going to remember how to exercise it, both on their own behalf ("Gray Power!") and in the service of a generally reawakened social conscience. In concert with their seniors in the Private Generation, Woodstockers will finally force Congress to pass meaningful health care reform, although it might not be anything too radical. In February 2007, in polling for UPI, we asked a large sampling of adults to pick from among four possible health care insurance systems. The choices were: a publicly funded nationalized and universal program, a publicly funded "single-payer" system, and two private-sector-based programs—one where individuals are responsible for choosing their own plan and paying for it, and the other a private "health savings" account coupled with a high-deductible plan to cover catastrophic care. The youngest and oldest adults had no doubt about their choices. By wide margins, First Globals favored the two publicly funded systems over the two private plans. By lesser margins, Privates went in exactly the opposite direction. The tiebreaker, in this case, belonged to Woodstockers, who narrowly favored the private-sector pick-and-pay program over a nationalized and universal health insurance system.

Health care, though, will be just one of many causes for Woodstockers. Like the star athlete who has long since retired but never forgotten the roar of the crowd, we Woodstockers keep asking ourselves the same questions. Is this all there is? What have we done lately? What's next for us? I think "living with limits" will provide the answer. Environmentalism, cutting down on waste, making do with less—they're a way back into the game, a chance to get the revolution right and not be so stoned or juiced that whatever happened is a vague memory in the morning. For Woodstockers, "small is beautiful" is that rarest of commodities in public life: a second act. As a practical matter, the Woodstock Generation also will demand and receive legalized medical marijuana.

The Nike Generation sometimes seems to be drifting like a ghost through the American landscape, but what it mostly has been doing is creating an alternative world in which it feels comfortable. The indie film and music scenes both owe their strong market penetrations primarily to Nikes and their distrust of the major studios and recording labels. Nikes are disproportionately large consumers of various forms of yoga and alternative medical disciplines such as acupuncture and chiropractic. They read food labels far more closely than the generations above them and are willing to pay the premium for organic fruits and vegetables. Understandably, even admirably, this is the age cohort most likely to prefer being a "scientist who strives to make sense of the world" to being a "police officer who preserves order and establishes safety and security." Given the world in which they were born and came of age, Nikes seek explanations for what they see around them, and find "preserving order" less compelling in a world where the status quo made little sense in the first place.

Scarred by their parents' divorces, these thirty- to forty-five-year-olds often resist marriage, but they tend to be deeply devoted to their partnerships. From them, we are learning commitment without ritual. The abiding sense of loss that so many of them have carried forward from childhood also explains, I think, why Nikes are more likely than other age cohorts to be Secular Spiritualists. This, too, is a form of commitment without ritual, or liturgy, or even doctrine. Nikes are alienated from institutions, but they hunger for food for the soul and are ready to make sacrifices to achieve the balance in their lives they never knew growing up.

This is not a generation out to save the world. Revolution is for someone else, a cohort that cares more than they do. But Nikes are deeply interested in preserving their families—the absence they feel most deeply from the past and the one institution they are now devoted to in their adult years. Indeed, families give Nikes one of the few causes they really do care about: charter schools, homeschooling, and other nontraditional alternatives to public education, another paradigm that began to implode under their feet as they were passing through it.

For their part, the First Globals are already leading us into a new age of inclusion and authenticity. These are our internationalists, our multilateralists. For Privates, the old adage that all politics is local holds true. For First Globals, it's just the opposite: All politics is global. The difference between the two vantages is huge, especially as it spreads out into the future. Politics, though, is only one way in which First Globals look outward rather than inward. More than half of all First Globals and 64 percent of those with passports tell us they are likely or very likely to use the Internet to listen to music from all around the world. Better than 60 percent of all First Globals and almost three in four passport holders do the same to view art from Africa, Asia, Latin America, the Middle East, and other distant points on the compass. Roughly one in three Privates told us in polling that globalization is bad because it breaks down traditional forms of nationalism and will eventually threaten Western traditions of education and democratic culture. Only one in ten First Global passport holders agreed. That difference, too, is huge going out into the future.

For this cohort, bullshit detectors are set on high all the time; like guild merchants of yore, they bite every metaphorical coin they are handed to see if the metal is real or false. That's one of the things they've learned from growing up online: the ease with which everything can be counterfeited, including emotion. Almost a third of them (32 percent) have broken up with someone using e-mail or a text-message—media that let the sender control the emotional content. The only other age cohort that even breaks into double digits on this front, and that at only 10 percent, is Nikes.

Yes, like all other generations, First Globals will change as they age. A twenty-year-old does not see the world the same way a fifty-year-old does, and a fifty-year-old does not see it through the eyes of an eighty-year-old. Marriages and commitment ceremonies, births, retirement, serious illness, the death of a loved one—each of these seminal events along life's ladder inevitably alters us. In time, perhaps, First Globals will be the sea anchor dragging against change at the other end of the age continuum. That time, though, is a long way off. For now, First Globals are the jumping-off point for where the future begins. The sections below describe where my polling indicates the vectors are leading us.

ON WORK: FROM JOB-DEFINED TO OTHER-DEFINED LIVES

Back when careers were stable and jobs often lifetime commitments, finding primary fulfillment in work only made sense. The office, the factory, the salesroom floor—that's where much of an adult life was played out, where friends were found, and where self-definition came from. You were what you did: a banker, a shop foreman, a rising junior executive, a company man. No more. Virtually every job today is potentially temp work, and maybe half the careers as well. Coworkers are for a season, not for life, or maybe they're not at all. Telecommuters know their colleagues mostly as names at the bottom of e-mails; their support staff is found at the all-night Kinko's, not down the hall.

Today's First Globals still are what they do, but they are far more likely than Woodstockers and Privates to define that in terms unrelated to their primary source of income—they play in an alternative rock band, they're painters or marathoners or kickboxers, or they get piercings and tattoos—because that, not the day job, is where they find fulfillment and self-definition. The results below are from our 2005 consumer profile poll.

	GLOBAL	NIKE	WOODSTOCK	PRIVATE
"My work is very fulfilling to me." STRONGLY AGREE	41%	48	53	61
"I have other things more fulfilling than my job." STRONGLY AGREE	78	75	71	55

To be sure, First Globals have many more choices available than Privates did at their age—in work, in living arrangements, and in many cases in parental support. Privates for their part are mostly retired. Many jobs are more fulfilling when you no longer have to show up at the door to do them. But our own and other polling consistently shows that, except for the paycheck, work is moving down the list of Americans' priorities. The Pew Research Center recently updated research it had done in the late 1990s on the attitude of mothers toward work. The results: In 1997, 32 percent of working mothers said that their ideal situation was a full-time job. A decade later, that number slipped to 21 percent. At the same time, the number of working mothers favoring a part-time job grew by 12 points, to 60 percent, and the number wanting to leave the workforce altogether held steady at about one in five. Among at-home mothers, the desire for a full-time job fell from 24 percent to 16 percent over the decade; the number wanting part-time work dropped 4 points, to 33 percent; and the number saying that their ideal situation was not working at all rose 9 points to 48 percent, nearly half of all at-home mothers.

Does all that spell the end of the feminist movement? I don't read it that way, but I do think that what we are seeing is a sea change in Americans' attitudes toward work and the workplace. When employers come and go, when résumés are patchwork quilts and the workforce largely nomadic, people have to look elsewhere to find out who they really are. When we asked respondents in the same consumer profile poll cited above for their opinion on the statement "I work at my job only to make money to live," 33 percent of First Globals either agreed or strongly agreed, while 43 percent went the other way. (The rest were undecided.) That same rough spread can be found among other demographic groups, including men generally, renters, those making less than twenty-five thousand dollars a year, single people, and non-churchgoers. Collectively, this is not a resounding vote for the self-validation to be found in work in these new times.

ON CAREERS: FROM RISK TAKING TO FANTASY ESCAPING

In that same 2005 surveying, we asked participants to choose which of two hypothetical careers they would prefer—one as an actor in fantasies, the other as a police officer, the ultimate in harsh reality.

Our immediate purpose was to measure how commitment to public service was changing from generation to generation. We were also curious about the long-range effect on younger participants of being exposed through TV, movies, videos, and video games to a nearly constant diet of escapist entertainment—that's why we phrased the question as we did. At a gut level, I also wanted to gauge the effect of well-publicized instances of police abuse in Los Angeles, New York, and elsewhere. When I was a kid in Utica, the beat cop was a role model. Was he still? I can't say the results surprised me. Karaoke machines, air-guitar contests, and webcams have already turned most teens into stars in their own fantasy dramas. But I do think it is going to be harder for municipalities—and Uncle Sam, for that matter—to find the price point at which young people are willing to act in the real dramas of police work, firefighting, and war making. Police, firemen, and soldiers, after all, risk their lives; actors risk only their reputations.

WHICH WOULD YOU RATHER BE?

	GLOBAL	NIKE	WOODSTOCK	PRIVATE
An actor who entertains us with fantasy escapism	57%	40	39	27
A police officer who puts his life on the line to protect others	42	49	49	58

ON STEM CELLS: FROM WORD WARS TO THERAPIES

Only in the minds of liberals and conservatives is stem cell research a settled matter: Just one in twenty liberals strongly agrees that it is immoral to create human embryos to harvest stem cells, while two in three conservatives say that is so. And even that strong majority position on the conservative side starts to break down when a loved one could potentially be helped by stem cell transplants. But if we are still a long way from resolving this prominent battle of the cultural wars—see especially the "not sures" in the bottom table below—the generational momentum on the subject is clear. More comfortable with the relevant technology and especially with biotechnology, which didn't exist in the school curricula of their elders, First Globals are both less prone to condemn the research on moral grounds and more inclined to contribute to it. This data comes from a June 2007 Interactive survey.

IT IS IMMORAL TO CREATE HUMAN EMBRYOS IN ORDER TO ISOLATE HUMAN EMBRYONIC STEM CELLS FOR RESEARCH.

	18–27	28–41	42–61	62–80	81+
Strongly agree	31%	35	36	37	31
Strongly disagree	44	29	24	26	23

IF GIVEN THE OPPORTUNITY, WOULD YOU DONATE UNFERTILIZED EGGS OR SPERM FOR THE DEVELOPMENT OF AN EMBRYO THAT WOULD BE USED TO ISOLATE HUMAN EMBRYONIC STEM CELLS?

	18–27	28–41	42–61	62–80	81+
Yes	40%	35	36	38	30
No	36	45	47	43	41
Not sure	24	20	17	19	29

ON THE INTERNET: FROM THE FCC TO UNCENSORED CYBERSPACE

It's probably a sign of the lack of faith Americans have in the efficacy of government that a majority of absolutely no one wants federal regulation of Internet content. Only a third of born-agains and just 38 percent of those who identify themselves as "very conservative" argue for applying the FCC model to cyberspace. In fact, the only group that tops even 40 percent are those who attend church more than once a week (41 percent). That doesn't stop congresspersons from railing periodically against the wide-open airwaves of the World Wide Web, but results like those below—and particularly the opposition from those most intimate with the Internet—should assure that fulmination doesn't turn into legislation in the years ahead. Only self-described libertarians (8 percent), liberals (7 percent), and progressives (3 percent) were equally or even less likely than First Globals to agree with the statement.

THE FEDERAL GOVERNMENT PLACES RESTRICTIONS ON WHAT CAN OR CANNOT BE BROADCAST ON RADIO OR TELEVISION. DO YOU AGREE OR DISAGREE THAT THE GOVERNMENT SHOULD PUT THE SAME REGULATION ON THE CONTENT OF THE INTERNET AS IT DOES ON RADIO AND TELEVISION PROGRAMMING?

	GLOBAL	NIKE	WOODSTOCK	PRIVATES
Agree	7%	18	22	33
Disagree	87	72	67	54

In a related question, we asked who should be responsible for controlling content available on the Internet to children. First Globals were less likely than any other age cohort to select the FCC or Internet service providers and more likely to say "no one," but the runaway winner across all age groups was "parents/family."

ON ENERGY USAGE: FROM WASTERS TO INNOVATORS

Just as most Americans are against letting the Feds regulate the Internet, so just about everyone is for cleaner air and water. That's true whether they think Al Gore is a god, a blowhard, or the devil incarnate. But one thing I've come to especially like about First Globals is their willingness to step up to the plate—the ways in which they translate attitudinal shifts, which polls can measure, to behavior on the ground, where the marketplace is the great statistician. Maybe First Globals are tired of seeing the slackers above them shrug their shoulders and move on. Maybe their willingness to take personal responsibility is part of their expansive worldview: Unlike in Vegas, what happens here environmentally doesn't always stay here. Whatever the reason, when we asked more than four thousand adults in June 2007 about their energy consumption, the young were the ones most willing to change their ways.

"I NEED TO USE LESS ENERGY BECAUSE MY ENERGY USE CONTRIBUTES TO DANGEROUS CARBON EMISSIONS."

	18–27	28–41	42–61	62–80	81+
Strongly agree	29%	24	22	19	12
Somewhat agree	36	30	27	26	21
Somewhat disagree	12	16	20	21	35
Strongly disagree	22	28	30	31	23

We also asked about alternative fuels and again got a resounding response from young adults, far more enthusiastic than from any other age group. To be sure, a certain amount of naïveté factors into that. Youths like the thrill of the new, and they are less inclined than their elders to worry about where the money is going to come from to create the infrastructure that will support alternative fuels. But when more than half of any age group strongly agrees with a statement like the one below, a movement is under way that will eventually translate itself into funding, research, exploration, and, with a little luck, reality.

ALTERNATIVE FUELS LIKE SOLAR, WIND, AND GEOTHERMAL CAN CREATE HUNDREDS OF THOUSANDS OF NEW JOBS.

	18–27	28–41	42–61	62–80	81+
Strongly agree	52%	37	38	30	19
Somewhat agree	29	37	34	40	45
Somewhat disagree	8	9	13	13	15
Strongly disagree	4	4	5	6	6

ON GUILT: FROM MINE TO THEIRS

Energy usage and carbon footprints are just one of the guilt goads for First Globals. They also are more inclined than other generations to feel guilty about indulging themselves generally. Money plays a role in that, of course: The young have less of it. But as our first global citizens, they also are more acutely aware of and empathetic with places such as Darfur, where suffering and want are severe. As we have seen in other polling results, they also are more willing to bring American interests in line with global ones if that will alleviate suffering in distant lands. Note particularly in the table below how far the generations have migrated from Privates to First Globals on every element of this question except for money.

HAVE YOU DEPRIVED YOURSELF OF ANYTHING . . . ?

	GLOBAL	NIKE	WOODSTOCK	PRIVATE
Because of guilt	73%	69	61	42
Because of lack of money	96	93	92	85
Because of fear of a negative response from a loved one	51	54	48	31

It's not that the young don't covet and envy. They do. As we have seen in previous data, they can be slaves to brands, but their global perspective has given them a larger-than-myself aesthetic that has rarely before surfaced in people their age. My hunch is that these young globals will be the first generation since the GI's of World War II to give freely of themselves to make the world a better place.

ON RELIGION: FROM PRODUCTION VALUES TO BACK-TO-BASICS

As the mainstream media tells the story, the future of Protestantism is mostly to be found in megachurches. More than twelve hundred such churches—commonly defined as those with congregations of two thousand or more regular attendees—are scattered across the United States, mostly in the South and West. A 2005 survey by the Hartford Institute for Religion Research found that megachurches average twenty full-time paid ministerial staff persons, twenty-two full-time paid program staff persons, and nearly three hundred volunteer workers who give five or more hours a week to the church. That's more regular volunteers than many mainstream Protestant churches can get to walk through their doors on Christmas and Easter combined. Houston's Lakewood Church, one of the largest of the congregations, operates out of the old Compaq Convention Center, where—at a cost of some $100 million—it has converted the old basketball arena into a chapel with waterfall displays, cascading seats, and all sorts of lighting displays.

I have no doubt that the effect is tremendous, perhaps even awesome, and I certainly don't think that megachurches are in any danger of disappearing in the immediate future. But I see a powerful countervailing trend in the authenticity movement and its emphasis on content over package. I see a countervailing trend, too, in the ways in which the evangelicals are spacing themselves from their putative leaders, and not just on the environment. Health care and child care advocates on the religious right are demanding to be heard whether their pastors and church elders are interested in the message or not. In the small but fast-growing house-church movement, I also see compelling evidence that the push back against megachurches is already well under way.

Much as the Amish have been doing for centuries, indeed just as early Christians did when the Church still had to operate underground, house-churchers meet for worship not in soaring glass cathedrals or on sprawling religious campuses but in worshipers' homes. Production values are nil. Hierarchy is flattened of necessity: These are not staff-rich environments. As one leader said of the house-church movement, "It is about authenticity. Church services have succeeded at being more characterized by excellence, but one of the consequences of that excellence is artificiality and the feeling that everything is produced and that it is a show." Or as another participant told the L.A. *Daily News,* "What is so exciting about doing small-group house church is just the chance to be real." In a culture filled with fake and overblown events, that's a powerful force. Estimates are that the house-church movement has grown tenfold over the last decade, to about twenty million participants attending either full-time or occasionally. I project that number to grow even more dramatically in the years ahead.

ON CAMPAIGNING: FROM RED STATE–BLUE STATE TO MICRO-PRECINCTS

Useful formulations die hard, which is why commentators during the 2008 presidential election cycle will still be talking about red states and blue states, but the fact is red state–blue state is already a blunt tool. As we saw earlier, retail shopping destinations are just as accurate a barometer of how people are likely to vote, and the voters in them are in many ways far easier to reach. That, though, is only the beginning of the forthcoming segmentation of the electorate. By the 2020 election cycle—only four presidencies away—political strategists will be counting voters one micro-precinct at a time: sports fans, pet owners, international travelers, early risers, cancer survivors, heart-bypass veterans, Catholic school alumni, science majors compared to humanities majors, Mac users compared to PC users, American-car owners compared to foreign-car owners, Yahoo! browsers compared to Google browsers, single moms compared to married moms, and on and on. Will all this be ultimately useful? For my business, yes, certainly! For voters, likely, it will mean a barrage of e-mails, calls, junk mail, and other forms of canvassing. But whether it's useful or not, micro-precinct campaigning has already begun because (a) we are at the point of being able to achieve that kind of granularity, and (b) once the possibility exists, no campaign will be able to resist putting it to use. This is a genie that's out of the bottle and will only grow and grow.

ON ISRAEL: FROM PARTISAN TO HONEST BROKER

The phrase runs like a heavy-handed leitmotif through the memoirs of ex-presidents, former secretaries of state, retired CIA chiefs, and other similar Washington bigwigs: America's role in the Holy Land has always been to be a "fair and honest broker" between the Israelis and the Palestinians. The words sound noble, but the American people for the most part think they are baloney. When we asked in December 2006 if the phrase accurately described the United States' current role, a plurality of every age group except for the oldest—and a whopping majority of First Globals—answered in the negative.

DO YOU AGREE OR DISAGREE THAT THE UNITED STATES IS CURRENTLY ACTING AS A FAIR AND HONEST BROKER IN THE MIDDLE EAST CONFLICT?

	GLOBAL	NIKE	WOODSTOCK	PRIVATE
Agree	24%	37	36	44
Disagree	62	48	50	40
Not sure	15	15	14	16

What would make the United States a fair and honest broker, in deed as well as word? In December 2006, we gave nearly sixty-three hundred adults several statements concerning both Israeli settlements and Jerusalem, and asked them to choose which ones came closest to their views. Those answers follow. Not surprisingly perhaps, the percentage of respondents answering "neither" was very high—these are complicated, emotionally charged issues. But going down the generations, the trend lines clearly point to a more balanced approach toward the two involved groups.

Statement A: The settlements are necessary for the security of Israel, and Israeli citizens have the right to build on land in the Palestinian West Bank.

Statement B: Israeli settlements are built on land confiscated from Palestinians and should be torn down and the land returned to Palestinian owners.

	GLOBAL	NIKE	WOODSTOCK	PRIVATE
Statement A	18%	24	25	29
Statement B	48	46	49	46
Neither	17	14	11	12
Not sure	16	16	15	13

Statement A: The city of Jerusalem should be partitioned with one part of the city as the Israeli capital and one part as the Palestinian capital. Division should be based on both the local population and the location of and access to holy sites.

Statement B: The city of Jerusalem should remain under the control of the Israeli government, with the Israeli government controlling access to the city. Palestinians currently living in the area of East Jerusalem would be allowed to remain in the city, but their access to holy sites would be controlled by the Israelis.

	GLOBAL	NIKE	WOODSTOCK	PRIVATE
Statement A	40%	33	34	31
Statement B	26	31	33	34
Neither	22	24	24	23
Not sure	13	12	10	11

One other thing the trend lines clearly point to in the Middle East: an end to trying to broker an "American peace." Roughly half of all the other age cohorts back a multinational approach to resolving the Israeli-Palestinian dispute, while 80 percent of First Globals do.

ON INTERNATIONAL ALLIANCES: FROM NATO TO THE U.N.

The North Atlantic Treaty Organization and the United Nations both trace their roots to the end of World War II. The U.N. was the realization of Woodrow Wilson's dream, from a war earlier, of a League of Nations that would help bring order to a discordant world. NATO had a more specific purpose: to halt the Soviet Union's westward expansion at the border of its Warsaw Pact satellite nations. Ultimately, both served their purpose. Russia is reemergent, but this time as a putative democracy stripped of its larger empire. Despite far too much discordance, the world order has survived as well. Sometimes, it even seems to prosper.

One might think that, given those track records, both NATO and the U.N. would be riding a rising tide of public opinion, but that's not entirely the case. The U.N. is highly esteemed in large and even small cities, where the population is more likely to be as varied as the U.N. General Assembly; among all religious groups, especially American Muslims; among liberals and moderates; and almost equally across all age groups. Conservatives and libertarians are, as always, opposed to the international body, but this is another case where the political and religious right wings part ways. By a 50–44 margin, those who identify themselves as born-again say the U.N. is more relevant than ever, while the "very conservative" disagree by a huge 82–17 margin.

NATO's problem is more age-related and is therefore more likely to erode support for the alliance in the decades ahead. First Globals still say the alliance is relevant, but as you will see in the tables below, the enthusiasm wanes sharply as we proceed down the generation ladder. Why? Lack of historical memory perhaps—the youngest First Globals weren't even born when the Soviet empire began to implode, and they were still in grade school when NATO forces intervened decisively to end the carnage in the former Yugoslavia. Or maybe the reason is that their worldview is less Eurocentric than that of older generations. These results are from polling we did for the Foreign Policy Association.

SOME SAY THAT THE UNITED NATIONS HAS BEEN REDUCED IN ITS INFLUENCE AND IS LESS RELEVANT TODAY IN GLOBAL MATTERS. OTHERS SAY THAT THE U.N. IS NEEDED NOW MORE THAN EVER TO REPRESENT A GLOBAL PERSPECTIVE IN ISSUES THAT ARISE. WHICH OF THOSE STATEMENTS COMES CLOSEST TO YOUR OWN VIEW?

	GLOBAL	NIKE	WOODSTOCK	PRIVATE
U.N. is less relevant	35%	37	45	32
U.N. is needed more than ever	63	59	52	61

SOME ARGUE THAT NATO HAS BEEN REDUCED IN ITS INFLUENCE AND IS LESS RELEVANT TODAY IN U.S. FOREIGN POLICY. OTHERS SAY THAT NATO IS NEEDED NOW MORE THAN EVER TO REPRESENT A GLOBAL PERSPECTIVE IN ISSUES THAT ARISE. WHICH OF THOSE STATEMENTS COMES CLOSEST TO YOUR OWN VIEW?

	GLOBAL	NIKE	WOODSTOCK	PRIVATE
NATO is less relevant	41%	32	34	22
NATO is needed more than ever	56	64	59	70

ON TRADE: FROM CLOSED DOORS TO OPEN DOORS

Free trade is another of those political issues that seem to have been settled for the future in the minds of everyone but the politicians. When we asked a thousand adults if free trade is good for America, all age groups, all ideologies, all religious affiliations, and all education levels said yes. Even among those with less than a high-school education—low-wage workers most likely to be affected by lifting trade protections—a plurality (47–45, with 8 percent not sure) favored getting rid of barriers. More intriguing and telling to me, though, was the answer to our follow-up question. When we asked if free trade benefited the respondents and their families, the answers were still on the positive side, but less so, and decidedly less so for First Globals.

DO YOU AGREE OR DISAGREE THAT FREE TRADE IS GOOD FOR AMERICA?

	GLOBAL	NIKE	WOODSTOCK	PRIVATE
Agree	89%	78	78	77
Disagree	9	17	15	13

DO YOU PERSONALLY FEEL THAT FREE TRADE BENEFITS YOU AND YOUR FAMILY?

	GLOBAL	NIKE	WOODSTOCK	PRIVATE
Agree	55%	70	66	56
Disagree	21	23	24	27

Why such support for free trade and open markets even when the benefits aren't being felt at home? In July 2007 Interactive polling we did for IBM, seven in ten respondents said they believed open trading markets around the world increased tolerance and friendship among countries. Predictably, respondents age seventy and older tended to look at the issue through strictly American eyes: Six in ten of them strongly agreed that the growth of the U.S. economy depends on the government's aggressive work to open markets abroad for American products and services. The youngest respondents meanwhile took a whole-earth view: 35 percent of those age eighteen to twenty-four strongly agreed that open markets can pave the way to peaceful international relations.

ON GLOBAL COMPETITION: FROM THE AMERICAN
CENTURY TO . . . SOMEONE ELSE'S

Of all the questions we've asked in recent years about U.S. foreign policy and international standing, the ones that evoke the greatest generational differences almost always involve America's rivals on the world stage. The fundamental fact is that First Globals view the other nations of the world in terms dramatically different from their elders. Militarily and economically, they are much less China-phobic. To them, if there's any Chinese hegemony to worry about down the road, it's cultural. Probably because First Globals were raised on video games and remain in their twenties so oriented toward electronics generally—from high-definition TVs to hand-held music players—they are also far more prone to cite the Japanese as economic rivals than even the Nikes are, in the age group just above them. Militarily, what scares First Globals most is the same nuclear nightmare that terrified schoolchildren in the 1950s, but this time the starring role goes not to the Soviets but to North Korea.

WHICH POWER POSES THE GREATEST THREAT TO THE U.S. MILITARILY?

	GLOBAL	NIKE	WOODSTOCK	PRIVATE
China	12%	25	22	26
EU	2	1	1	1
Japan	2	0	0	0
Russia	0	2	1	2
Iran	15	15	19	21
North Korea	49	37	39	30
None	16	13	15	8

WHICH POWER POSES THE GREATEST THREAT TO THE U.S. ECONOMICALLY?

	GLOBAL	NIKE	WOODSTOCK	PRIVATE
China	31%	52	55	64
EU	24	11	9	4
Japan	26	13	6	4
Russia	0	4	1	0
None	10	15	22	14

WHICH POWER POSES THE GREATEST THREAT TO THE U.S. CULTURALLY?

	GLOBAL	NIKE	WOODSTOCK	PRIVATE
China	23%	13	12	14
EU	12	12	11	8
Japan	4	2	1	3
Russia	0	0	1	2
None	56	66	66	54

One final batch of numbers: As you will see, First Globals are also much less likely than older age cohorts to assume continuing American domination in cutting-edge sciences. This table breaks the results down by generation and, within generations, by those with and without passports. The differences between passport holders and those without passports are significant within all generations, but notice especially how vast they are within First Globals. More than perhaps any other point of distinction, travel seems to be the one experience from which there is no backing away.

WHICH COUNTRY OR REGION WILL BE THE WORLD LEADER IN THE NEXT TEN YEARS IN BIOTECHNOLOGY? (RESULTS ARE SHOWN BY GENERATION WITH AND WITHOUT PASSPORTS.)

	GLOBAL		NIKE		WOODSTOCK		PRIVATE	
	W/	W/O	W/	W/O	W/	W/O	W/	W/O
United States	40%	57	53	49	55	48	59	59
Europe	24	7	7	16	17	14	13	7
China	9	14	5	7	6	10	8	10
India	5	3	6	4	7	4	5	3
Asia	15	5	10	10	6	9	6	5

Is any of this set in stone? Obviously not. As I wrote at the beginning of this book, nothing is a given in polling. Wars intervene. Charismatic individuals arise to alter the public chemistry, for good and ill. (Think Roosevelt, Churchill, Jack Kennedy, Martin Luther King, Jr., and Nelson Mandela; but also remember Hitler and Stalin.) Cataclysmic natural events skew the trend lines no matter how entrenched they might seem, laying bare hidden faults. Our polling consistently shows that Hurricane Katrina had precisely that effect on the vaunted "permanent Republican majority." Stuff happens, in life and in predictions.

What are clear are the meta-movements that are pushing us forward. The America of 2020 will be a more tolerant nation. Our people by then will have lived for two decades in a new world of less. We will have gotten comfortable with the limitations on us and embraced the Zen of more minimal lifestyles and consumption patterns. We will expect our leaders to talk straight: Hype, hokum, and hooey—in politics, in advertising, wherever it appears—will be punished. So will those who tell us to sacrifice, then refuse to make sacrifices of their own; of that, perhaps more than anything else, Congress and presidents must be aware. We'll care about this fragile planet in hitherto unseen ways, and along with our global brethren, we'll vote with our pocketbooks for goods and services that serve the environment rather than destroy it. That's the new reality we are headed for, and truth told, it sounds pretty good.

A GUIDE TO MARKETING TO THE WAY WE'LL BE

- Don't write off the Private Generation (born 1926–45). They've got decades of healthy living ahead of them, and they're going to fill those golden years with volunteering, mentoring, and lifelong learning opportunities.
- Woodstockers (born 1946–64) will finally get tired of trying to look and act like their children. This is a generation that needs a second act—something with more social utility than an endless obsession with self. Write the script, and they will come.
- Nikes (born 1965–78) made "Just Do It" their mantra, but as they age, they're going to bond with their own families as no generation before them has, and they are going to spearhead the search for greater fulfillment that the Secular Spiritualists have begun.
- First Globals (born 1979–90) are ready to go anywhere, experience everything, and work and live in exotic places; and they pillage cyberspace for information that will allow them to do all those things. If you can't market successfully to this amazing crew, find another line of work.
- Americans will continue to define themselves less and less by paid work. It's "who I am," not "what I do."
- In the battle between science and anti-science, science wins. No more Terri Schiavos, and no more global warming denial idiocy. Alternative fuels *will* heat and light our world.
- The church of the future will be a bungalow on Maple Street, not a megastructure in a sea of parking spaces. It's intimacy of experience people long for, not production values.
- The nation of the future will be in a strange way more intimate, too. Americans want to live in a world *with* other people, not in a walled empire surrounded by enemies.

A C K N O W L E D G M E N T S

This book has not only taken a long time, perhaps my entire life of observations; it has also been helped along the way by many people who have molded my thinking and helped me see the goodness in the American people. Here is the short list:

Rafe Sagalyn is a literary agent extraordinaire: tenacious, respected, a cocreator of this project.

Howard Means has been a brilliant, sensitive, and savvy wordsmith who has guided this book to its final form. Above all, he is a good friend and a fellow believer. He has been Henry Higgins to my humbling Liza Doolittle. His wife, Candy, assisted in many ways to organize random thoughts and ideas.

Tim Bartlett, a very patient editor, transformed this raw work into a credible piece of literature.

Several members of my staff at Zogby International played critical roles in researching, editing, and creating ideas to survey: Grace Ren, Joe Mazloom, John Bruce, Karen Scott, Marc Penz, Rebecca Wittman, Fritz Wenzel, Chad Bohnert, and Janine Bohnert all deserve special gratitude. But my entire staff should take a bow. They made the difficult work of writing surveys, managing the call-center work, doing the telephone and online sampling, and crunching the statistical data look a whole lot easier than it actually is.

A very special thanks to my administrative assistant, Janet

Clements, who handles my schedule and runs the details of my life with a smile, especially when there is nothing to smile about.

Ben Loehnen has been a good editor, a good friend, and a supporter of this project. Christine Cipriani read and edited the first few drafts and made the raw ideas come alive. Carl De Santis, friend and adviser, was present at the creation of many of the ideas in this book. And special thanks to David H. Bennett, professor of history at the Maxwell School of Syracuse University, for a wonderful parable on the American dream.

But it all comes down to family.

I can never forget from whence I have come. My father, Joseph Rachid Zogby, was an immigrant from Lebanon who worked six days and evenings a week in the grocery store he cofounded with his brothers. A gentle man of profound wisdom, he was always generous to those less fortunate. When he passed away in 1961, we found a ledger he kept in the store's safe with hundreds of names of customers who were extended "credit" for food during the Great Depression.

My mother, Celia Ann Zogby, was an incredible teacher, an independent woman long before it was acceptable. She spoke on women's rights at her 1924 high school graduation, a surprise to all because it wasn't the prepared speech they had approved. And she spoke and taught three languages, as well as math, social studies, and literature, even though she took only a few college courses. A woman of strong faith and enormous intelligence, she rallied her young family after Dad died and served as mentor to four generations of extended family until she passed away at the age of ninety-two.

Selwa Stemmer, my sister, helped Mom carry the family load during the tough times and has gone on to raise six of her own children with her husband, Richard. She is deeply rooted in the values of faith, community, and social justice taught to us by our parents.

James Zogby, my brother Jim, is the smartest person I know. Guided by a strong faith that he shares with his wife, Eileen, Jim is a longtime Washington presence, strongly committed to the cause of Palestinians, Arab Americans, and human rights everywhere. He is recognized as one of the most effective communicators of everything that is right. He and I also are mistaken for each other all the time, so I hope he gets only great reviews for this book.

Kathy Zogby, my wife, is now a retired special-education teacher, but she still hears lovingly from her students and stays connected with them. They were lucky to have her, and so am I.

Our boys, now men—Jonathan, Benjamin, and Jeremy—are just so smart about so many things. They share a passion for learning, for justice, and for the people of the wider world. I am very proud of them.

I have learned from everyone I have mentioned and so many more. But any screw-ups in these pages are not borrowed. They bear my own mark of creativity.

JOHN ZOGBY
Utica, New York

A

ABC News, 7, 83–84
abortion, xii, 27, 30, 52–54, 65,
    103–5, 190, 193
    conflicting values and, 6,
        52–53
    stem cell research and, 53–54,
        200–201
Abramoff, Jack, 151
actors, career, 199–200
Adams, Henry, 28
Adams, John, 29
adoption rights, 95
advertising, 9, 12–13, 123, 155,
    178–83, 192
    Benetton's United Colors, 115,
        182
    Cisco's The Human Network, 182
    Coca-Cola, 178–79
    Dove Campaign for Real Beauty,
        181
    Ford's "Bold Moves," 180
    GM's This Is My Country, 76
    of Hummer, 75, 181–82
    of Kellogg's cereals, 183
    of Land Rover, 73
    people featured in, 179
    political campaign, 9, 182–83
    "What Happens in Vegas Stays in
        Vegas," 180

Advertising Age, 115
Afghanistan, 68, 156, 157
African Americans, 12, 13, 14–16,
    96–97, 118, 158
    authenticity of, 164–65
    at integrated social events, 98
    in investor class, 39, 40, 41
    as national election voters, 19
    as U.S. presidents, 100–102
    as work supervisors, 98
age cohorts, 11, 18–19, 21–22,
    23, 31–32, 34, 36, 53, 60, 64,
    68, 71, 74, 76, 81, 86, 92–93,
    98, 100, 139–40, 153–54,
    185–215
    see also elderly people; First
        Globals; Nike Generation;
        Private Generation; Woodstock
        Generation
Agnew, Spiro, 28
Ahmadinejad, Mahmoud, 67
Alfred P. Sloan Foundation, 81
Alien and Sedition Acts
    (1798), 29
Al Jazeera website, 54–55
all-day calling, 7
Allen, George, 84
alternative fuels, 203, 215
alternative medicine, 196
American-Arab Anti-Discrimination
    Committee, 150

American dream, 24, 36, 41–42, 47, 49, 120–47
  goals of, 121–24
  as material success, 121, 122, 123–27, 128, 139–40, 142–43, 193
  as spiritual fulfillment, 121, 123–47; *see also* Secular Spiritualists
American Enterprise Institute, 95
Americans for Tax Reform, 39
Amish, 205
Amnesty International, 93
Anderson, Sherry Ruth, 171
Anderson Analytics, 115, 116
AOL, 10, 14, 79
Arab American Institute, 150
Arabs, 54–55, 67, 113, 150
  Palestinian, 207–9
Arctic National Wildlife Refuge, 64
Arkansas, 22–23
"Armageddon" elections, 31–35
armed forces, U.S., 43–44, 45, 46, 187
  distrusted leaders of, 153–54
  homosexuals in, 95, 97
  veterans of, 146
Asian Americans, 29, 98, 110
Atlanta, Ga., 13–14, 103
authenticity, xvi, 137, 148–83, 196, 214
  in aspects of life, 164
  of celebrities, 164–67
  in consumer shopping, 162–63, 172, 173–76
  in content vs. package, 162–63, 205
  corporate ethics in, 172–76, 181
  definition of, 161
  in desirable opposite-sex attributes, 168–71, 183
  in exterior design, 162
  honesty and integrity in, 154–55
  of house-church movement, 205–26
  inauthentic events vs., 155–59, 206
  Internet transparency in, 158–61, 168
  in lifetime companion, 164
  in marketing, 163, 178–83, 205
  of other people, 161, 164–71
  personal ethics in, 172, 176–78
  in political campaigns, 171–72
  trait selection issue and, 161–62
  untrustworthy leadership vs., 151–55
auto industry, 71–77
  Big Three manufacturers of, 71–72, 75–77
  patriotism in marketing of, 60, 74, 76–77
  see also cars

B

baby boomers, 141, 189–90
Ball, Lucille, 10, 11
Baltimore *Sun*, 86
basketball players, 116–18
Baum, L. Frank, 5
BBC website, 55
beer industry, 71
Benetton, 115, 182
Bennett, William, 91, 92–93
Benny, Jack, 10
Bernstein, Carl, 171
Big Idea with Donny Deutsch, The, 168
Big Lots, 49
billionaires, 136–37
  "tax relief" for, 152
Bill of Rights, 29–30
biotechnology, 213–14
blogs, 83, 84–85, 86–88
  investing in, 87
  traditional media vs., 87–88
  Wal-Marting Across America, 180
Bloomingdale's, 8, 13, 175
body mass index, 181
"Bold Moves" ad campaign, 180
Bollinger, Lee, 67
Bolton, John, 51
Bonds, Barry, 151
born-again Christians, 43, 44, 53, 127, 146, 190, 201, 209
Born to Buy (Schor), 91–92
Boscov's, 8, 173
Boston, Mass., 77–78

BOTOX, 168, 169, 189
Bowling Alone (Putnam), 138
BP, 59
Brand-Intel, 115
brands, 92, 115–16, 204
    beer, 71
brand value, 115, 116
Bremer, L. Paul, 146
Brinkley, David, 83
Brokaw, Tom, xiii
Brown, Michael, 157
Buchanan, Pat, 6–7
Budweiser, 71
Buffett, Warren, 36, 137
Burns, James MacGregor, 35–36
Bush, George H.W., 7, 30, 100, 166
Bush, George W., xi, xiii, 25, 30, 51,
    100, 166, 167
    administration of, 39, 58, 64, 68,
        151–52
    approval ratings of, 6, 8, 9, 35, 152
    "axis of evil" concept of, 67
    Christian values of, 52
    dishonesty of, 151–52
    foreign policy of, 51–52, 60, 66, 68
    global warming as viewed by,
        59, 65
    Hurricane Katrina and, 155, 157,
        158
    Iraq War and, 4, 66, 155
    Libby's sentence commuted by, 152,
        157–58
    in 2000 election, 4–6, 7, 190
    in 2004 election, 6, 8, 31–35,
        39–40, 52, 71, 133, 145, 182,
        190
Business for Diplomatic Action,
    51–52
BusinessWeek, 115

C

Cabrera, Angel, 117
Caraviello, David, 118
Carnegie, Andrew, 144–45
Carrier, Carolyn, 118
cars, 71–77
    environmentally friendly, 74–76, 77

gas-guzzling, 65, 75, 181–82
    gasoline mileage standards for,
        75–76
    gasoline prices and, 69, 76, 78
    hybrid, *see* hybrid cars
    pickup trucks, 76–77
    time-share travel in, 79
Carter, Jimmy, 30, 165, 166, 167
Case, Steve, 79
CBS News, 83
cell phones, 20–21, 119, 162
Census Bureau, U.S.,18, 86, 122, 140,
    148
Center for American Progress, 128
charitable activities, 131, 142, 144–45
Cheney, Dick, 152
Chevy Silverado pickup truck, 76–77
Chicago, Ill., 14, 77–78
Chicago Markets, 49
Chicago Tribune, 86, 97
children, 183, 205
    controlling Internet exposure of,
        202
    qualities taught to, 131–32
    trait selection of, 161–62
China, 29, 109, 110, 212, 213
Chinese Americans, 110
Christianity Today, 65
Christian right, 26, 35, 52, 90, 205
Christians:
    born-again, 43, 44, 53, 127, 146,
        190, 201, 209
    evangelical, 53, 64–66, 69, 190,
        204–5
    house-church movement of, 205–6,
        215
    megachurches of, 204–5
    Roman Catholic, 60, 152, 191
    values of, 35, 52, 132, 133–35
Christians for the Mountains, 65
Christmas holiday spending, 124
Chrysler, 71–72
church attendance, 8, 33, 34, 44, 123,
    127, 146, 201
CIDAC, 109–10
Cisco, 182
civil liberties, 35
civil rights movement, 30

civil unions, 43, 95–96
Civil War, 27, 29, 30, 31, 33–34
Cizik, Richard, 65
Clinton, Bill, 30, 32, 33, 51, 53, 118,
    159, 166, 171, 186, 189–90
  Lewinsky scandal and, 83–84, 151,
    156, 158
Clinton, Hillary, 32, 50, 84, 118, 166,
    167, 171–72, 190
  as presidential candidate, 101–2
CNBC, 168
CNN, 6–7, 34
Cobain, Kurt, 136
Coca-Cola, 115, 178–79
coffee cup quotes, Starbucks, 25–26
coffees, 93–94
  fair-trade, 48
coffee shops, 34
Colbert, Stephen, 172
cold war, 56, 184, 186
colleges and universities, 36, 42, 89,
    94, 111
  Internet access to, 60, 80–82, 87
  lifelong learning programs of, 142
  as personalized choices, 80
  state, 80–81, 82
  students of, 92, 115–16
  time-share travel on, 79
  traditional, 82, 87
  tuition fees of, 45, 80, 82
Colorado, 9, 22–23
Columbia University, 67
comedic performers, 10–13
Committee of 100, 110
Congress, U.S., 23, 29, 32, 34, 68,
    110, 151, 152, 158
  decreased approval rating of, 57
  health care reform enactment by,
    195
  public distrust of, 153–54
  2006 elections to, 22, 40, 41, 65,
    69, 84
conservatives, 6–10, 12, 26, 35,
    53–54, 85, 90, 100, 105–6, 118,
    141, 145, 146, 172, 193, 200,
    201, 209
Constitution, U.S., 29–30, 96
consumer polling, 3, 7–10, 12–13, 17,

    34, 41, 72–77, 91, 136–37, 143,
    150, 162, 172–77, 192, 198, 199
consumer shopping, 47–49, 77, 192
  authenticity in, 162–63, 172,
    173–77
  functionality vs. form in, 48–49
  luxury, 23–24, 48–49, 55, 192
  personalized choices in, 69–71
  political alignments linked to, 7–10,
    12–13, 26, 34, 206
  social responsibility in, 48–49, 55
corporations, 86, 89, 117, 152, 160,
    171
  environmentally sensitive, 38,
    48, 59
  ethics of, 172–76, 181
  multinational, 110
  public distrust of, 153
  small companies vs., 60
  social responsibility of, 38, 48
Cosby, Bill, 10, 11–13, 15, 99, 165,
    167
Costco, 49, 162–63, 175, 176
Couric, Katie, 167
craft beers, 71
credit card debt, 25, 37, 43–44, 45
Cronkite, Walter, 83
Cultural Creatives, The: How 50
    Million People Are Changing the
    World (Ray and Anderson), 171
cultural lag, concept of, 49
Cunningham, Randy "Duke," 151

D

Dalai Lama, 166, 167
Daltrey, Roger, 181
Danko, William D., 36
Darfur, xii, 204
dating, interracial, 98–99
Dean, Howard, 7
debt, 42–44
  credit card, 25, 37, 43–44, 45
  education, 45, 193
Declaration of Independence, 42
Deferred Dreamers, 122–23, 125
defined-benefit pension plans, 37
Deloitte & Touche poll, 177–78

Democracy in America (Tocqueville), 27–28
Democratic party, xi, 18, 21, 31, 40–41, 44, 50–51, 106, 151
  see also specific elections
Democratic Vistas (Whitman), 28
Democrat-Republican party, Jeffersonian, 28–29
Denmark, 95, 115
Diana, Princess of Wales, 137
Diebold, 34
dinosaurs, 184
  re-creating of, 105–6
Dobbs, Lou, 34
Dobson, James, 53, 166
Dole, Bob, 33
"dollar" retailers, 49, 173, 176
Donaldson, Sam, 83–84
Don't Think of an Elephant (Lakoff), 4
Dove, 181
Dreamless Dead, 122–23, 125
Drudge, Matt, 84
Du Bois, W.E.B., 28
Duke University lacrosse team case, 34
Duncan, Tim, 116
Dunkin' Donuts, 34

E

Easterbrook, Gregg, 23, 137
education, 13–16, 45, 193, 197
  indebtedness for, 45, 193
  levels of, 11, 36, 71, 177, 210–11
  for retired persons, 142, 194, 215
  see also colleges and universities; schools
Eduventures, 81
Eisenhower, Dwight D., 25, 30
elderhostels, 142
elderly people, 44, 54, 77, 90, 140–44, 193
  long-term care of, 140–41, 142, 194
  retirement of, 141–42, 186, 194, 198

volunteerism of, 142, 194, 215
  see also Private Generation
elections, ix–x, 18–19, 185
  "Armageddon," 31–35
  micro-precincts in, 206
  predicting results of, 21, 22–23
  primaries of, 6–7, 32–33
  red states vs. blue states in, 6, 7–10, 31, 33–34, 118, 206
  undecided voters in, 32–33
elections, U.S.:
  of 1800, 29, 31
  of 1860, 31, 33–34
  of 1972, 190
  of 1984, 122
  of 1988, 122
  of 1992, 6–7, 189–90
  of 1994, 23
  of 1996, 7, 100
  of 2008, 9, 50–52, 206
  of 2020, 206
elections of 2000, xiii, xiv, 4–6, 33, 190
  Florida vote recount in, 31–32
  primaries of, 7
elections of 2004, xi, 6, 8, 22, 23, 41, 71, 127, 133, 145, 190
  as "Armageddon" election, 31–35
  Christian values as issue in, 52
  investor-class voters in, 39–40
  political campaigns of, 182–83
  primaries of, 7
elections of 2006, xi, 52
  congressional, 22, 40, 41, 65, 69, 84
  gubernatorial, 22–23, 40
Emergency Quota Act (1921), 148
Emerging Democratic Majority, The (Judis and Teixeira), 41
energy usage, 58, 59, 61–64, 72, 78, 180, 202–3
  alternative fuels for, 203
  costs of, 61–62
  oil consumption in, 61, 62–64
Enron, 152
"enthusiasm gap," 81–82

environment, environmentalism, 57,
61, 121, 171, 180, 187, 189,
194, 203, 215
approval ratings on, 58
cars and, 74–76, 77
corporate sensitivity to, 38, 48, 59
evangelical supporters of, 64–66,
69, 205
global warming and, 24, 58, 59,
64–65, 68, 78, 90, 215
marketing and, 90
oil production and, 64
personal measures taken for, 13
of Woodstock Generation, 195
Esty, Daniel C., 59
ethics, 172–78
corporate, 172–76, 181
personal, 172, 176–78
of retail stores, 173–76
ethnicity, 14–16, 41, 96–97
European Union, 95, 212, 213
evangelical Christians, 53, 64–66, 69,
190, 204–6
Evangelical Environmental
Network, 65
Excelsior College, 82
exit, surveys, 7
ExxonMobil, 65

F

Facebook.com, 107, 159
fair-trade coffee, 48
Falwell, Jerry, 64
families, importance of, 130, 131,
196, 215
fashion models, 179, 181
Fastow, Andrew, 152
federal government, 63–64, 161, 211
decreased approval rating of, 57–59
potential Internet regulation by,
201–2
public distrust of, 151–55
Federalist party, 28–29
feminist movement, 199
Filene's, 8, 13, 173
First Globals, x–xii, xiv, 91–119, 146,
182, 186, 188, 191–94, 196–97
aging of, 197
American values as viewed by, 92–93
committed partnerships of, 193
distrusting attitude of, 197
diversity embraced by, xvi, 91,
94–97, 114, 115, 117, 119, 193
energy usage of, 202–3
foreign travel of, 94, 110–14,
213–14
as global citizenry, 23, 93–94,
113–14, 116, 117
guilt feelings of, 204
as Internet congregation, 107–8,
115, 119, 197
job insecurity of, 117, 193–94
liberalism of, 92, 102–6, 119, 190
marketing bombardment
experienced by, 91–92
marketing to, 114–19, 215
moderate position of, 103, 105–6
multilateralist worldview of,
108–10, 193, 196–97, 203
opinions of, 187, 191–92, 195,
198–214
spending habits of, 192, 204
sports figures and, 116–18
and third political party, 106
tolerance of, 97–102
flash polls, 17
Flexcar, 79
Florida, xiii, 6, 9, 129–32
2000 election vote recount in,
31–32
Focus on the Family, 53
Fogel, Robert, 140, 142
foot ointment, forms of, xiii–xiv
Forbes, 164
Ford, Gerald, 30
Ford Motor Company, 71–72, 73, 76
"Bold Moves" ad campaign of, 180
foreign policy, 51–52, 60, 66–69, 110,
186, 209–10
Foreign Policy Association, xi, 67–68,
210
foreign travel, 94, 110–14, 213–14
401(k) plans, 37
463 Communications, 159
FOX News, 34

Foxworthy, Jeff, 10
France, 67
    as U.S. ally, 191
Franken, Al, 25
Franklin, Benjamin, 133
Frederick Miller Classic Chocolate
    Lager, 71
free trade, 109–10, 210–11
Friedman, Thomas, 116
Frost, Robert, 184
Frum, David, 25
fuels:
    alternative, 203, 215
    gasoline, 65, 69, 75–76, 78, 181–82
    oil, 61, 62–64

G

Gallup Organization, 24–25, 48,
    57–58, 61, 99, 101
gasoline, 65, 69, 75–76, 78, 181–82
Gates, Bill and Melinda, 137, 144–45,
    165, 167
gay issues, *see* homosexuals
Geldof, Bob, 93
gender, 11, 34, 41, 48, 71, 126–27,
    130, 172
    and desirable opposite-sex
        attributes, 168–71, 183
gender gap, 33
General Motors (GM), 71–72,
    75–77
Gen X, 191
geographic variables, 43
geopolitics, 61, 62, 78, 193
geothermal power, 203
German Americans, 29
Germany, 115–16, 191
gerontology, 194
Gibson, Mel, 151
Gilmor, Dan, 88
Ginobili, Manu, 116
Girl Scouts of the USA, 181
Giuliani, Rudy, 9, 50–51
global community, 108–9, 167
global competition, 212–15
global consciousness, 47, 55
globalization, 117, 197

"globally integrated enterprise," xii
global poverty, 93, 119
global warming, 24, 58, 59, 64–65,
    68, 78, 90, 215
    Kyoto treaty on, 64, 108–9, 112
God, views on, 132–33, 147
Goldberg, Lucianne, 84
Gore, Al, xiii, 4–6, 33, 166, 202
Greenfield Online poll, 89
greenhouse gas emissions, 24
Green to Gold (Esty and Winston), 59
grief, stages of, 136
guilt feelings, 143, 147, 204
gun owners, 33

H

Hamilton, Alexander, 28–29, 30
Hamilton, Lewis, 118
Hamilton College, x, 94–97, 103
Hardaway, Tim, 117–18
Harris Interactive poll, 52, 60, 89
Hartford Institute for Religion
    Research, 205
Hawn, Goldie, 25
health care system, 35, 90, 174, 194,
    205
    low approval rating of, 58
    reform of, 195
Healthy Forests Restoration Act
    (2003), 152
Higher Grounds Trading
    Company, 94
Hilton, Paris, 136
Hispanics, 8, 96–97, 158
    English-speaking, 47
    in investor class, 39, 40, 41
    as work supervisors, 98
homeland security, 68
home ownership, 42, 43
homeschooling, 60, 196
homosexuals, 26, 27, 53, 94–97,
    117–18, 186
    in armed forces, 95, 97
    in same-sex marriages, 35,
        94–96
    as work supervisors, 98
Hope, Bob, 10, 11

house-church movement, 205–6, 215
House of Representatives, U.S., 30
  bitter partisanship in, 51
  Select Committee on Hunger of, 135
How (Seidman), 160–61
Huffington, Arianna, 23, 83
Huffington Post, 83
Human Network, The, 182
human rights, 24, 29–30, 119, 194
Hummer, 75, 181–82
Huntley, Chet, 83
Hurricane Katrina, 20, 35, 58–59, 122, 152–53, 155, 157, 158, 214
Hussein, Saddam, 68, 100, 152
hybrid cars, 61
  Toyota Prius, 48, 74–75, 77, 79

I

IBM, xii, 94, 115, 116, 211
Iliad, The (Homer), 13–16
Illich, Ivan, 86
immigration, 29, 34, 45, 47, 111, 121, 148–50, 186
  illegal, 47, 149–50
Immigration Act (1924), 148–49
income levels, 11–12, 36, 98, 127, 141, 145
  reduction in, 43, 127–28, 135–36, 147, 190
  Secular Spiritualists and, 135–40, 143
  see also poverty
independents, 19, 44, 51, 52, 106, 146
Interbrand, 115–16
International Criminal Court, 68, 108, 112
Internet, 69–70, 93, 170, 186
  colleges and universities accessed on, 60, 80–82, 87
  e-mail users on, 21–22
  First Globals and, 107–8, 115, 119, 197
  government regulation of, 201–2
  Netflix on, 70, 77

  in news industry, 84, 85, 86; *see also* blogs
  popular music downloaded from, 70
  privacy negated by, 108, 158–61, 168
  sexually explicit websites of, 108
  surveying on, 17, 21–23, 89
  values influenced by, 54–55
investor class, 36–42, 55, 126, 172–73
Investors Next Door (IND), 36–37, 38, 40, 117, 124
Iran, 30, 61, 67, 212, 213
Iraq War, xi, 4, 20, 35, 51, 59, 66, 68, 69, 146, 152, 155–56, 157
IRAs, 37
Is God Green?, 65
Israel, 191
  Jerusalem, 207, 208
  Palestinians vs., 207–9

J

Jackson, Jesse, 122, 166
Japan, 115, 212, 213
Japanese Americans, 29
JCPenney, 8, 175
J. D. Power and Associates, 73
Jefferson, Thomas, 28–29, 30, 133
Jensen, Christopher, 76
Jerusalem, 207, 208
Jews, 34
jobs, 47, 127–28, 135–36, 147, 186, 203
  added, 143, 145
  fulfillment in, 198–99
  goals for, 138–39
job satisfaction, 60
job security, 45–47, 117, 130, 131, 193–94
John Paul II, Pope, 165
Johnson, Lyndon B., 30
Jordan, Michael, 99
Josephson Institute of Ethics, 178

Judis, John, 41
Junior Achievement, 177

K

Kaufmann's, 8–10
Keillor, Garrison, 87
Kellogg's cereals, 183
Kennedy, John F., 30, 55, 182, 214
Kennedy, Paul, 56–57
Kerry, John, xi, 6, 7, 8, 12, 32–34, 41, 71, 127, 129, 133, 182, 190
King, Martin Luther, Jr., 30, 214
KKR private equity company, 49
Kohl's, 8, 9
Kravis, Henry, 49
Kübler-Ross, Elisabeth, 136
Kyoto global warming treaty, 64, 108–9, 112

L

Labor Department, U.S., 124
labor unions, 40, 41, 42, 43, 141, 155, 173
Lakewood Church, 205
Lakoff, George, 4
Landis, Floyd, 151
Land Rovers, 73
Las Vegas, Nev., 180
Lay, Kenneth, 151, 152
League of Nations, 209
Lebanon, 148–49
Lewinsky, Monica, 83–84, 151, 156, 158
Lewis, Jerry, 10
Libby, Lewis "Scooter," 152, 157–58
liberalism, liberals, 12, 28, 34–35, 85, 127, 141, 145, 146, 200, 202, 209
   definitions of, 102
   First Globals as, 92, 102–6, 119, 190
   retail politics of, 8–9
libertarians, xi, 12, 13, 35, 145, 172, 191, 193, 202, 209
Lichtman, Jim, 153
life-cycle issues, 44

life expectancy, 140–42, 187–88, 194
lifelong learning programs, 142, 194, 215
Lincoln, Abraham, 31, 34, 55, 183
Live Aid rock concerts, 93
living with limits, xvi, 42–49, 59, 71, 88, 89, 195, 214
   consumer shopping habits in, 47–49
   indebtedness in, 42–44, 45
   job insecurity in, 45–47
   lowered expectations in, 24, 36, 37, 40, 49, 66
Lohan, Lindsay, 136
Los Angeles, Calif., 14, 200
Los Angeles Times, 86
LRN, 160
Luntz, Frank, 92–93
Lynch, Jessica, 155–56, 157, 158

M

McCain, John, 7, 51, 166
McCaskill, Claire, 22
McGovern, George, 190
Macy's, 7–10, 175
Madrid, Spain, 181
margin-of-sampling error (MOE), 18, 22, 50, 123
marijuana, legalized medical, 195
marital status, 33, 36, 43
Mark, Gospel according to, 34
marketing, 9, 90, 123–24, 189, 195–96, 215
   to American values, 55, 179
   authenticity in, 163, 178–83, 205
   of cars, 71–77
   to elderly, 194
   endless bombardment of, 91–92
   to First Globals, 114–19, 215
   manipulative, 179
   micro-targeting, 55
   niche, 55
   patriotism as tool for, 60, 74, 76–77
   to Secular Spiritualists, 147

marketing *(cont'd)*:
    social responsibility in, 55
    worldwide, 186
    Zogby Champs and Chumps in,
        178–83
marriage, 196
    gay, 35, 94–96
    interracial, 98–99
Marshall's, 8–9, 173
Martin, Steve, 11
Maryland, 31
mass transit, 77–79
    European, 78
    time-share travel in, 79
Maupin, Armistead, 26
meaning of life, 139–40, 142, 147,
    192
media, 9, 25, 83–89, 136, 153, 173,
    185, 197, 204
    Arab, 54–55
    see also news industry
Medicaid, 141
megachurches, 204–5
mercury poisoning, 65
MetLife, 190
Mexico, 109–10
Miami, University of, 85
microbrews, 71
micro-precincts, 206
Miller Lite, 71
mining, 65
Minneapolis, Minn., 14
miscegenation, 98–99
Missouri, 22
moderates, 12, 13, 51, 103, 105–6,
    145, 146, 209
money, *see* income levels; spending
    habits
moral behavior, 133–35, 172
    Internet transparency and,
        160–61
    see also ethics
Morris, Ted, 115
Motorola, 22
MoveOn.org, xii
Moyers, Bill, 65
Muslims, 67, 209
MySpace.com, 107

N

NAFTA, 109–10
NASCAR races, 33, 118, 141
National Association of
    Evangelicals, 65
National Basketball Association
    (NBA), 116–18
National Do Not Call Registry, 21
National Football League (NFL), 118,
    156
National Guard, 45
Natural Resources Defense Council,
    152
NBC News, xiii, 7, 83–84
Neiman Marcus, 8, 173
neoconservatives, 56–57, 146
Netflix, 70, 77
Netherlands, 95
Network, 151
New Hampshire, 107
    1992 primary election in, 6–7
New Mexico, 6
news industry, 60–61, 83–89
    cable in, 84
    global, 88–89
    Internet in, 84, 85, 86; *see also*
        blogs
    radio in, 85–86
    TV networks in, 83–84, 85, 86–88,
        153
newspapers, 83, 84–85, 86–90,
    153
Newsweek, 67
New York, 9–10, 40, 171–72, 189
New York, N.Y., 77–78, 148, 149,
    160, 200
New Yorker cartoons, 37
New York Times, 76, 83, 85
New York Times Magazine, 161–62
Nike Generation, 186, 193, 195–96,
    197
    characteristics of, 190–92
    committed partnerships of, 196
    importance of families to, 196, 215
    opinions of, 191–92, 198–214
Nixon, Richard, 28, 30, 57–58, 190
Norquist, Grover, 39

North Atlantic Treaty Organization
(NATO), 60, 67–68, 209–10
North Carolina, University of (UNC),
80, 81
North Korea, 68, 212, 213
nuclear weapons, 184, 212

O

Obama, Barack, 51, 53, 101
Odyssey, The (Homer), 14–16
Ohio, 34
oil, 61, 62–64
Olympic Games, 116–17
of 2000, 103
OPEC, 1973 embargo of, 61
Ottoman Empire, 148, 149
overnight polls, 16
Ownership Society, 39–40
Oxfam, 93–94
Oz, land of, 4–6

P

Pace, Peter, 97
Palestine Human Rights Campaign,
150
Palestinians, 207–9
Parker, Tony, 116
party identification ("party ID"), 8,
19–20, 21, 66
passports, 111–12, 197, 213–14
patriotism, 60, 74, 76–77, 92–93
PBS, 37–38, 65
Pennsylvania, 31
Perot, Ross, 33
Pew Forum on Religion and Public
Life, 64–65
Pew Research Center, 199
Philadelphia, Penn., 77–78
Philadelphia Inquirer, 86
Phoenix, University of, 81
Pigs at the Trough (Huffington), 23
police officers, career, 196, 199–200
political campaigns, 206
advertising of, 9, 182–83
authenticity in, 171–72
political correctness, 92, 117

political polling, 3–10, 17, 54,
171–72, 182, 185
all-day calling in, 7
comedic performers and, 10–13
consumer shopping habits and,
7–10, 12–13, 26, 34, 206
exit surveys in, 7
of investor voters, 36
monthly, 16–17
question formation in, 3–6
rolling average in, 20
weighting for party identification
in, 19–20, 21
see also elections, U.S.
polling, polls, ix–xvi, 3–26, 184–85,
214
door-to-door, 89
education and, 13–16
e-mail users as registered
participants in, 21–22
face-to-face, 89
flash, 17
generational divides revealed by, xv
Internet surveying in, 17, 21–23, 89
overnight, 16
questions asked in, 3–16, 17, 114,
188
reading results of, 26
telephone surveying in, 20–21,
22–23, 50, 89
text-message, 22–23
trailer variables in, 19
underlying motivation sought in, 3,
4–6, 17
see also sampling, probability
popular music, 70, 93, 195–96
poverty, 16, 44–45, 53, 122–23
attributed reasons for, 145–46
global, 93, 119
hunger produced by, 135
Powell, Colin, 100, 157, 158, 164,
166
president, U.S., 30, 53, 151
first black, 100–102
first woman, 101–2
qualities voters desire in, 50–52
privacy, Internet negation of, 108,
158–61, 168

Private Generation, 185–88, 194, 195, 196–97, 215
  characteristics of, 186–88
  life span expected by, 187–88, 194
  opinions of, 186–87, 191–92, 193, 195, 197, 198–214
progressives, xi, 12, 202
Progress Paradox, The (Easterbrook), 23, 137–38
Pryor, Richard, 10–13
public transportation, 77–79
Putnam, Robert D., 138

Q

Quindlen, Anna, 150
QVC television network, 143

R

race, 14–16, 28, 36, 41, 71, 96–102
racism, 28, 34–35
radio, 85–86
Radiohead, 70
Ray, Paul H., 171
Raymond, Lee, 65
Reagan, Ronald, 30, 36, 55, 100, 189, 191
RealClearPolitics.com, 83
recording industry, 70, 185–86
red states vs. blue states, 6, 7–10, 31, 33–34, 118, 206
religion, religious practice, 33, 43, 44, 64–65, 127, 128, 204–6, 209
  God as defined in, 132–33
  of Secular Spiritualists, 130–31, 132–34, 147
religious leaders, 165, 166, 167
religious right, 13, 28, 53, 64–66, 205, 209
Report Card on the Ethics of American Youth, 178
Republican party, 9, 19, 23, 39–40, 44, 50–51, 60, 64, 66, 100, 106, 145–46, 151, 214
  see also specific elections
residency, identification of, 113–14
retail politics, 7–10, 12–13, 26

retirement, 141–42, 186, 194, 198
Reuters, xiii, 38, 88
Rise and Fall of the Great Powers, The (Kennedy), 56–57
Roberts, Cokie, 83
Rock, Chris, 10, 11
rock bands, 70, 93
Rock the Vote, 22
Roe v. Wade, 53, 103
role models, 137, 200
rolling average, 20
Roman Catholic Church, 60, 152, 191
Roosevelt, Franklin D., 36, 55, 183, 214
Roper Reports, 99
Russert, Tim, 83–84

S

Salinger, J. D., 160
sampling, probability, 16–20, 26
  correct selection of, 18–19, 21
  margin-of-sampling error (MOE) in, 18, 22, 50, 123
  randomness of, 18, 21
  weighting of, 19–20, 22–23
San Antonio Spurs, 116–17
Saudi Arabia, 191
Schiavo, Terri, 35, 53, 215
schools, 58
  nontraditional alternatives to, 60, 196
  racial integration of, 97–98, 99
Schor, Juliet, 91–92
Sears, 71, 175
Secular Spiritualists, 123–47, 167, 215
  characteristics of, 126–27, 129
  charitable activities of, 131, 142, 144–45
  family as important to, 130, 131
  generosity of, 144–47
  God as viewed by, 132–33, 147
  income levels and, 135–40, 143
  increased life expectancy of, 140–42
  international issues as viewed by, 146–47

job security of, 130, 131
lowered expectations of, 127–28
marketing to, 147
meaning of life for, 130–40, 142, 147
moral behavior and, 133–34
Nike Generation as, 196
personal attributes favored by, 143–44
qualities taught to children by, 131–32
religious practice of, 130–31, 132–34, 147
retirement goals of, 141–42
simpler life desired by, 128
spending habits of, 127–28, 142–43, 147
Traditional Materialists vs., 124–27, 139–40, 142–43
values of, 128–35, 144
wealth as viewed by, 136–37
Seidman, Dov, 160–61
Seinfeld, Jerry, 10, 11
self-identification, 36–37, 38, 51, 85, 102, 105–6, 127, 172
as investor class members, 36–42
political party, 8, 19–20, 21, 66
Seligman, Martin, 137–38
Senate, U.S., 22, 30, 51, 84
September 11, 2001, terrorist attacks, 6, 20, 59, 68, 122, 152, 156, 179, 186
shopping, see consumer shopping
Simpson, Jessica, 136
Simpsons, The, 13–16
Skelton, Red, 10–13
smear-and-smash political campaign, 171–72
Smith, Wesley J., 25
Smith, Will, 99
social responsibility, 37–38, 40
in consumer shopping, 48–49, 55
of investor class, 38, 55
Social Security, 42, 44
solar power, 203
South Korea, 192
Soviet Union, 56, 209, 212
Spears, Britney, 136

spending habits, 47–49, 150–51
at Christmas, 124
guilt engendered by, 143, 147, 204
of Nike Generation, 192
of Secular Spiritualists, 127–28, 142–43, 147
Spitzer, Eliot, 40
sports figures, 116–18, 164, 166
SRI (Socially Responsible Investing) mutual funds, 38
Stanley, Thomas J., 36
Starbucks, 34, 93
"The Way I See It" coffee cup quotes of, 25–26
State Department, U.S., 111
stem cell research, 53–54, 90, 200–201
Stern, David, 117–18
Stewart, Jon, 172
stock-market stakeholders, 36–42
Stokke, Allison, 87
success, 128, 142
investors' definitions of, 37
material, 121, 122, 123–27, 128, 139–40, 142–43, 193
superpowers, era of, 56–57, 59, 66
Supreme Court, U.S., xiii, 29, 31, 32
Sweden, 95

T

Talent, Jim, 22
Target, 8, 9, 13, 71, 175
Teen Ethics Poll, 177–78
Teixeira, Ruy, 41
telemarketing, 21
telephone surveying, 20–21, 22–23, 50, 89
average response rates to, 20
Teresa, Mother, 165, 166
text-message polling, 22–23
"This Is My Country" ad campaign, 76
Thoreau, Henry David, 120–21, 128–29
Tiffany, 162–63
Tillman, Pat, 156, 157, 158
timber industry, 152

time-share travel, 79
Tocqueville, Alexis de, 27–28, 42
Tommy Hilfiger, 115
Toyota, 76, 77, 115, 116
Toyota Prius, 48, 74–75, 77, 79
Traditional Materialists, 123, 124–27,
 139–40, 142–43
trailer variables, 19
trait selection, 161–62
Trans Am band, 75
travel:
 foreign, 94, 110–14, 213–14
 by retired persons, 142, 194
 time-share, 79
Trump, Donald, 137, 150
Tudor, Frederick, 120–21, 123

U

UCLA, 97
unemployment rate, 45
"United Colors" ad campaign, 115,
 182
United Nations (UN), 51, 108,
 209–10
 General Assembly of, 67, 209
 Powell's speech to, 157, 158, 164
 sharing power with, 60, 66–69
United Press International (UPI), 58,
 62, 195
United States:
 as biotechnology world leader,
  213–14
 as broker in Israeli-Palestinian
  conflict, 207–9
 citizens' collective wisdom in,
  23–26
 countries allied to, 191–92
 as force for good, 57, 60
 foreign image of, 51–52, 55, 59,
  187
 global competitors of, 212–15
 international cooperation and
  power sharing by, 58, 60, 66–69,
  186
 mega-institutions of, 57–59,
  69–70
 as meritocracy, 24–25, 42

 national character of, 27–28, 42
 national destiny of, 56–57
 optimism of, 27, 42, 43
 see also values, American
USA Today, 25
Utica, N.Y., 46, 49, 108, 148–50,
 200

V

values, American, xiv–xv, 23–26,
 27–55, 90, 171, 186, 190–91
 in Bill of Rights, 29–30
 centrist, 35–36, 51, 52, 53
 Christian, 35, 52, 132, 133–35
 conflicting, 6, 52–53
 divide in, 6, 27, 28–35
 ethical, see ethics
 generational divide in, xv, 31–32
 Internet influence on, 54–55
 of investor class, 36–42, 172–73
 marketing to, 55, 179
 other nations' and cultures' values
  vs., 92–93, 112–13
 polarized, 33–34
 of Secular Spiritualists, 128–34,
  144
 shared, 30, 45
 social responsibility in, 37–38, 40,
  48–49, 55
 of Woodstock Generation, 189
 see also living with limits
Venezuela, 67
Versace, 115
veterans, military, 146
Vietnam War, 20, 30, 58, 190
Virginia, 9, 84, 99
vital center, 35–36
volunteerism, 142, 194, 215
voting machines, 34

W

WakeUp Wal-Mart, 173
Walden Pond, 120–21
Wall Street Journal, 85
Wall Street Week with FORTUNE,
 37–38

Wal-Mart, 7–10, 12–13, 34, 35, 44,
        49, 52, 118, 162–63
    marketing by, 179–80
    public image of, 173–76, 179–80
Wal-Marting Across America blog,
        180
Walton, Sam, 175
war on terror, 33
Warren, Rick, 25, 53, 166
Washington, George, 55, 133
Washington Post, 87
"wasting asset," 79
Watergate scandal, 20, 30
"Way I See It, The," coffee cup
        quotes, 25–26
wealth, 136–37
    inequitable distribution of, 35, 136
weighting, 22–23
    for party identification, 19–20, 21
Weinberger, Caspar, 100
We Media conference, 85
"What Happens in Vegas Stays in
        Vegas" ad campaign, 180
"What Would Jesus Drive?" ad
        campaign, 65
Wheeler, Patti, 118
Whitman, Walt, 28
Whole Foods, 93
Williams, Robin, 10, 11
Williams Institute, 97
Wilson, Woodrow, 55, 209
wind power, 203
Winfrey, Oprah, 99, 164, 165
Winston, Andrew S., 59
women, 41, 76, 123, 157, 179, 186,
        199
    discrimination against, 174
    as fashion models, 179, 181
    as NASCAR drivers, 118
    political values in consumer
        decisions of, 48

    in presidency, 101–2
    see also gender
Woods, Tiger, 100, 117, 164, 166,
        167
Woodstock concert, 189
Woodstock Generation, 186, 194–95,
        215
    characteristics of, 188–90
    opinions of, 191–92, 195,
        198–214
woolly mammoths, re-creating of,
        105–6
work, 47, 60, 138, 190, 215
    fulfilling, 198–99
    minority supervisors at, 98
    see also jobs
workforce, 42, 45–47, 80, 199
working mothers, 199
WorldCom, 152
World Editors Forum, 88
World War I, 24, 29, 149, 165
World War II, 24, 29, 42, 186, 204,
        209
WSJ.com, 180

Y

Yao Ming, 117
YouTube.com, 107, 108, 159, 172

Z

Zogby, Jim, 150
Zogby, Joseph Rachid, 148–50
Zogby Interactive, 17, 21–22, 39, 43,
        58, 62, 75, 89, 92, 99, 123, 141,
        145, 153
Zogby International, xiii, 16, 85, 150,
        182, 188
    Utica headquarters of, 46
Zyman, Sergio, 178

ABOUT THE AUTHOR

JOHN ZOGBY is the president and CEO of Zogby International, whose many media and business clients include Reuters, NBC News, MSNBC, the *New York Post,* C-SPAN, Gannett News Service, IBM, MetLife, and Microsoft. He is a regular contributor to network television news broadcasts and has been a frequent guest on *Today, Hardball with Chris Matthews,* and *The Daily Show with Jon Stewart.* His writing has appeared in many publications, including *The New York Times* and *The Wall Street Journal.* A frequent lecturer and panelist, he is married to Kathleen Zogby, a retired special education teacher, and has three sons, Jonathan, Benjamin, and Jeremy. He lives in Utica, New York.

ABOUT THE TYPE

This book was set in Sabon, a typeface designed by the well-known German typographer Jan Tschichold (1902–74). Sabon's design is based upon the original letter forms of Claude Garamond and was created specifically to be used for three sources: foundry type for hand composition, Linotype, and Monotype. Tschichold named his typeface for the famous Frankfurt typefounder Jacques Sabon, who died in 1580.